ETHICS IN
QUALITATIVE
RESEARCH

SAGE has been part of the global academic community since 1965, supporting high quality research and learning that transforms society and our understanding of individuals, groups and cultures. SAGE is the independent, innovative, natural home for authors, editors and societies who share our commitment and passion for the social sciences.

Find out more at: **www.sagepublications.com**

ETHICS IN QUALITATIVE RESEARCH

CONTROVERSIES AND CONTEXTS

MARTYN HAMMERSLEY AND **ANNA TRAIANOU**

Los Angeles | London | New Delhi
Singapore | Washington DC

First published 2012

SAGE Publications Ltd
1 Oliver's Yard
55 City Road
London EC1Y 1SP

SAGE Publications Inc.
2455 Teller Road
Thousand Oaks, California 91320

SAGE Publications India Pvt Ltd
B 1/I 1 Mohan Cooperative Industrial Area
Mathura Road
New Delhi 110 044

SAGE Publications Asia-Pacific Pte Ltd
3 Church Street
#10-04 Samsung Hub
Singapore 049483

Library of Congress Control Number: 2011936589

British Library Cataloguing in Publication data

A catalogue record for this book is available from the British Library

ISBN 978-0-85702-140-3
ISBN 978-0-85702-141-0 (pbk)

Typeset by C&M Digitals (P) Ltd, Chennai, India
Printed in India at Replika Press Pvt Ltd
Printed on paper from sustainable resources

'The only safe way to avoid violating principles of professional ethics is to refrain from doing social research altogether.' (Bronfenbrenner 1952: 452)

CONTENTS

About the authors   viii

Introduction   1

1   What is ethics?   16

2   The research ethos   35

3   The risk of harm   57

4   Autonomy and informed consent   75

5   Privacy, confidentiality and anonymity   99

Conclusion: challenging moralism   133

References   145

Index   171

ABOUT THE AUTHORS

Martyn Hammersley is Professor of Educational and Social Research at The Open University. He has carried out research in the sociology of education and the sociology of the media. However, much of his work has been concerned with the methodological issues surrounding social inquiry. He has written several books, including: *Reading Ethnographic Research* (Longman 1991); *What's Wrong with Ethnography?* (Routledge 1992); *The Politics of Social Research* (Sage 1995); *Taking Sides in Social Research* (Routledge 1999); *Educational Research, Policymaking and Practice* (Paul Chapman 2002), *Media Bias in Reporting Social Research* (Routledge 2006), *Questioning Qualitative Inquiry* (Sage 2008), and *Methodology, Who Needs It?* (Sage 2011).

Anna Traianou is Senior Lecturer in the Department of Educational Studies, Goldsmiths, University of London. She has carried out research into the nature of teacher expertise, and, in particular, the ways in which knowledge and learning are implicated in educational practice. This resulted in her book, *Understanding Teacher Expertise in Primary Science: A Sociocultural Approach* (SENSEpublishers 2006). Anna has also worked on the relationship between research evidence and practical wisdom, exploring some of the problems facing any notion that effective teaching can simply be an application of the results of scientific research. She has a particular interest in qualitative research methodology and theories of science.

INTRODUCTION

- What is ethical and unethical in qualitative research?
- What does it mean to be ethical or unethical?
- Who should judge whether or not qualitative researchers are behaving ethically?
- How is this to be done?

These are some of the questions we will be addressing in this book. We will argue that answering them can be more difficult than is often supposed, and our own answers will be controversial in some respects, for example as regards the severity of the ethical dangers involved in qualitative inquiry and how we should approach them.

All social research involves ethical issues, but the character and importance of these varies. This book focuses on qualitative research, broadly conceived as research that employs relatively unstructured forms of data, whether produced through observation, interviewing, and/or the analysis of documents. The production of such data can involve researchers in quite close, and sometimes long-term, relationships with people. Indeed, the ethos of qualitative research tends to emphasise the need for such closeness if people's perspectives are to be understood adequately, and perhaps also if the full relevant range of their activities is to be documented. Furthermore, data collection usually takes place in 'natural' settings, rather than in situations specifically set up for research purposes. These features have considerable significance when it comes to thinking about ethical issues, and we will be focusing especially on ethnographic or participant observation research for this reason, though our discussion will be relevant to most other kinds of qualitative work.

Any discussion of 'research ethics' must begin by addressing the meaning of that phrase, and this will be our focus in Chapters 1 and 2. There is a common tendency to treat research ethics as primarily or even exclusively about how researchers should treat the people they study, this often being conceptualised in terms of protecting rights and interests, for example avoiding causing harm, respecting people's autonomy, and preserving their privacy. We will argue that, while such matters are important, they do not identify the primary obligation placed upon researchers, which is to pursue research in ways that answer worthwhile questions to the required level of likely validity. Other ethical considerations, we suggest, must be evaluated against this background.

Here in the Introduction we will begin by outlining why research ethics has become such a prominent issue in social science in recent years. In the final part, we will outline the contents of the other chapters.

THE RISE AND RISE OF RESEARCH ETHICS

Research ethics has long been a topic for methodological reflection, and occasionally for intense discussion and disagreement, among social scientists. However, in recent years it has come to be given even more attention than previously. There are several reasons for this.[1] One is the use of new technologies (from digital photography and audio- and video-recording to the analysis of virtual materials from the Internet). This has introduced some distinctive problems, or at least it has given old problems a new form (Prosser 2000; Buchanan 2004; Wiles et al. 2008b; Markham and Baym 2009). Another factor is data protection legislation, in the UK and elsewhere, which carries implications for how researchers store and report data, and for its deposition in archives and its re-use.[2]

Later in the book we will examine the issues raised by these developments, but here we want to look more closely at two other factors that have led to increased attention to research ethics: the growth of ethical regulation, and the fragmentation of qualitative research along philosophical and political lines.

Professional codes and ethics committees

The move towards ethical regulation of social science began many years ago with some social science subject associations establishing codes to guide the behaviour of their members. This was stimulated in part by earlier developments within medical research after the Second World War, these being prompted by the appalling experiments carried out by Nazi doctors on people in institutions and in concentration camps. The Nuremburg Code of 1947 specified ethical principles that should guide medical experiments, these later being applied more widely, notably in psychology. They were subsequently clarified, developed and supplemented in the World Medical Association's Helsinki Declaration of 1964, and in the Belmont Report of 1979 in the USA. The last of these was prompted by further scandals, for instance the Tuskegee project in the southern United States, in which African-American men

---

[1]Writing over 30 years ago, Barnes (1979: Ch. 1) also noted a growth of interest in research ethics, explaining this in terms of long-term socio-political trends.

[2]For interpretations of the implications of this legislation in the UK, see Akeroyd (1988); SRA (1995); Le Voi (2006); Alderson and Morrow (2011: 36–7). On ethical issues and archiving, see Corti et al. (2000); Thompson (2003); Erdos (2011a, 2011b); Williams et al. (2011).

were not given treatment for syphilis, in order to allow researchers to understand the variable course of the disease.[3]

The production of ethics codes by social science associations also stemmed more directly from controversies resulting from the involvement of social scientists in work for external organisations, especially governments. For example, during the Second World War, some anthropologists in the United States were employed by a US government agency that was responsible for the internment of people of Japanese descent in California (Opler 1986; Starn 1986; Mills 2003: 40; see also Price 2008), and this led the Society for Applied Anthropology to produce a code of ethics in 1948, probably the first social science association to do so. In the 1960s and 1970s, there were a series of further controversies around anthropologists' and other social scientists' involvement in government-sponsored projects concerned with military operations and counterinsurgency in Latin America and East Asia (Wakin 2008: Ch. 2).[4] The one that caused most debate was Project Camelot, where anthropologists, sociologists, political scientists, and psychologists were to be funded as part of a proposed CIA project concerned with 'assessing the potential for internal war within national societies' and identifying 'those actions which a government might take to relieve conditions which are assessed as giving rise to a potential for internal war' (Horowitz 1967: 5). This, along with some anthropologists' involvement with CIA activity in Thailand (Wakin 2008), and demands that social science associations take a stand against the Vietnam War, led the American Anthropological Association to set up an ethics committee, and eventually to produce a statement on ethics in 1968 and a code in 1971. This code declared that: 'Anthropologists' paramount responsibility is to those they study. When there is a conflict of interest, these individuals must come first'. In the same spirit, it was argued that 'anthropologists must do everything in their power to protect the physical, social and psychological welfare and to honour the dignity and privacy of those studied' (AAA 1971).

Similar developments occurred in other associations; for example the first version of the American Sociological Association ethics code was adopted in 1970, being prompted by many of the same events and issues. Of course, while some social scientists denounced all involvement in government projects concerned with foreign policy, others argued that, in this area as in others, they had a responsibility to offer their expertise for use by governments, or to seek to modify government policy through advising on its formulation and implementation.[5]

---

[3]The Tuskegee case is one of several 'atrocity stories' (Dingwall 1977) used in discussions of research ethics, particularly in justifying ethical regulation. However, it is open to conflicting interpretations: see Cave and Holm (2003) and Shweder (2004). Kimmel (1996) provides an account of the development of ethics codes in US psychology; see also Diener and Crandall (1978: 17–22).

[4]More recently, there has been concern over the involvement of anthropologists in the invasions and occupations of Iraq and Afghanistan; see Fluehr-Lobban (2008) and Lutz (2008).

[5]It ought to be noted that the positions taken on this issue often reflected the attitudes of commentators towards particular governments or policies at particular times, and towards the people affected by them, even though the debates were formulated as disagreements about fundamental ethical principles.

Codes in other social science associations in other countries arose rather differently. For example, the British Sociological Association (BSA) established a code of ethics in 1968 as a result of concern about the huge increase in the number of people engaged in sociological work outside universities, and specifically about their competence and level of experience (Mills 2003: 46; Platt 2003: 34). Here, the emphasis was on establishing and maintaining professionalism: it was stated that 'the professional sociologist, while insisting that only persons properly trained or skilled should do social research, should himself [*sic*] recognise the boundaries of his professional competence' (quoted in Platt 2003: 162). It is worth noting, however, that this emphasis on professionalism was closely related to a concern to defend academic freedom. In fact, during the course of dealing with an individual case that raised this issue, the BSA's Ethics Committee came to be replaced in 1971 by a Committee on Academic Freedom in Teaching and Research (Platt 2003: 116), though a 'professional ethics committee' was re-established later.

As should be clear from this brief account, the production of codes has involved some variation in motives. Furthermore, the resulting codes served different functions at different times, not necessarily those intended or anticipated. They could be designed or function to protect the people studied, to preserve or promote the image of social science, and/or to defend it against unrealistic expectations and complaints. Occasionally, the aim seems to have been to ward off external intervention. For example, Homan claims that the BSA revised its code in the early 1980s in order to avoid government intervention prompted by official reports into privacy issues (Homan 1991: 38). As regards change in the functioning of codes over time, Caplan (2003: 19) has noted that, in the case of anthropology, 'from the 1960s until the end of the 1980s, support for ethical codes was seen as support for a politically radical version of anthropology, while, by the 1990s, ethics had for some become a politically conservative part of audit culture'. Partly as a result of this variation in function, codes also differed, across associations and over time, in how abstract or specific, and how prescriptive, they were.

It should be said that the introduction of these codes did not go unopposed. They were challenged for reasons that anticipated later complaints about ethical regulation. For example, when the American Sociological Association published its ethics code, this was criticised on the grounds that it inevitably oversimplified complex issues, that it presumed a consensus that did not exist, and was unnecessary given that sociologists do not deal with a clientele, in the manner of most service professions (Becker 1964a; Freidson 1964; Roth 1969; Galliher 1973; see also Ladd 1991). In addition, Payne et al. (1981: 249) have argued that codes 'put a premium' on forms of research that can be easily policed, as well as undercutting the 'sense of personal accountability and, hence, of the importance of personal integrity'. Along similar lines, Pels (2005: 82) has suggested that since the 1990s ethical codes have introduced a form of 'legalism' which shifts the emphasis of ethics 'away from research practice to the practice of rule making'.

However, in social science the codes that were developed did not amount to ethical regulation, strictly speaking, by contrast with medicine, where codes were generally accompanied by procedures through which complaints could be made, and punishment administered. While medical associations could often prevent a member continuing to practise, at least within their jurisdiction, this was rarely if ever possible for social science associations. In short, their codes were largely advisory in function, with little or no policing to ensure compliance.

In recent decades, however, there has been a major shift towards the ethical regulation of social science. One aspect of this is that the locus has moved from professional associations to the organisations in which social scientists work, or with which they must deal in carrying out their research: universities, research institutes, and research sites like hospitals. This process began in the United States, with the introduction of Federal regulations in the early 1980s which required the establishment of Institutional Review Boards to assess research proposals within all institutions receiving funds from what was then the Department of Health, Education and Welfare. What forced universities to comply in setting up these boards was that future Federal funding for projects was dependent upon this. While the review board system was primarily concerned with medical research, the remit of these boards covered social science as well. And their flexibility in interpreting ethical principles across research fields has varied considerably (Israel and Hay 2006: 41–5). Furthermore, over time, there has been a process of 'ethics creep' involving an intensification of regulation and its extension to examine all aspects of the research process (Haggerty 2004).

In the UK, the shift towards this kind of ethical regulation was more recent. Here, too, it began in the field of health, with the Department of Health requiring hospitals to set up research ethics committees, and later providing guidelines for the establishment and operation of these. And more recent changes have led to much tighter regulation through the NHS Research Governance Framework (RGF), which was introduced in 2001, and now covers most research conducted in healthcare settings in the UK, not just medical research. Dixon-Woods and Ashcroft (2008: 383) describe what is involved as follows:

> The RGF defines research governance as improving research quality and safeguarding the public by: enhancing ethical and scientific quality; promoting good practice; reducing adverse incidents; ensuring lessons are learned; and preventing poor performance and misconduct. Its aim is the continuous improvement of standards and reduction of 'unacceptable variations'. It formalizes structures and responsibilities, specifying arrangements to define and communicate clear quality standards, mechanisms to ensure these standards are met, and arrangements to monitor quality. [...] The RGF clarifies the responsibilities of those conducting and those 'hosting' research, so that all NHS trusts (healthcare organizations) are now legally required to have, as a core standard, systems to ensure that the principles and requirements of research governance are consistently applied. [...] Any research conducted in the NHS [National Health Service] must comply with the requirements of the RGF, which include having the approval of a REC [Research Ethics Committee].[6]

---

[6]Quotations here are from the Research Governance Framework.

These changes in the health field were important factors in stimulating increased regulation across UK social science. There had previously been ethics committees in some universities, but these had usually been concerned with medical research, and/or with the treatment of animals by biologists, and of children by psychologists. However, in 2005 the Economic and Social Research Council published its *Research Ethics Framework* (2005) and this was formulated very much in the language of 'research governance'. In effect it required that most research proposals coming to it be subject to vetting procedures within universities before they could be funded. In the wake of this, universities extended the remit of existing ethics committees to deal with social research, or set up new procedures; although this continues to be done in a variety of ways, and with differing degrees of operational effect. More recently, regulation has been tightened up and extended through a revised framework (ESRC 2010; Stanley and Wise 2010).

The most significant aspect of this shift from codes to regulation is that whereas, even within professional medical associations, the application of codes had been retrospective, responding to complaints, the operation of the new institutional review boards and ethics committees was prospective, effectively determining whether particular research projects could go ahead. Furthermore, it frequently entails a 'mandatory requirement for the prior and meticulous review of social research proposals by groups that are representative of a wider constituency than the research community' (Homan 1991: 17). In other words, research proposals are to be judged not just by members of the relevant research community but by committees that include academics from across diverse disciplines and, increasingly, lay representatives as well.

It is no accident, perhaps, that this move to ethical regulation took place at a time when the organisational character of universities, in the UK and elsewhere, was changing quite rapidly: away from a broadly collegial towards a more managerial model (Deem et al. 2007; Tuchman 2009). The aim of many governments in funding universities was increasingly to bring their mode of operation into some sort of correspondence with the presumed character of business firms, the aim ironically often being to make them more effective instruments of government policy, where previously they had been regarded as relatively autonomous. This resulted from the application of 'new public management' ideology, according to which an insufficiently accountable and therefore (it was supposed) inefficient public sector was to be transformed through the introduction of regulatory practices that mimicked the 'discipline of the market' and forms of internal organisation parallel to those characteristic of contemporary large-scale commercial organisations (Hammersley 2011: Introduction). One aspect of this was the development of policies and structures for the strategic management of research, designed to maximise external income. And, over time, the operation of ethics committees came to be integrated into these in many universities. Indeed, in the UK this is a requirement laid down by ESRC.

The reorganisation and tightening of ethical regulation has had particularly sharp consequences for qualitative research, because the model of inquiry on which regulatory guidelines and arrangements have come to be based is usually at odds with its character. This biomedical model assumes clear specification of objectives and means of achieving them at the start of the research process, followed by the testing of hypotheses, and the scheduled production of promised outcomes. It also presumes that research consists of the administration of research instruments in researcher-controlled environments (Reiss 1979). By contrast, qualitative research generally operates on the basis of a flexible and emergent mode of research design: in which the task – in the early stages of data collection at least – is to clarify and develop understanding of the research problem. As a result, it is difficult for qualitative researchers to anticipate, at the beginning, what sorts of data will need to be collected. Furthermore, qualitative research typically takes place in 'natural' settings, over which researchers have little control. Even when interviews are involved, these are usually relatively unstructured in character, and carried out in territory that is not controlled by the researcher. All these features make it difficult to anticipate what contingencies might arise at various stages of the research process, and to plan in any detail how ethical issues will be dealt with.

This mismatch between regulatory procedures based on bio-medical or experimental psychological models and qualitative research has sometimes been recognised by regulatory authorities. But the result has usually been the introduction of only marginal flexibility into procedures, or even the recommendation of more detailed regulation. For instance, the ESRC's *Framework for Research Ethics* states that: 'Where a study design is emergent, the REC [Research Ethics Committee] should agree procedures for *continuing* ethics review (for example through a Project Advisory Group) [...] as a condition of approval' (ESRC 2010: 17, point 1.11.2, emphasis added). In other words, those engaged in qualitative studies are required not simply to submit proposals to an ethics committee prior to starting the investigation, *but there must also be continual external monitoring during the rest of the research process*. At present, this recommendation does not seem to be widely implemented, but it may be in the future.

The establishment of ethics committees has been closely associated with specification of *principles* of research ethics by regulatory organisations and their sponsors. For example, the ESRC's *Framework for Research Ethics* (p. 3) lists the following 'six key principles':

1 Research should be designed, reviewed and undertaken to ensure integrity, quality and transparency.
2 Research staff and participants must normally be informed fully about the purpose, methods, and intended possible uses of the research, what their participation in the research entails and what risks, if any, are involved. Some variation is allowed in very specific research contexts [...].
3 The confidentiality of information supplied by research participants and the anonymity of respondents must be respected.
4 Research participants must take part voluntarily, free from any coercion.
5 Harm to research participants must be avoided in all instances.
6 The independence of research must be clear, and any conflicts of interest or partiality must be explicit.

It is no accident that these 'principles' have the character of injunctions, using words like 'should', 'ensure', and 'must', since this is effectively demanded by the sort of accountability regime they are intended to implement. But there are serious questions to be raised about this approach to research ethics, as we will make clear in subsequent chapters.

The growth in ethical regulation has generated a considerable literature. Some of this has concerned the principles on which regulation should be based, some has been designed to assist researchers in thinking about research ethics in ways that allow them to navigate the requirements of ethics committees, and a considerable amount has been concerned with the negative effects of ethical regulation for qualitative work.[7]

Qualitative research and ethics

Qualitative inquiry raises distinctive ethical issues because, as already indicated, it generally involves emergent and flexible research designs, and usually entails collecting relatively unstructured data in naturalistic settings. Furthermore, since the middle of the twentieth century, there has been much discussion of these ethical issues. To some extent, this was stimulated by particular studies that attracted adverse publicity or were seen as involving severe problems. (See Box 1 for some of the qualitative studies that have generated controversy.)

BOX 1

STREET CORNER SOCIETY

In the late 1930s Whyte studied a poor Italian-American community in Boston, USA, living with a family there and hanging out with young men on the street. Some issues raised:

1 Whyte broke the law by engaging in 'repeat' voting. Is it ever legitimate for a researcher to break the law?
2 There were negative reactions from some participants towards their portrayal in the book that Whyte published. What responsibilities do researchers have regarding their portrayal of others?

(See Whyte 1992, 1993a, 1993b; Barnes 1977: Ch. 2; Boelen 1992; Denzin 1992.)

WHEN PROPHECY FAILS

In this study, researchers joined a small apocalyptic religious group, covertly observing and interviewing them, in order to study their reactions when the world was not destroyed on the date predicted. Some issues:

1 Is covert observation of private meetings in people's homes an invasion of privacy?
2 Was it legitimate to deceive the participants by pretending to share their beliefs?

(See Festinger et al. 1956; Riecken 1956; Erikson 1967; Bok 1978.)

---

[7]For references, see Traianou and Hammersley (2011).

SPRINGDALE

This was a study of a small town in upstate New York in the 1950s. It emerged out of a larger investigation published independently. It was specifically intended to counter the 'positive', 'bland' account of the town portrayed by the main study, focusing instead on conflicts within the community and on the power of some key community members. Some issues:

1 What are the responsibilities of individual researchers where they participate in larger teams and projects?
2 What constraints, if any, should operate on how researchers portray individuals, communities, or organisations that they have studied; particularly when some of these are easily identifiable?

(See Vidich and Bensman 1958 and 1964; Bell and Bronfenbrenner 1959; Becker 1964b.)

COVERT RESEARCH ON ALCOHOLICS ANONYMOUS

Lofland and Lejeune (1960) recruited graduate students to attend open meetings of Alcoholics Anonymous (AA), these students being required to present themselves as alcoholics, and to behave in ways that supported this impression; as well as dressing in different styles in order to assess variation in initial acceptance according to social class. Some issues:

1 How far is covert observation in 'open' meetings, and deception of members of this type of organisation, ethically acceptable?
2 Did Lofland and Lejeune ask their graduate students to behave in an unethical way?
3 Was this research also unacceptable because it could result in Alcoholics Anonymous and other organisations becoming wary of sociological researchers and refusing to cooperate with future research?

(See Davis 1961; Lofland 1961; Lofland and Lofland 1969: 299–301; Erikson 1967; Denzin 1968.)

TEAROOM TRADE

Laud Humphreys carried out a covert study of male homosexual encounters in public restrooms/ lavatories ('tearooms') in the US, acting as a look-out for the men. He later traced them to their homes and interviewed them without disclosing that he had observed them. Some issues:

1 Covert observation of very private, and illegal, behaviour, albeit in a 'public' place.
2 Illegal obtaining of addresses from car number plates.
3 Putting participants at risk of legal prosecution through contacting them.

(See Humphreys 1975 – this includes the original study, some critical articles, and Humphreys' response; see also Nardi 1999; Galliher et al. 2004; Horowitz 2004.)

(Continued)

(Continued)

RESEARCHING OLD-TIME PENTECOSTAL RELIGIOUS GROUPS

As part of his research in the sociology of religion, Homan spent 18 months as a regular worshipper in a Pentecostal community. He adopted a covert strategy on the grounds that the community would have been unlikely to agree to his carrying out research, and if they had known of his research their behaviour would have been significantly altered in his presence. Some issues:

1   Was a covert strategy essential in this case?
2   Given the methods employed, should his article have been published in a reputable sociology journal?

(See Homan 1978, 1980a, 1980b; Barbour 1979; Dingwall 1980; Bulmer 1982.)

SEXUAL RELATIONS WITH PARTICIPANTS

Goode carried out research on the National Association for the Advancement of Fat Americans (NAAFA). In gaining access to the organisation it was made clear to him that his participation should be as a 'fat admirer' not primarily as a researcher, and therefore that he must be prepared to date women within the organisation. During the course of his research he had sexual relations with some of the women, including one who had his child. Some issues:

1   What conditions of entry should and should not be accepted in negotiations with gatekeepers?
2   Are sexual relations between researcher and researched ever legitimate? And, if so, under what conditions?

(See Goode 1999, 2002; Hopper 1999; Bell 2002; Manning 2002; Saguy 2002; C. Williams 2002; and Zussman 2002.)

IRE IN IRELAND

Scheper-Hughes studied social relations in a village in rural Ireland, arguing that these generated mental illness on the part of some family members. Following publication of the book, a journalist was able to identify the village and subsequently published articles in the *Irish Times*. When Scheper-Hughes returned to the village twenty years later in order to collect data for a second edition she was received with hostility and was quickly forced to leave. Some issues:

1   Do researchers have a responsibility to produce an account that is appealing, or at least acceptable, to those whose behaviour they describe?
2   How far does the responsibility of the researcher extend when anonymisation procedures fail to protect participants' privacy?

(See Scheper-Hughes 1979, 2000a.)

THE EL DORADO SCANDAL

This was prompted in 2000, when an investigative journalist (Tierney) published a book that included criticism of a very well-known US anthropologist (Chagnon) for behaving unethically in relation to the Yanomamö people in Brazil, whom he had studied over a long period of time. Central was the charge that he did not do all that he could have done to deal with a measles epidemic that killed large numbers of Yanomamö. But it was also claimed that, on his own account, Chagnon had violated some of the principles of the American Anthropological Association ethics code, and that his work had been used against the interests of the Yanomamö by Brazilian mining companies. Some issues:

1 What level of responsibility do researchers have for intervening to counter the effects of local catastrophes?
2 Does the distribution of money or goods to participants by researchers itself cause harm, for example generating conflict?
3 What counts as the 'staging' or 'fabrication' of data?
4 Is it legitimate for researchers to use deceitful means to obtain information, in this case about names and genealogy, that are matters which participants regard as private or secret?
5 What responsibility do researchers have for how their work is used by others?

(See Tierney 2001; Geertz 2001; Pels 2005; Hill n.d.; Fluehr-Lobban 2003a; Borofsky 2005.)

SCANDALOUS STORIES AND DANGEROUS LIAISONS

Sikes carried out an in-depth qualitative study about consensual romantic and sexual relationships between male teachers and women (over the legal age of consent) who had been their students. Her research findings challenged stereotypical views that such relationships always involve the abuse of power. In 2005 Sikes agreed to give a pre-publication copy of her article to a journalist who was writing a report on the topic. As a result, her research was misreported and misrepresented in the wider press as promoting sexual relationships between teachers and students. Some issues:

1 The right of the researcher to study 'sensitive' or 'taboo' topics.
2 What are the responsibilities of researchers as regards the dissemination of their findings via the mass media?

(See Sikes 2006a, 2006b, 2008, 2010; Sikes and Piper 2010.)

Besides debates around particular studies, increasing attention to research ethics has also been generated in recent years by the proliferation of sharply discrepant approaches to qualitative research. There are now deep divisions within the research community, relating not just to the means to be employed, but also to what is seen as the goal of and rationale for qualitative research.

In debates about quantitative versus qualitative approaches, one sort of criticism made of quantitative work concerned ethics. It was argued that it tends to force people's responses into categories determined by researchers, thereby reducing them to objects that can be counted and represented as statistics, rather than portraying them as persons and agents (see, for example, Mills 1959: Ch. 5). These features were seen as closely associated with the practical functions served by quantitative research, notably in being used by governments and big business to control and manipulate employees, citizens, and consumers.

However, with the rise in influence of qualitative work, and its fragmentation into competing approaches, ethical criticisms came to be directed at some forms of this work as well. For instance, the involvement of early anthropological ethnography in the operation of European colonialism was highlighted, with the suggestion that it continues to serve as an arm of neo-colonialism (Asad 1973). Furthermore, there was the claim that qualitative research is, if anything, even more capable of intruding into people's private lives than quantitative work. Through participant observation, researchers can gain direct access to people's lives, observing what they say and do at firsthand, which has sometimes been denounced as surveillance (Nicolaus 1968; see also Barnes 1979: 22) or voyeurism (Denzin 1992). Similarly, open-ended interviewing was criticised, notably by feminists, on the grounds that it could encourage people to disclose aspects of their past and of their experience that they might wish to keep private, as a result of false rapport strategically developed by interviewers (Finch 1984). More fundamentally, the asymmetrical roles played in the research process by researchers in relation to those they are researching came to be challenged as constituting a 'hierarchical' relationship that involves the exercise of power, and that is fundamentally exploitative in character (Stacey 1988).

Besides these charges, there were also criticisms that much qualitative research is politically trivial, in the sense that it has little or no impact in changing the world and therefore is of little or no value. For example, at the height of the Vietnam War, when radicals were challenging their profession to take a stand against it, Gjessing (1968: 397) suggested that unless the whole direction of anthropological inquiry were changed anthropologists would be 'playing an intellectual game in which nobody outside our own tiny circle is interested'.

In order to remedy these defects, it was insisted by many that qualitative research must be aimed directly at emancipation, in other words at challenging oppression, social inequalities, or human rights abuses. Thus, over the course of the 1970s and 1980s there were calls for a 'liberation anthropology' (Huizer and Mannheim 1979) and for qualitative inquiry to 'become critical' (see Hymes 1972). Sometimes it was argued that what is required is a form of participatory action research (Hall et al. 1982), one which recognises the agency of those who need political support in overturning the status quo. Not surprisingly, these criticisms and proposals were often formulated in ethical terms.

Later, these differences in attitude about the methods and goals of social research, and about what counts as ethical research practice, deepened and diversified. For example, some feminists criticised mainstream social research for its commitment to abstract ethical principles, proposing instead an ethics of care that gives central concern to the *interdependence* of human beings and their responsibilities to each other; for adopting Western conceptions of the subject; and/or for maintaining a distinction between researchers and researched that reinforces power differences, and thereby undermines the production of 'authentic' data (Mauthner et al. 2002). Within disability studies, there was growing resistance to research by non-disabled researchers (Oliver 1992; Barnes 2009), just as under the influence of anti-racism there were challenges to whites studying blacks. Similarly, in the field of childhood studies, which emerged in the 1980s, there has been an insistence that research must be designed to secure children's rights, that it must represent their voices, and, increasingly, that children should themselves carry out research (Alderson 2000; Kellett 2010). Parallel developments have also taken place in relation to research on 'indigenous communities' (see Smith 1999; Denzin et al. 2008; Chilisa 2009).

While these developments have been strongly shaped by socio-political changes, and 'new social movements' like feminism and disability activism, they have also been influenced by changes in ideas about the nature and value of social scientific research. Whereas qualitative researchers in the 1960s and 1970s generally insisted on the scientific character of their work, from the 1980s onwards many began to distance themselves from this model, looking more towards the Humanities and Arts. In part this reflected wider cultural challenges to the status and character of science, and also attacks upon Enlightenment thinking, inspired by Critical Theory and post-structuralism. Indeed, it came to be argued that this legitimates oppression and disguises Western interests behind a veil of objectivity and universalism (see, for example, Clifford and Marcus 1986).

In important respects, these developments transformed research ethics and gave it heightened relevance. Indeed, for some it moved centre-stage. For example, Caplan (2003: 3) has argued that 'the ethics of anthropology [...] goes to the heart of the discipline: the premises on which its practitioners operate, its epistemology, theory and praxis'. In other words, it is concerned with '*What* is anthropology for? *Who* is it for?' Many qualitative researchers outside of anthropology would concur that what is at issue here is the whole rationale for and orientation of qualitative inquiry (see Denzin and Lincoln 2011).

AN OUTLINE OF THE CHAPTERS

We argue in this book that there needs to be careful attention paid to the meaning of the terms used in talking and writing about research ethics, and this begins with the words 'ethics' and 'ethical' themselves. In Chapter 1 we look at ambiguities in these, and at their relations with other relevant, and equally problematic, concepts, such as 'morality' and 'politics'. We also examine some of the different kinds of argument that are employed in thinking about ethical matters, drawing on the philosophical literature.

Chapter 2 proposes that research ethics is a form of occupational ethics, and explores the implications of this. The most important one is that a distinction needs to be made between those intrinsic values that constitute the goal of research, or derive from this, and extrinsic values, for example about how the people studied should be treated. We insist that the only operational goal of research can be the production of knowledge, that this is what distinguishes it from other activities. Of course, there are many reasons why we might believe that producing knowledge is important, and why we should devote ourselves to this task, but these do not themselves constitute the goal of research. So, knowledge as justified true belief is the goal, and the primary value guiding research is truth: every effort must be made to try to ensure that the knowledge claims produced are justified. In this chapter we explore the implications of this, outlining several virtues that qualitative researchers must exercise. Towards the end we outline some of the key extrinsic values that should operate as a constraint on research, these being the focus for subsequent chapters.

Chapter 3 is concerned with a value that has been central to most discussions of research ethics: the minimisation of harm. We argue that identifying what constitutes harm is by no means entirely straightforward, and we highlight the different kinds of harm that have been given attention, exploring how there can be significant variations in degree and likelihood of harm, and how these can be assessed. Against this background, we suggest that there is the potential for causing harm, as well as for producing benefits, in all research, so that what can reasonably be expected of researchers is only that they try to avoid serious harm. The danger of this varies, of course, across different forms of qualitative research, and we explore this by considering the case of research with children that employs visual data. One of the problems is that research rarely if ever causes harm on its own; other factors in the situation will also play a role, and there can be reasonable uncertainty about what caused what and about where responsibility lies, as well as attempts to displace blame on to others. Moreover, researchers are usually faced with the task of assessing the risk of harm prospectively, an even more uncertain business. Finally, we consider the range of people who could be harmed by research, including researchers themselves.

In the next chapter we examine the principle of respect for the autonomy or freedom of the people studied. Autonomy is a central value in Western societies and in other societies too, and we explore some of the complexities surrounding it. This value underpins what is the main procedural requirement often believed to be central to research ethics: informed consent. We consider when consent is required, from whom, and for what; as well as the question of whether consent can ever be unconstrained, and what this might mean. In addition, being informed is usually seen as essential for autonomy, but there are issues to do with what information can and should be provided about qualitative research projects, especially at their start; about what being informed amounts to; and about what is possible in this respect, given the constraints under which qualitative inquiry is typically carried out.

Another value commonly given a central place in discussions of research ethics is privacy, and this is the topic of Chapter 5. It is often argued that researchers must not intrude into the private sphere of the people they are studying, or that they should minimise such intrusion. Privacy is, of course, a general issue in society, but it is one that is subject to conflicting pressures, with growing trends towards making the private public, and demands for 'transparency'. Furthermore, there is uncertainty surrounding which settings or parts of settings are public and which are private, and what this means. Another aspect of privacy concerns the control of information, some of which may be treated as sacred or personal. The issues involved here are present in all qualitative inquiry, but they take on distinctive features in online research, and we explore this as an example. We also look at the strategies that qualitative researchers employ to maintain confidentiality, including anonymisation of people and places in data records and publications, and at some of the debates surrounding this.

The three extrinsic value principles to which we have devoted chapters in this book by no means exhaust those that researchers take into account in doing their work, or that could be relevant in evaluating research proposals or assessing completed studies. Other values mentioned in the literature include trust, reciprocity, and equity. While we do not have the space to discuss these principles in our book, we believe that the sort of approach we have adopted in Chapters 3, 4, and 5 applies to them too.[8]

In the Conclusion we summarise our arguments and draw them together, contrasting them with currently influential views about research ethics and about the character and purpose of social research. In particular, we challenge what we see as the moralism that informs much discussion of research ethics by qualitative researchers today, and that underpins the spread of ethical regulation.

---

[8]Trustworthiness is a very widely valued personal attribute, and is of considerable significance in many of the contexts in which qualitative researchers carry out their work, especially given that the researcher often enters as a stranger. By 'reciprocity' we mean the idea that participants ought to be rewarded for any costs the research imposes upon them. Relevant here would be arguments about the exploitative character of research (see Hammersley and Atkinson 2007: Ch. 10), and debates about whether or not there should be financial remuneration for participants (see McKeganey 2001; Sanders 2006: 210). By 'equity', we mean the extent to which researchers treat different people in the field in an equivalent way. Further extrinsic values include integrity (Macfarlane 2009) and authenticity (Guignon 2004).

1

WHAT IS ETHICS?

Much thought and discussion about social research ethics takes for granted that we already know what the word 'ethics' means. Yet, while most people will have a general idea of its meaning, there is no single agreed sense given to the term, either in everyday conversation or in more specialised usage. In this chapter we will examine some of the ambiguities and complexities surrounding the words 'ethics' and 'ethical', and their relations with associated terms like 'morality' and 'politics'. We will also consider the range of considerations that people take into account when making ethical judgments, and some of the main philosophical views about ethics.

THE MEANING OF 'ETHICS' AND 'ETHICAL'

'Is it ethical?', or (perhaps more commonly) 'Is it *un*ethical?', is a question that can always be asked about both research proposals and actual pieces of research, as well as about the use of particular methods, the publication of particular findings, or even about the adoption of particular theoretical perspectives or the study of particular topics. But we need to consider what this question means, and what weight it should be given in various circumstances, as well as how to answer it.

The word 'ethics' can have at least two meanings. It can refer to:

A field of study, concerned with investigating what is good or right and how we should determine this. On this interpretation, 'social research ethics' means *the study of* what researchers ought and ought not to do, and how this should be decided.

Alternatively, 'ethics' or 'ethic' can mean:

A set of principles that embody or exemplify what is good or right, or allow us to identify what is bad or wrong. These principles may be general in character, relate to some particular domain (for example, medical ethics or media ethics), or come from some particular perspective (for example, liberal, Muslim, or Christian ethics). In these terms, the phrase 'social research ethics' means 'the set of ethical principles that should be taken into account when doing social research' or 'the set of ethical principles held by social researchers'.

A similar, and perhaps even more confusing, ambiguity surrounds the adjective 'ethical'. This can refer to:

The realm of considerations relevant to determining what is good or bad, right or wrong. Here, the contrast is with *non-ethical* matters, for example those concerned with what would be efficient, effective, prudent, expedient, conventional, or good etiquette.

Alternatively, 'ethical' can mean:

What is good or right, as contrasted with the *unethical* – what is bad or wrong.

So, if it is said that something is ethical, we need to be clear whether what is meant is that it is an ethical issue or that it is good or right. Allowing funders to decide whether or not the results of a study will be published might be judged an ethical issue, but at the same time we could reasonably conclude that this practice is unethical, in the sense of being wrong. It is also important to emphasise that to act primarily on non-ethical grounds in some situation is not necessarily unethical, in the sense of being wrong.

Bringing these various meanings of 'ethics' and 'ethical' together, we can say that our discussion in this book falls into the field of ethics, as an area of study, that it will be concerned with the relationship between ethical and non-ethical aspects of research, and that it will examine how we should judge what is ethical and unethical, in the sense of what is good/bad or right/wrong in research contexts, thereby offering a research ethics, in the sense of some core principles along with ideas about how these relate to the practice of research.

There are some other terms that are closely related in meaning to 'ethics' and 'ethical', and that therefore need to be mentioned here. One of these is 'morality'. This is often used as a synonym for 'ethics', where that term refers to a set of principles. Similarly, 'moral' can be used as a substitute for 'ethical', in both of the senses we outlined above. However, some writers draw a sharp distinction between the two sets of terms, albeit doing this in different and even conflicting ways. For example, Reynolds (1979: ix) formulates his discussion of social research ethics in terms of 'moral dilemmas' facing researchers precisely because he wants to emphasise that they should not be preoccupied with applying ethical codes.[1] Homan, on the other hand, distinguishes between ethics as specifically relating to research, treating 'morality' as having a broader reference to ideas about what people in general ought and ought not to do. Meanwhile, the philosopher Bernard Williams rejects what he refers to as 'the morality system', which he conceives as having its central focus on obligations. In place of

---

[1]Though in the title to his book he uses the phrase 'ethical dilemmas'.

this he adopts a broader conception of the ethical sphere that recognises a variety of concepts and considerations, a diverse landscape as opposed to the flattened out one that he believes the notion of morality portrays. So, he is against morality but insists on the importance of ethics (see Williams 1985: Ch. 10; Louden 2007).[2]

Given this background of diverse usage and confusion, in our discussion here we will not make any distinction between these two sets of words, treating them for the most part as synonyms. While we will draw on Williams's work in questioning moralism, for our purposes the ideas and practices to which this term refers could just as well be labelled 'ethicism' (Hammersley 1999). And, while we will take a similar line to Reynolds in recognising the necessary role of judgment in research decisions, we will often refer to any dilemmas involved as ethical.

Also of importance is the relationship between ethics and politics. Some have insisted on the priority of politics, since they regard separate treatment of research ethics as indicating an undesirable 'bifurcation of values' (Whitt 1999). Others have sought to draw a clear line between ethics and politics, requiring that social scientists should *not* be engaged in politics, but that their work *should* be guided by ethical considerations. However, the word 'politics' suffers from its own problems of ambiguity. In narrow terms it can be used to refer to the struggle among parties to achieve power within an organisation of some kind, or within a nation-state. However, it is often employed in a much more general way, as in the well-known feminist slogan 'the personal is political'. On this usage, it is difficult to identify what would *not* be a political matter. A broad interpretation of the term is also involved in the notion of 'micropolitics', which refers to the kinds of conflict, persuasion, negotiation, and coercion that occur within almost all forms of social interaction and all institutional contexts.

While research might not be political in narrow terms — though it can get caught up in battles among political parties and interest groups, and researchers may face decisions about whether or not to obey the law of a particular nation-state or local authority — it is inevitably political in the broader senses. Yet even here there are further distinctions that need to be drawn. It is quite possible to argue that research is unavoidably political in important respects but is not, or should not be, political in others. For example, it can be argued that research is inevitably political in that its focus will be motivated by value-commitments of some kind, that it depends on the acquisition and deployment of scarce public resources, and involves negotiations with gatekeepers and people in the field. Furthermore, the publication of the findings may have consequences for the interests of various people, groups, and institutions. But even those who accept all this can still reasonably insist that research should *not* be political in the sense of pursuing any immediate goal beyond the production of value-relevant knowledge (Hammersley 1995). This is an issue that we will examine in the next chapter. Here, we simply note the ways in which different interpretations of the words 'ethics' and 'ethical' may overlap with, or set up a contrast to, various

---

[2]An older philosophical critique of 'the moral point of view' is to be found in Hegel; see Walsh (1969: Chs 5 and 6) and Wood (1990: Ch. 12 and *passim*). Further highlighting the diversity of viewpoint, Caputo (1993: ix) claims to follow Kierkegaard and Derrida in rejecting ethics in favour of obligation.

interpretations of 'politics' and 'political'. As a result, considerable care is required in handling all these terms.

These semantic ambiguities do not exhaust the uncertainties surrounding the notion of ethics and what is ethical/unethical. This is because there are a variety of ways in which we can seek to determine what is good or right, and these by no means always produce the same conclusions in particular cases.

DIFFERENT WAYS OF DETERMINING WHAT IS GOOD OR RIGHT

We need to begin by noting that, when considered outside of specific contexts, the words 'good' and 'right' are very abstract or 'thin' in meaning, they mean little more than 'should be approved of'. In other words, when we use them to describe some specific course of action, person, or situation, much of their meaning derives from the particular context. What it is about the objects concerned that should be approved of, and why, it is not conveyed by these words themselves.[3]

We need to take a step back here in order to recognise that ethical judgments are just one sort of evaluation. Making evaluations is central to all aspects of human life – we are continually engaged in judging things, including ourselves and other people. Furthermore, our evaluations can vary in several important respects; notably according to *what sort of thing* is being evaluated (for example, persons, courses of action, outcomes, institutions, cultures, societies, etc.), and in terms of *what standard* (for instance, in the case of actions this may be according to what is needed, what is pleasurable, what is fair, what is courageous, etc.). Furthermore, in applying a standard we can use a variety of benchmarks: in particular, we might judge something in relation to a required threshold, or alternatively assess it comparatively in relation to alternatives or competitors. For instance, we could describe a piece of research as 'too theoretical' (which implies a threshold) or as 'more reliable than other studies in the field' (a comparative evaluation). Similarly, when it is insisted that researchers should abide by 'high ethical standards', as is quite common, what is probably implied is some threshold, one that is presumably considerably above that which is adequate or satisfactory. By contrast, when it is suggested that researchers should adopt the 'highest standards' it may be that a comparative evaluation is involved: that researchers are required to be 'more ethical' than other people.

Some of the standards that we use in evaluating things are taken to be ethical in character (in other words, ethical rather than non-ethical), while others would not generally be given this label. And this may vary depending upon whether we are evaluating an action, a person, or an institution. It is common for people to contrast ethical considerations with matters of etiquette or convention, or with an interest in the efficiency with which some goal has been pursued, as we did earlier. However,

---

[3]The terms 'good' and 'right' are also sometimes given distinctive meanings, for example with the former being used to refer to states of affairs and the latter more commonly applied to actions. 'Right' is also sometimes used specifically to refer to what should be done irrespective of the consequences, whereas 'good' may be taken to refer to the results of an action (see Ross 1930).

on different occasions these contrasts may pick out rather different features of the ethical, and in fact in common usage we tend to employ multiple overlapping contrasts to distinguish the ethical from the unethical. Here are some of the main ones:

1   To do with what is of ultimate value rather than what is only of instrumental value.
2   Concern for the interests, feelings, or rights of others versus following self-interest.
3   Consistently observing principles or rules rather than acting in the most expedient way in the circumstances.
4   Concern with 'higher values', such as self-realisation, the common good, or the interests of science, rather than other considerations, such as financial return or social status.
5   Acting from duty versus responding to desire or inclination.
6   Behaving thoughtfully as against impulsively.

Generally speaking, the first option in each of these contrasts is more likely to be treated as ethical, in the sense of being good or right, than the second. However, it should be fairly obvious that while these various notions of what would be an ethical orientation overlap, they by no means match one another perfectly. For example, in an emergency situation we might put the interests of others before our own interests without thinking about it. This would be ethical in terms of the second criterion but unethical according to the last one, and perhaps others too. Similarly, there are people who insist that one's first duty is to follow self-interest because if everyone does this the best of all possible worlds will result, for example because of the 'invisible hand' of the market. While this would be unethical in terms of the second criterion, it could be regarded as ethical in terms of at least some of the others, depending upon exactly how these are interpreted. We might also act in the interests of others in a desire to please them, rather than from duty or on the basis of principle. Here, we would meet the second criterion but not the third, fourth, and fifth.

So, we can expect that people will make ethical judgments about actions, and will expect others to do this, in a variety of ways. At a rather higher level of abstraction than the list of contrasts we have just discussed, it is possible to identify two widely influential types of ethical argument. First, judgment may be made in terms of the extent to which an actual or proposed course of action conforms to relevant rules and expectations about what type of act is required given the type of situation; for example, that if a promise has been made it should be kept. The other mode of ethical judgment involves assessing actions according to whether the intended, the likely, or the actual *outcomes* are judged to be good (in terms of some standard). In these terms, people are not only expected to have good intentions, in the sense of aiming for good outcomes, but also to be aware of the likely consequences of particular actions, and to take precautions so as to avoid or minimise negative results: in short, they can be held to account for negligence, for causing a negative outcome that they could have anticipated and avoided.

Two of the most influential views about ethics in Western philosophy differ precisely in the priority they give to these two types of judgment. Deontological views insist that intentions must be evaluated in terms of conformity to general rules about right action, whereas consequentialist positions require that actions be assessed in terms of the desirability of outcomes. Each of these philosophical views has a long history, though their most fully developed versions emerged in the nineteenth century. We will outline them briefly here, before looking at some other philosophical views about ethics, particularly those that became influential during the twentieth century.

Deontology

Strictly speaking, 'deontology' means 'the study of duty' (from the Greek words for 'duty' and 'science', 'deon' and 'logos'). So, deontological arguments focus on whether or not an action – proposed or performed – corresponds to some command or general rule that an agent has a duty to obey. However, both the content and the source of the duty can vary considerably, so it is by no means the case that all of those advocating a deontological approach to ethics will agree about what would be ethical or unethical action in any particular situation.

In most societies there are rules of one sort or another that specify duties. Many of these will be prohibitive – ruling out certain types of action as illegal or immoral – while others will be prescriptive, indicating what *ought to be* done in a particular type of situation. There may also be some that are permissive in character, concerned with what is allowed under given circumstances. The first two types are the most common. Thus, the Decalogue, or Ten Commandments or Sayings – central to Judaism, Christianity, and Islam – consists of prohibitive and prescriptive commands, for example 'thou shalt not kill' and 'honour thy father and mother', respectively.

However, the rules underpinning deontological ethics are not necessarily religious in character; they may instead be laws enacted by a secular state, 'laws of nature' (d'Entrèves 1994; Oderberg and Chappell 2004), or they may just be the customary morality within a society, group, or locality. Moreover, while in some communities there may be little room for discretion on the part of ordinary individuals in making ethical judgments, in many modern societies there are diverse sources of rules that have to be negotiated, and there may also be considerable scope for individuals to interpret these rules for themselves; in religious terms, the emphasis may be upon the exercise of individual conscience rather than on 'obeying the law'.

The most influential philosophical version of deontology since the Enlightenment, that of Immanuel Kant, requires each individual to derive her or his duties from Reason; more specifically, these are to be determined by a process of rational deliberation using a principle that (Kant claims) any rational agent would adopt *simply by virtue of being a rational agent*. This principle is universalisability: 'act only on that maxim through which you can at the same time will that it should become a universal law' (Kant 1785: II 421; Paton 1948: 84). In other words, maxims for action must not be accepted if they apply only to a particular agent at a particular point in time; they must be justifiable as obligatory for any agent facing a situation of the same general kind. Kant labels the sort of injunction that results from this principle a 'categorical imperative', by contrast with 'hypothetical' or instrumental imperatives, which take the form 'if you will this goal, then you must will these means'. The notion of a categorical imperative necessitates that something be treated as of absolute or intrinsic value, and for Kant this can only be human beings. He therefore concludes that we should never treat people simply as means to achieving our goals, but also always as ends in themselves (see Caygill 1995: 99–102).

To a considerable degree, the sorts of more specific duties that Kant derives from the analysis of Reason are similar to those laid down by other sources. As well as ruling out murder, they include, for example, that one must never lie to or deceive other people. For Kant, given that these are *categorical* imperatives, not obeying them is *always* wrong. He writes: 'By a lie a man throws away and, as it were, annihilates his dignity as a man. A man who himself does not believe what he tells another ... has even less worth than if he were a mere thing' (MdSVI 428). It is characteristic of Kant that what is involved here is portrayed as a betrayal of Reason, this being precisely the feature of human beings that distinguishes them from animals and makes them of absolute value.

In summary, for Kant duties are to be identified by individuals, who derive them rationally from *a priori* principles; in other words, principles that can be shown to be true independently of (prior to) any knowledge we have of the world, for example about what sorts of consequence will follow from a particular type of action. Given their character, these are ethical rules that any rational person would and should adopt, and must therefore treat as specifying duties.

While, as we saw, etymologically, 'deontology' refers to duties, in broader terms it also covers rights. On some interpretations, these are simply two sides of the same coin: one person's rights are another's obligations, in the sense that if a person has a particular right then others have an obligation to respect that right (Pinkard 1982: 264; Faden and Beauchamp 1986: 6–7). However, in Western societies the notion of rights has gradually come to be given greater emphasis than duties, from the days of Thomas Paine's *Rights of Man* (1791), through Mary Wollstonecraft's corrective in her *Vindication of the Rights of Woman* (1792), to the United Nations Universal Declaration of Human Rights (1948), or the more recent Convention on the Rights of the Child (1990).[4]

The research ethics codes that we discussed in the Introduction often seek to lay down duties for researchers, and these frequently relate to respecting the rights of the people they are studying. As such, they have a deontological character. However, the codes also often require researchers to assess likely harm, and perhaps also the benefits, that might result from any course of action proposed or adopted. This points to a very different philosophical view of ethics.

Consequentialism

In its simplest form, consequentialism involves a radical rejection of all forms of deontology. Rather than being guided by general rules specifying duties and rights, actions must be judged, prospectively, in terms of how well designed they are to produce good outcomes, and, retrospectively, according to whether or not they actually produced such outcomes.

---

[4]For a useful discussion of the concept of right and of the various arguments surrounding it, see Waldron (1984).

So, from the consequentialist point of view we should decide what to do in a particular situation on the basis of what will produce the best outcome, on balance. Of course, this leaves open the question of how we are to judge the goodness or badness of consequences. In principle, the criterion could be whether they serve our own interests or those of some community or organisation to which we belong. However, many people would not regard this criterion as ethical in character, but rather as non-ethical or even unethical. Instead, it is usually argued that the desirability of consequences must be judged in terms of what is best for people in general, or for all of those who might be affected by the action.

This is certainly the assumption behind the most influential consequentialist position in philosophy: utilitarianism. Jeremy Bentham, who first elaborated this view, argued that in acting we should seek to maximise 'the greatest happiness of the greatest number', or more broadly what he called 'utility' (Bentham 1789 [1907]). He assumed that we can calculate the balance of utility between positive and negative consequences, so as to be able to assess which course of action would be the best overall in its consequences, in the sense of maximising the amount of good in the world and/or minimising harm. A similar approach, cost–benefit analysis, has been institutionalised within economics, and applied to many policy decisions (Layard and Glaister 1994; Adler and Posner 2001).[5] Here, as the name implies, the costs and benefits of some proposed course of action are to be calculated and weighed against one another, in order to determine whether or not the proposal, for example building a new airport in a particular location, should go ahead. Various difficulties as regards conceptualising the nature of utility – whether it should take the form of happiness, welfare, well-being, or benefit of specific kinds, and also whether it is unitary or plural – have been raised, and there are also challenging measurement problems involved.

Bentham's main focus was on legislators formulating laws and policies, rather than on the decisions of individuals, and this shows that consequentialists need not be against the idea that ethical behaviour requires conformity to rules. What is crucial is that these rules must be based on sound judgments about what will generally produce desirable outcomes, rather than being determined by what is right 'in itself'. In other words, they should be determined by empirical evidence, not a priori argument, whose validity Bentham rejected; indeed, he famously dismissed the notion of natural rights as 'nonsense-on-stilts'.[6]

A distinction has often been drawn between two kinds of utilitarianism: act-utilitarianism, where the costs and benefits of each possible course of action must be weighed up in each case before a decision is made about what to do; and rule-utilitarianism, which requires us to act according to whatever *general rule* would usually produce the greatest utility for the greatest number. Where the former seems to exclude any following of general substantive rules about what ought and ought not to be done, in favour of decisions that calculate the relevant costs and benefits in relation to the situation concerned, the latter emphasises the importance of following

---

[5]For a discussion of cost–benefit analysis in relation to research ethics, see Diener and Crandall (1978: 24–6).

[6]For a history of natural rights theories, see Tuck (1979).

rules, *albeit of the right kind*. Furthermore, these provide guidance, rather than being absolute obligations in the manner of Kant.

Another important area of difference among consequentialists concerns whether there is just one kind of good that is to be maximised or harm to be minimised, or whether there are different sorts of good and harm that can be evaluated differentially, these perhaps even being incommensurable. For Bentham, utility was the ultimate, single form of what is good/bad, and he regarded it as unitary and quantifiable. However, later developments in utilitarianism saw attempts to distinguish higher from lower forms of pleasure or happiness. Thus, John Stuart Mill famously denied Bentham's claim that 'prejudice apart, [...] pushpin [a children's game] is of equal value with the arts and sciences of literature and poetry' (Bentham 1830: 206; Mill 1859a: 389).[7] Other utilitarians, notably Sidgwick (1967), believed that there were multiple forms of good, or utility principles, that cannot be weighed against one another in any straightforward way. This brings utilitarianism into somewhat closer alignment with our intuitions as to what would be good or bad, acceptable and unacceptable, but it introduces considerable potential indeterminacy as regards what should be judged the best course of action, in general or in particular cases.

Situationism

A feature of many deontological and consequentialist positions has been the assumption, or aspiration, that conclusions about what ought or ought not to be done can be determined definitively, either through being derived *logically* from principles, or produced by means of *calculation*. In other words, the idea is that there must be a *procedure* by which a single, right conclusion can be produced, one about which there would or should be general agreement. The motivation behind this is a desire to eliminate or at least to minimise the role of *judgment* about what is good or bad, right or wrong; where judgment is seen as potentially involving error or uncertainty, as well as leading to disagreement. However, not only do deontology and consequentialism involve competing ideas about how this is to be done, but the project of reducing ethical judgment to processes of logical inference or calculation is now generally regarded as futile.

As we saw, some utilitarians recognised that there are incommensurable kinds of goodness; and, while Kant sought to identify a single set of harmonious duties, it is not hard to recognise that the duties people recognise may often conflict in practice, forcing them to sacrifice one for another, or at least to find some compromise amongst them. Furthermore, in our everyday lives, most of us draw upon *both* deontological and consequentialist considerations, and this too will be a source of conflicting imperatives, and therefore of uncertainty and disagreement in judgments. For example, imagine a situation where a researcher has promised an informant that what he says will remain confidential, but that in the course of the interview the informant indicates

---

[7]This continues to be a tension within current discussions of happiness and well-being; see Bailey (2009).

that he is going to commit a violent crime. Or consider the more complex case faced by Tourigny (1993:18) who, interviewing a woman with HIV/AIDS, discovers that she is working as a prostitute in order to support her children, and that most of the men she comes into contact with refuse to wear condoms. In all circumstances like these, a deontological approach might require the researcher to keep her promise and not disclose the information to others, but consequentialism could imply that she should break her word in order to ward off harm to others; though, in Tourigny's case, there are conflicting considerations – the woman asks 'you ain't gonna turn me in, are you?', and Tourigny comments 'If I did, who would care for her children, two of whom are HIV-positive?'. In general terms, consequentialism recommends that we only keep promises where the result of doing so would be beneficial, or at least that we should *not* keep promises where the outcome is likely to be undesirable. By contrast, many deontological positions insist that keeping promises is good in itself, so that we have an absolute duty to do this.

It has often been concluded from this that plurality and conflict among value implications is unavoidable (Larmore 1987, 1996; Gray 1995; Crowder 2002). This means that there will often be cases where a course of action is justified or even obligatory from one point of view but at the same time is still wrong in terms of some other value principle to which we are also committed, a situation that is often referred to as the 'problem of dirty hands' (Stocker 1990). In the example we used earlier, about an informant who discloses to a researcher a plan to commit violence, the researcher may well feel that her hands would be 'dirty' whichever decision she took.

It is important to stress that this does not necessarily mean that we are continually faced with excruciatingly hard choices, or with conflicting imperatives between which we find it impossible to decide, either in everyday life or in research. Much of the time, despite value plurality and conflict, we will be relatively confident in our judgments about what ought, or ought not, to be done; and other people will often agree with us. It is, nevertheless, important to recognise that there is always scope for dilemmas that are hard to resolve, and therefore for disagreement about what is good or bad, right or wrong, in particular situations.

Some philosophers have been so impressed with this that they have sought to understand ethics in a very different way from Kant and Bentham: instead of seeking some general principle or means by which what would be right or good can be determined, they have started instead from what they judge to be ethical or unethical in particular situations, assuming that these judgments will often be shared with others. Sometimes they have then attempted to move 'up' from these cases to more general principles that can summarise or systematise our ethical intuitions. An example from the middle of the twentieth century is David Ross. Using this approach, he identified six or seven 'prima facie' duties – including to bring about good, to avoid harm, to practise self-improvement, and to try to be just. Several of these principles were incorporated into one of the most influential attempts to clarify research ethics, the Belmont Report in the United States, though the subtleties of Ross's position were generally lost in how that Report was interpreted and the forms of regulation that resulted (Small 2001).

There is, however, a much older tradition of ethical thinking that emphasises case-by-case judgment, and often resists the attempt to derive general principles. This is called casuistry, and two of the contributors to the Belmont Report went on to explore it (Jonsen and Toulmin 1988; see also Miller 1996). There have been casuistical traditions in most of the major world religions at one time or another. Probably the most highly developed emerged within Western Christianity in the Middle Ages; and, while it suffered major decline from the seventeenth century onwards, it retains influence within the Roman Catholic Church even today. The initial stimulus for casuistry within the Church was the need for priests to hear confessions of sins and to determine what penances were appropriate. It was recognised from early on that the seriousness, and even the wrongness, of the same act, such as killing someone, could vary according to circumstances; for example, whether it was premeditated or done in the heat of the moment, whether it was carried out in self-defence or as aggression, whether it was motivated by a desire for personal gain or was done in support of an important ideal, and so on.

Underpinning this casuistical tradition was the idea that reasonable judgments can be made, despite the multifarious nature of cases, if proper attention is given to relevant similarities and differences among cases. In some contexts this seems to have degenerated into decisions being made via consultation of tracts summarising authoritative views about various types of act and circumstance. The other extreme, which eventually led to the discrediting of casuistry in many quarters, was the tendency to use the fact that there are conflicting arguments to justify whatever decision seemed expedient to the parties concerned. However, for the Jesuits, who perhaps unfairly bore the brunt of the criticism, the whole point was to use arguments about particular cases, as preserved in the casuist literature, to educate people in the kind of thinking that would be required to resolve future cases fairly, *not* to provide a simple means of deciding what is right by 'weighing' the views of different casuist authorities, even less to exploit conflicting arguments to serve personal interests.

A rather similar approach of more recent origin, also arising within the Christian tradition, was given the label 'situation ethics' or 'situationism' (Cunningham 1970). In his influential account, Fletcher (1966) presents this position as located between 'legalism', on the one hand, which is the view that moral judgments can be logically derived from some set of principles, and 'antinomianism', on the other, this implying that decisions can be no more than a matter of whim, of doing 'what comes naturally' in the specific situation, with no attention to general considerations. So, situationism does not ignore all principles, but at the same time it insists that rules cannot tell us conclusively what it is good or right to do in particular cases. Indeed, the principles recognised by situationists tend to be very abstract, and therefore require considerable interpretation if they are to be used. From Fletcher's religious point of view, ethical judgments must be guided by the requirement to love God and one's neighbours, and also by all the various more specific principles that have arisen within the Christian tradition. But his central point is that 'circumstances alter rules and principles', so that the key consideration is always the particular features of the situation faced. Fletcher specifically describes situationism as a form of casuistry, but insists that it is one that resists the idea that what to do can be read off from some 'book of cases' of the sort that was produced within the casuistic tradition.

A rather more radical position, but along the same lines, has been developed much more recently within academic philosophy, this time being given the label 'particularism'. According to Dancy, 'particularists think that moral judgment can get along perfectly well without any appeal to principles, and indeed that there is no essential link between being a full moral agent and having principles' (Dancy 2004: 1).[8] Dancy's argument is that in making ethical judgments we are often faced with a range of 'contributory reasons' on each side, and that the 'weight' and even the direction in which they point will vary depending upon the features of the situation concerned, rather than being fixed independently.

As this makes clear, one of the issues that arises in debates between casuists, situationists, or particularists and their opponents concerns exactly what the term 'principles' means (see Little 2000 and Nussbaum 2000). There is a tendency for these to be dismissed by situationists as always degenerating into purported absolute rules, so that any exception to them automatically undercuts their value. However, there are more subtle positions: principles may be seen as embodied in exemplary cases where what is the right decision is relatively straightforward, while most cases deviate from these paradigm cases, with the result that much of the time no principle can usually tell us *on its own* exactly what ought to be done, but principles *can* guide careful judgment by identifying what might count as relevant considerations.

Interestingly, a moderate form of situationism can be found even earlier than most of the casuistical religious traditions, in Aristotle's *Nichomachean Ethics* (1976).[9] He writes:

> Matters concerned with conduct and questions of what is good for us have no fixity, any more than matters of health. The general account being of this nature, the account of particular cases is yet more lacking in exactness, for they do not fall under any art or set of precepts, but the agents themselves must in each case consider what is appropriate to the occasion, as happens also in the art of medicine or of navigation. (II.2.1104A)

This view was part of a more general argument by Aristotle that there cannot be a science of human affairs, conceived on the model of geometry and physical science, whereby abstract, determinate conclusions can be reached by logical inference. Rather, this is a realm where understanding situations, and what would be appropriate action within them, depends upon a capacity, acquired through experience and reflection upon it, to identify what is relevant and to distinguish what is significantly similar and what is significantly different. In this way, and others, Aristotle combined a form of situationism with some other distinctive assumptions, resulting in a position that has come to be called 'virtue ethics'. This is a view that was revived in the twentieth century, and has had some influence on recent discussions of research ethics (Iphofen 2009: 4–5; Pring 2001; Macfarlane 2009).[10] By contrast, casuistry, situationism, and particularism have had little explicit impact on those discussions (for an exception, see Simons and Usher 2000).

---

[8]Particularism can take a variety of forms, but here we will focus for the sake of exposition on Dancy's radical particularism, perhaps its most influential version. See Hooker and Little (2000).

[9]However, there are those who challenge the idea that Aristotle can be appealed to in support of a particularist position, see Irwin (2000).

[10]The revival of virtue ethics is generally ascribed to the influence of Anscombe (1958); see also Foot (1978).

Virtue ethics

What distinguishes virtue ethics from the approaches previously discussed is that while the latter are primarily concerned with evaluating actions – whether in terms of intentions, consequences, or situations – virtue ethics focuses on evaluating *persons* (Crisp and Slote 1997; Slote 2000). As its name implies, it aims at identifying virtues that people should develop, and vices they should avoid. Indeed, the starting point for ancient virtue ethics was not the question of what actions are right or wrong, or even how to determine this, but rather what is the best form of life for a human being and how this can be achieved. And it is important to recognise that this was often linked both to a particular conception of society and to a view of the universe that ascribes a proper place and role to every type of thing that exists within it, including human beings. From this point of view, virtue amounts to serving the natural tendencies built into the world; though it was not assumed that these would automatically guide the behaviour of individual people – it was usually recognised that there is always much scope for deviation through ignorance and weakness of will.

Virtue ethics – like situationism and particularism – is in sharp conflict with those ethical views that see right action as deriving from obligatory compliance with general rules, or as involving the strict calculation of what it would be best to do. As we saw, Aristotle denied that what would and would not be an ethical course of action can be determined on the basis of any principle or set of principles; whether these relate to intentions or to consequences. Rather, deciding what to do in a particular case necessarily relies upon the *capacity* of the agent to recognise what needs to be taken into account *in the situation*, to give proper attention to the various considerations that are relevant, and (just as importantly) to have the *character* to act on this basis. In other words, what is crucial from this point of view is that the person concerned has developed the virtues necessary for making sound, situated judgments and for acting on them; and has avoided acquiring vices that might lead in the wrong directions.

Like the ancient Greeks more generally, Aristotle identified a range of virtues – including, justice, fortitude, courage, and temperance. Moreover, he regarded many of these virtues as representing a mean between contrasting vices. For instance, courage occupies a middle position between the excesses of timidity and recklessness. Macfarlane has applied this approach to research ethics, identifying multiple virtues – especially courage, respectfulness, resoluteness, sincerity, humility, and reflexivity – though he emphasises above all the ideal of integrity, which he defines as 'the integration of a person's true self and linking of their values and identity as a person with their practice as a researcher' (Macfarlane 2009: 45).

While virtue ethics has become quite influential in recent times, after a long period when it was neglected, it is important to recognise that the identification of virtues in ancient Greek thought took place against a social background that is very different from that which exists for most of us today. In particular, Aristotle was primarily concerned with what were virtues for men who were citizens of Athens, or for those who formed an equivalent political class in other societies; his account was *not* intended to apply to women, slaves, or children, for example. While the virtues and vices identified by him, and by subsequent influential authors in this tradition, such as Cicero (1991), have wide relevance, they do not take much explicit account of the differences in role that people play within societies. Instead, as with deontological and consequentialist views, a universalist image is presented but in this case one that assumes implicitly a particular identity and role on the part of the agent; one that in fact is *not* universally applicable but rather is specific to a particular type of past society.

Feminists, in particular, have highlighted such background assumptions in much ethical theory, and, given this, have sought to develop ethical ideas that take account of the distinctive position of women. They have argued that much modern ethical theory takes masculine experience as the norm, and thereby devalues women's interests and points of view. While not all feminist theorists have rejected the influential ethical theories we have discussed up to this point, since the 1980s many have been preoccupied with developing an approach that takes women's experiences as the starting point for ethical deliberation, often given the label 'the ethics of care'.[11] Where Aristotle focused on one particular sort of person – a man who was head of a household and who played his part in political decision-making – these feminists have taken a very different model as central: that of a mother caring for her children. This is one example of what have come to be characterised as relational conceptions of ethics.

Relational ethics

So, the ethics of care elaborates a moral perspective which is said to arise from women's distinctive experiences of nurturing and mothering (Gilligan 1982; Noddings 1984; Ruddick 1989; Held 1993). This involves a relationship that is characterised by asymmetrical dependence rather than mutual independence, and the concept of need, rather than right or even obligation, comes to prominence. Furthermore, supporters of care ethics often reject the notion of general moral principles or abstract rights, and insist that 'relations, not individuals, are ontologically basic' (Noddings 2003: xiii). Noddings claims that the caring attitude expresses both 'our earliest memories of being cared for' and also our subsequent 'growing store of memories of both caring and being cared for'. She claims that while, generally speaking, these experiences are more central for women than for men, the caring attitude can and should be central for men too (Noddings 1984: 5).

The ethics of care has been particularly influenced by the work of the psychologist Carol Gilligan, who argued that women tend to differ from men in the character of their ethical judgments, emphasising interpersonal relations rather than abstract notions like what action is right in its own terms, what will maximise utility, or what is socially just (Gilligan 1982). She claims that girls tend to see themselves as connected to others and to fear isolation and abandonment, whereas boys typically regard themselves as separated from others and fear connection and intimacy. In her research on how young girls and boys approach moral dilemmas, Gilligan found that

---

[11]It can be argued that, nevertheless, the ethics of care is a form of virtue ethics (see Crisp and Slote 1997; Slote 2000, 2007). What this illustrates is that the categories used here and elsewhere to distinguish different approaches to ethics are by no means hard and fast, even if they do provide useful orientation.

girls place values such as care, trust, attentiveness, and love for particular others above impersonal principles of equality, respect, rights and justice.

The ethics of care views what is involved in caring as a *process* that fosters the intellectual and emotional growth of those participating in it; especially, but not only, those who are most vulnerable (see Meagher and Parton 2004). So, care ethicists stress that we should make decisions about what would be right or wrong, good or bad, in ways that take account of our own relationship to the people who would be affected by the decision and their level of vulnerability. They insist not only that we feel different obligations to different people, but also that it is right to treat them differently on this basis, rather than adopting a universalistic orientation.

In a manner that is somewhat similar to virtue ethics, many advocates of the ethics of care treat caring as a *disposition*: they argue that moral subjects are expected to attend to others with emotional sensitivity, with compassion and empathy, with trust and intimacy. At the same time, there is an emphasis upon reciprocal relationships – on the contribution of the cared-for as much as that of the carer. A key concern is with the conditions that make it possible for caring relationships to flourish. Furthermore, like situationists, advocates of the ethics of care recognise that each moral decision takes place within a specific context.[12]

The ethics of care shares something in common with other relational forms of ethical thinking. Two influential examples here are the Jewish philosophers Martin Buber and Emmanuel Levinas. Both take as a starting point the immediate contact between one person and another. For example, Buber (1958) argued that the 'I' emerges through encountering other people, and that its character depends upon the quality of the relationship with the other. He distinguishes between two kinds of relationship, what he refers to as I–It and I–Thou relations. To act ethically is to treat the other as Thou rather than as It: this involves entering into a mutually affirming relation, in which each person becomes open to the other. Moreover, he sees this as simultaneously a relation with God, the 'eternal Thou'. When applied to people, the I–It relationship amounts to treating them solely as means to an end, rather than also as of value in or for themselves. Buber accepted that we cannot entirely avoid treating other people in an I–It manner but challenged what he saw as the tendency in the modern world for this sort of relationship to predominate. Furthermore, he insisted that the dialogic principle, the primacy of the I–Thou relationship, is not a philosophical conception but a reality beyond the reach of discursive language: it is a truth that can be discovered only directly in experience through our relations with others.[13]

For Levinas, too, the source of the ethical is the face-to-face relationship between two people, formulated as coming into contact with the Other. He sees this as placing an immediate demand upon us, namely the obligation to make ourselves available to

---

[12]The ethics of care has been given somewhat different formulations by different writers, and developed in various ways in response to criticism. In addition to the sources already cited, see, for example, Dancy (1992), Bowden (1997), Jaggar (2000), and Held (2006).

[13]In this respect, despite some agreement in substantive terms, his position is very different from that of Kant, who believed in the possibility and necessity of a rational demonstration of what is ethical and unethical. On Buber's ethics, see Schilpp and Friedman (1967).

the neediness (and especially the suffering) of other people. The experience of this, he suggests, breaks through all mediation: it is prior to all laws, rules, codes, or social roles. The emphasis here is on human vulnerability, by contrast with the Enlightenment picture, represented by both Kant and consequentialism, of humans as capable of taking control of their lives and their world.

In contrast to Buber, and closer to the ethics of care, Levinas stresses not reciprocity but the asymmetry of the fundamental moral relation: 'I see myself obligated with respect to the other; consequently I am infinitely more demanding of myself than of others' (Levinas, quoted in Putnam 2002: 39). For Levinas, to prioritise reciprocity would be to base ethics on similarity with the other person, rather than on difference and the infinite. The religious dimension of Levinas's thought is not hard to detect here. He writes: 'The dimension of the divine [or the infinite] opens forth from the human face' (Levinas 1999: 78). To some degree, as Putnam points out, Levinas is universalising Judaism, so that (at least in his philosophical writings addressed to gentiles) a conception of what is essential to humanity replaces the obligation attached to being a Jew, namely to look after all other Jews. Putnam (2002: 39) summarises Levinas's position here as: 'If you have to ask, "Why should I put myself out for him/her?", you are not yet human.'

A number of writers have sought to apply relational ethics of one sort or another, and especially the ethics of care, to thinking about social research ethics.[14] For example, Ellis (2007: 4) argues that a relational ethics recognises and values 'mutual respect, dignity, and connectedness between researcher and researched and between researchers and the communities in which they live and work' (see also Christians 2002 and Gunzenhauser 2006). This approach has been particularly influential where those being researched are judged to be vulnerable, for example children, or in contexts where the responsibility of caring is already prioritised, for instance in nursing research.

A more radical turn?

There are lines of philosophical thinking about ethics that are not primarily concerned with addressing the question of how we can and should decide what to do, what sort of person we should be, what kind of relationship we should have with others, and so on. Rather, they seek to explicate, or to put into question, one or another aspect of the whole character of current ethical thought.

One line of argument here arises from a major focus of attention in philosophical discussions of ethics in the twentieth century: whether ethical judgments can be true or false, and if so whether this indicates that they capture features of the objects (actions, people, or relationships) being evaluated that exist independently of ethical judgments about them. The battle lines here are sometimes described as lying between moral realism and moral expressivism, the latter being the view that ethical attributes (good, bad, right, wrong, harm, benefit, etc.) are simply expressions of our attitudes towards the

---

[14]There have been relatively few attempts to use the work of Buber and Levinas to think about research ethics, but see Miller (1996) and Usher (2000) respectively.

objects concerned (see Fisher and Kirchin 2006: Part 5). So, for expressivists, ethical judgments cannot be treated as true or false, any more than aesthetic ones can. According to this view, statements about what is and is not good, or right, do not tell us anything about the world, only about how someone feels about it or about some part of it (see Urmson 1968). In these terms, then, ethical judgments cannot but be irrational, or at least non-rational. There can be no reasonable deliberation about whether or not an ethical judgment is sound, nor can people come to reasoned agreement about what judgment to make. In its extreme form, this expressivist position leaves little scope for thought or discussion about any ethical issue, including those relating to research.[15]

There are also those who build on the central idea of situationism in ways that lead to doubts about the possibility of any ethical theory (Leiter 2001): some claim that the situations we face always potentially exceed the terms of any principles we have, in a way that challenges not just the role of ethical principles but that of any general ethical thought. This has been labelled, somewhat misleadingly, 'anti-theory' (see Clarke 1987), and has sometimes been taken to herald, even more misleadingly, 'the end of ethics' (Caputo 1993, 2000).

Thus, drawing on ideas from Levinas and post-structuralists like Derrida and Lyotard, Caputo argues that we do not, and could not, derive our ethical judgments from any theory; that there is an important sense in which any principle or theory comes *after*, or is secondary to, our intuitions about what is good or right. Moreover, contrary to those philosophers who have argued for an intuitionist theory of ethics, our intuitions are always necessarily situated and situational, rather than constituting some (actually or potentially) coherent set of premises that underpins, or can underpin, our judgments and actions:

> The end of ethics means that the premises invoked in ethical theory always come too late, after the fact. To this way of thinking, ethicians appear rather like the crowd that gathers around the scene of an accident to see what has just happened. An accident, of course, is something that no one saw […] coming, although afterwards everyone has something to say about it, up to and including insisting that the proper authorities should have seen that this would happen. So if there are 'cases' at the end of ethics, the cases are casualties […] stumbling over unforeseen difficulties and obstacles, the 'accidents' that strike at us in daily life, that sometimes strike us down. (Caputo 2000: 111)

Caputo playfully suggests that this position should be called 'accidentalism', a theory that is at the same time not a theory. And this position is close to Stanley Fish's 'unprincipled' approach to political and legal issues, which has been given the label 'postmodern sophistry' (Fish 1999; Olson and Worsham 2004).

A related position that also puts ethics into question stems from the idea that our current sense of what is ethical (perhaps both as regards what is ethical/unethical and what is ethical/non-ethical) may be a socio-cultural distortion. Rather than treating

---

[15]It is important to note that not all anti-objectivist/anti-naturalist views about the nature of ethical judgments have this result. For a sophisticated version of this position, see Mackie (1977).

all ethics as a matter of non-rational reaction, as expressivists do, these writers believe that current ways of thinking about ethics may not be *genuinely* ethical; indeed, that in a deep sense they may actually be unethical. In other words, it is argued that the way we think and feel about ethics may have 'a pathogenic dimension' and be 'composed of values that occasion human suffering in the pursuit of human well-being' (Scott 1990: 1). Seminal figures in this tradition are Nietzsche, Heidegger, and Foucault. It is important to note that what frequently motivates this position is not commitment to some already-understood notion of what a genuine ethics would be; instead this remains to be discovered, or will only emerge in the future.

For example, Foucault examined the history of ethical ideas and practices, as these had developed from antiquity, in order to help us to resist the way in which modern ethical practices tend to form us as people of particular kinds with particular preoccupations, aspirations, fears, and tendencies. Moreover, like Nietzsche he saw these practices as already in decline, so that his preoccupation was with what could replace them (Foucault 1984a, 1984b; Davidson 1994; O'Leary 2002). He draws on Graeco-Roman ideas, according to which ethics involves working on the self: coming to know oneself and how one's ideas and behaviour have been socio-culturally formed. So, Foucault's main emphasis is on the capacity that we have to reflect on how we have come to believe and feel the way we do, and engage in the practices that we do, *and above all to recognise that these could have been, and in future will be, different.* What is required, he argues, is an 'aesthetics of existence' (Foucault 1990: 49/732) in which the emphasis is on self-crafting or turning oneself into a work of art, an idea that is also derived from Nietzsche (Nehamas 1985), who suggested that what is needed is 'to "give style" to one's character' (Nietzsche 1887: section 290).[16]

The central ethical value underpinning Foucault's work, then, is that of freedom, conceived as applying aesthetic ideals to one's life. At the same time, he recognises that we can never fully escape being shaped by institutional practices that exercise subtle, and not so subtle, power over us. It seems that for Foucault the only genuine ethical principle exhorts us to resist the normalising tendencies that operate upon us, notably but not only those deriving from what Nietzsche referred to as the 'slave morality' promulgated by Christianity (Nietzsche 1886), such resistance being seen as of intrinsic value.

It is rare for ideas like these to be applied in the field of research ethics, but some use has been made of Foucault's work (Pels 2000; Faubion 2003; Cannella and Lincoln 2007). For example, it has been argued that ethics codes constitute part of the 'technologies of the self' implicit in academic disciplines, and that careful attention to these – through an exercise in reflexivity – can highlight the 'value-rich' rather than 'value-neutral' character of social research (Pels 2005: 78–9). Moreover, such reflexivity is conceptualised as part of a process of 'self care' in which researchers must identify and resist the normalising tendencies operating on and within them. What is to be resisted here is not just the idea that research can be neutral in relation to values but also that ethics can be a simple matter of checking whether or not some proposed action is in line with a set of rules or principles. Rather, there must be reflexive judgment

---

[16]For a discussion of Nietzsche's views about morality, one that challenges Nehamas's interpretation, see Leiter 2002.

about the whole situation in which action is taking place, including the identities of the researcher and of the researched, and the forces, of various kinds, operating upon and within this situation.

CONCLUSION

In this first chapter we have outlined some of the problems involved in defining 'ethics' and 'ethical', and sketched a range of very different philosophical approaches to the topic. Interestingly, all of these ideas are capable of generating doubts about what is commonly taken to be ethical or unethical, whether in general or in relation to research; and, as we have seen, there are those who question whether there can be any rational or reasonable way of making ethical judgments at all.

The approaches we have discussed involve some very significant differences, not just in ideas about how to determine what is ethical but also in whether the focus is on decisions about which action to choose, what sort of life to live, what kind of qualities are desirable in a person, which type of human relationship should be taken as the model for the ethical, or whether there can be rational answers to these questions. And there are some very sharp contrasts involved here: between those who regard ethics as about right action and those who treat maximising what is good or minimising harm as central; between those who believe that ethical judgments should be logically derived from abstract principles, or calculated via cost–benefit analysis, and those who insist on the always situated and judgmental character of ethical evaluations; between those who treat autonomy as the primary virtue and denounce conventional morality as slave mentality and those who emphasise human dependence and vulnerability; and so on. At the same time, there is considerable variation in view within each of the approaches, and also some overlap between them. For example, while Kantian ethics is one of the main positions against which advocates of virtue ethics have argued, there are interpretations that bring the two into quite close proximity; after all, Kant believed that it is a duty to cultivate appropriate emotions and virtues (see Louden 2007: 115 and 118).

The approach that we adopt in this book will be closer to some of the positions we have outlined than to others. For instance, we will certainly emphasise that any principle has to be interpreted in the light of particular situations – it is rarely if ever a matter of simply *applying* a rule, *calculating* what is best, or knowing directly what a situation requires. Furthermore, in judging what is ethical we are often faced with conflicting principles that we have to balance against one another, and doing this well in the context of interpreting particular situations always depends upon a process of learning, of acquiring relevant dispositions. Nevertheless, to a large extent, we see the various approaches we have discussed here as identifying forms of argument that we all use in our lives, at one time or another, in making or reflecting on ethical judgments, and that may need to be taken into account by qualitative researchers in the course of their work.

Having sought to clarify the meaning of 'ethics' in this chapter, in the next one we will address the equally problematic term 'research ethics'.

2

THE RESEARCH ETHOS

In the previous chapter we outlined a range of distinctive approaches to thinking about ethics. While each of these is of value, and we will draw on many of them in the remainder of this book, there is an important respect in which most of them tend to obscure a point that is of great significance for research ethics. The problem is especially obvious with deontological and consequentialist views. As we saw, these two approaches are primarily concerned with evaluating *actions*. Therefore, the particular characteristics of the agent, and of the people affected by the action, are usually treated as specifically irrelevant to ethical judgment: the focus is on how *people in general* ought to deal with one another; in other words, how we should treat people *as fellow human beings*. Yet, in fact, we rarely act simply as *people*, nor do we usually treat others simply as *people*.

Other approaches – situationism, virtue ethics, and relational ethics – do focus on the evaluation of persons and/or recognise situational variation, including different social relationships, so that their orientation is less universalistic. However, even they do not usually take sufficient account of the fact that when we engage in action we are almost always acting in one or more specific social roles. The ethics of care comes closest to this, but while it begins from an account of what is appropriate in a certain type of role, namely in the relationship between mother and child, it assumes that the virtues central to this context can and should be extended to other areas of social life (Bowden 1997). There is a danger with this that the requirements of other, very different, roles may be obscured; in effect, the ethics of care privileges one type of role or context over others. Worse still, other versions of relational ethics, and some forms of situationism too, treat any form of role-playing as inauthentic: their focus is on *personal* ethics.[1]

The importance of social roles for ethics was recognised many years ago by Dorothy Emmet in her book *Rules, Roles and Relations*, but has been rather neglected

---

[1]The notion of authenticity is, of course, central to existentialist ethics; see McBride (1997) and Guignon (2004).

since. She suggests that: 'What people think they ought to do depends largely on how they see their roles, and (most importantly) the conflicts between their roles' (Emmet 1966: 15). She defines a role as 'a capacity in which someone acts in relation to others. [...]. It [suggests] a way of acting in a social situation which takes account of the specific character of the relation, and what is considered appropriate in a relation of that kind, either for functional reasons or from custom and tradition' (pp. 13–14).[2]

Thus, people often act as incumbents of *occupational* roles, and as a result they take on certain primary tasks and responsibilities, downplaying other concerns and considerations. Moreover, they deal with others differentially according to these tasks and obligations. For example, doctors and nurses discriminate between patients, relatives, hospital managers, drug company representatives, and so on; teachers deal differently with children or students, parents, colleagues, caretakers, inspectors, and others. In this way, occupational practitioners make ethical judgments about their own behaviour and that of others *against the background of the roles involved*. Indeed, their actions may be guided by explicit codes of occupational ethics that are concerned with the principles that should govern the specialised work they do; though we should add that these codes tend to be interpreted and used in a variety of ways, and role theory need not assume that people playing roles follow well-defined 'scripts' (Turner 1962).

The point we are leading up to is that the term 'research ethics' refers to a form of occupational ethics: it is about what social researchers ought, and ought not, to do *as researchers*, and/or about what count as virtues and vices *in doing research*. This is not to suggest that general ethical principles about how human beings should treat one another – of the kind characteristic of deontology, consequentialism, and the ethics of care – are completely irrelevant, but it *is* to propose that what is and is not good behaviour *for a researcher* ought to be the main focus in any discussion of research ethics.

This carries with it a further, and very important, point: from the perspective of any occupational ethics, *the primary obligation placed upon a practitioner is to pursue the occupational task effectively*. Surprisingly, this requirement is rarely given priority, or even much attention, in the literature on research ethics.[3] Instead, the main, if not exclusive, focus has been on how researchers ought to treat the people they are studying, collecting data from, and/or writing about – so as to minimise harm, respect their autonomy, and so on. Moreover, these issues have generally been approached in universalistic or personalistic terms, rather than *viewed from the point of view of an occupational ethics for researchers*. This latter perspective requires that general ethical principles – about how people should be treated – are interpreted against the background of the goals, rights and responsibilities, virtues and vices, that are distinctive to being a social researcher.

Thinking about research ethics as a kind of occupational ethics leads us to differentiate between those values that are intrinsic to the task of research (what Shils 1997: 3

---

[2] Here she is drawing on a long, and now rather neglected, tradition of sociological work on role theory; see for example Biddle and Thomas (1966); Turner (1956, 1962); Goffman (1959); Banton (1965); and Biddle (1979).

[3] For partial exceptions see Dockrell (1990) and Macfarlane (2009).

calls 'inherent commitments'), and those that, while nevertheless very important, are extrinsic to it. Intrinsic values actually constitute, or they derive from, the goal towards which the activity is directed, and shape judgments about what is required for that goal to be pursued effectively. By contrast, extrinsic values are not integral to the research task in these ways but serve instead as *proper constraints* upon how that task ought to be pursued.[4] Most of this chapter will be concerned with the values that are intrinsic to research, but towards the end we will outline some relevant extrinsic values, in preparation for more detailed discussion of these in subsequent chapters.

THE TASK OF RESEARCH

In specifying the values that are intrinsic to an occupation, a first requirement is to identify its goal. Unfortunately, in the case of qualitative research this appears to be a matter of dispute. The predominant view in the past, and the one that we adopt here, insists that the sole operational aim of inquiry is to produce knowledge, albeit knowledge which is relevant to some general human interest, to a body of disciplinary knowledge, and/or to a public policy issue. This traditional view was always subject to challenge, and in recent decades it has come to be openly rejected by many qualitative researchers. Thus, today, many argue that the kind of knowledge that social science has typically claimed to produce is not possible and/or that social research should be directed at practical or political goals; notably, promoting social justice by challenging social inequalities or human rights abuses, or resisting and subverting dominant social arrangements and prevailing orthodoxies (see, for instance, Scheper-Hughes 1995; Usher 2000; Bourgois 2007; Mertens and Ginsberg 2009; Denzin and Lincoln 2011). It is important to recognise that these alternative conceptions of the goal of research not only represent a break with the traditional view but themselves point in divergent directions: for instance, much depends upon how social justice is conceived, what count as rights, which aspect of the status quo is to be challenged, and so on.

In rejecting these revisionist accounts of the task of research, we recognise that there are many reasons, besides simple curiosity, why people take up the occupation of researcher, or why they pursue particular research projects. These motives include the hope that the resulting knowledge will improve the world or transform it for the better. However, personal motives of this kind, while certainly legitimate and important, are distinct from the institutional goal of research: *they are the reasons why people adopt that institutional goal not that goal itself.* In our view, research as an institutionalised occupation is compatible with its practitioners having a wide variety of motives and political viewpoints, *but not with their pursuing under its auspices other operational goals than the production of knowledge.* In other words, the latter should be the only aim

---

[4] In an important way, this runs directly counter to MacIntyre's (1982: 175; see also MacIntyre 1993) claim that 'to invite the social scientist to consider the moral dimensions of social research is in no way to ask him or her to recognise some external, intrusive, limiting factor, threatening his or her freedom of inquiry from without'.

towards which researchers direct their actions *as researchers.* This is the distinctive goal of the activity – it is what marks it off from others – and commitment to it is an ethical obligation for anyone who calls her- or himself a researcher.

Rather confusingly, the position we are adopting here has often been formulated as adherence to the principle of value-neutrality or value-freedom – the demand that, in carrying out their work, researchers should attempt to remain neutral in relation to, or detached from, values other than those associated with the production of knowledge, so as to minimise the risk of these causing error.[5] While this label points to an important aspect of this position, what we will refer to later as objectivity, it obscures the parallel requirement that researchers must have a strong commitment to *epistemic* values; in other words, that they should be committed to the values centred on the pursuit of knowledge.

The main such value is, of course, truth. In an essay on the 'academic ethic', Shils writes that:

> the discovery and transmission of truth is the distinctive task of the academic profession, just as care for the health of the patient is the distinctive task of the medical profession, and protection, within the law, of the client's rights and interests is the distinctive task of the legal profession. [...] That truth has a value in itself, apart from any use to which it is put, is a postulate of the activities of the university. It begins with the assumption that truth is better than error, just as the medical profession accepts that health is better than illness and the legal profession begins with the belief that the assurance of rights under the law is better than to be at the mercy of arbitrary power. (Shils 1997: 3)

This implies that it is a constitutive assumption of academic research as an activity that discovering truths of relevant kinds is both possible and desirable. And we suggest that the same is true of other kinds of social inquiry as well.[6]

In the above quotation, Shils is using 'truth' as a synonym for 'knowledge', as the product of inquiry. In our view, the term 'truth' is more usefully employed to refer to the main standard in terms of which we should evaluate candidate knowledge claims as researchers. This is the respect in which it plays the central constitutive role

---

[5] The main source for this idea of value neutrality is the methodological writings of Max Weber. Weber's position is frequently misrepresented; for a detailed, accurate account, see Bruun (2007). The term 'neutrality' is very problematic; see Montefiore (1975: Part 1).

[6] A distinction can be drawn between academic and practical research. The former is aimed at contributing to the development of knowledge within some academic discipline or field of inquiry, whereas practical research is concerned with supplying information needed by a lay audience. For a more detailed discussion of this distinction, see Hammersley (2002: Ch. 6). In our discussion here we will focus primarily on academic research, though we believe that much of what we say will apply to practical inquiry too. We will have little to say about action research, which is in effect the subordination of inquiry to another activity (Hammersley 2003, 2004a). This raises distinctive ethical issues: see, for example, Morton (1999), Tickle (2001), McNamee (2001), Williamson and Prosser (2002), Miller (2007), Nolen and Vander Putten (2007), Brydon-Miller (2009), Jones and Stanley (2010), and *Action Research* (4, 1, 2006).

in research: a commitment to pursuing knowledge and evaluating knowledge claims in terms of their truth is an essential requirement. However, as we shall see, there are additional virtues required in the pursuit of knowledge.

In recent times many social scientists, and especially qualitative researchers, seem to have been in denial about, or at least have been extremely reticent in stating, this commitment to knowledge and truth, as evidenced by their placing words like 'true', 'false', 'reality', and 'fact' in scare or sneer quotes, or avoiding use of them completely. This reflects the influence of a number of epistemological, ontological, political, and ethical arguments whose implications are frequently taken to be that the pursuit of knowledge is either futile or, taken on its own, undesirable. We will examine these arguments briefly in the next section.[7]

CHALLENGES TO THE TRADITIONAL VIEW

When we refer to something as being true this can carry a variety of meanings, partly depending upon the object involved. We can talk about a plumb line being true, a map being true to scale, a picture or story as 'true to life', people being true (in the sense of being trustworthy) or as needing to be 'true to themselves', and so on. What is meant by 'truth' in the context of research is more prosaic and specific than some of these other senses: it refers to empirical propositional truth, in other words the aim is to produce propositions that are true answers to some set of factual questions about the world. These propositions may be descriptions, explanations, or theories, but not evaluations or prescriptions, since what it means for them to be true is that they correspond (in some sense) to relevant aspects of the phenomena to which they refer (Hammersley 2004b).[8] While this concept of truth involves some philosophical problems, we should note that it amounts to refinement of a usage that is routinely employed and largely taken for granted in everyday life, and in many other special-ised activities. Moreover, the problems with a correspondence theory of truth are no worse than those associated with competing epistemological positions, and are open to resolution (Haack 2009).

This view of truth as central to research was largely taken for granted as under-pinning their work by researchers during much of the twentieth century, but from the 1980s onwards, as a result of what Denzin and Lincoln (2005) have referred to as 'the crisis of representation', it has come under increasing challenge from a vari-ety of directions. These include scepticism not just about the possibility of scien-tific knowledge of the social world but also sometimes about any knowledge in the conventional sense of that word as representing reality. Occasionally, these arguments are presented in full-blown form, but their influence is much more

---

[7]For more detailed discussions, see Hammersley (1992, 1995, 2000, 2004b); Haack (2009); B. Williams (2002); Bridges (2003: Ch. 6).

[8]We do not believe that the normative components of normative claims correspond to features possessed by phenomena existing in the world, though the *factual* components of such claims may do so. Our position here is close to that of Mackie (1977).

pervasive, with commentators using them selectively, for example engaging in what Woolgar and Pawluch (1985) refer to as 'ontological gerrymandering'. Equally important, some commentators have insisted that, if it is to have any value, research must be directly geared to action aimed at bringing about social improvement of one sort or another – that knowledge in itself is worthless, and can only have instrumental value.[9]

While these two types of argument have led to widespread rejection of the traditional view about the purpose of research, it is worth noting that they are incompatible with one another, so that what is involved here is not a debate between two sides but a much more complex discussion. We will briefly examine these alternative positions.

Scepticism

As already noted, there is now widespread nervousness among social researchers about using words like 'truth', 'knowledge', and 'fact'. One reason for this is an insistence that we can never be *absolutely* certain that a knowledge claim is true or false, or that something is a fact. Yet usage of these terms carries no such implication: we can aim at truth, or put claims forward as true, or believe something to be true, without claiming to be able to achieve, or to have achieved, absolute certainty about the matter. To frame this point the other way round: the fact that all knowledge claims are fallible does not imply that they are all false, nor that they are all equally likely to be true.

Often, though, scepticism goes deeper than this. Some commentators reject the possibility of propositional knowledge, in general or specifically about the social world, because knowledge claims necessarily rely upon untested assumptions, so that doubts can always be raised about their validity. As a result, it is suggested, we are faced with multiple incompatible views; in effect, with 'multiple realities' (see Smith 1987). These conflicts in viewpoint are seen as deriving from the discrepant social locations and the incompatible interests of different social groups. In addition, underpinning this sceptical or relativist orientation is often an ethical or political argument to the effect that researchers must not make any claim to authoritative knowledge, since to do so involves a denial of others' rights to claim knowledge about their world – a denial that they are 'experts on their own lives'.

One effect of such scepticism has been to encourage a shift in the focus of research towards investigating how conflicting accounts are constructed, how epistemic disagreements are negotiated, whose interests particular accounts serve, and so on. Thus, in many areas of social science, there has been a growth of interest in examining the discursive strategies through which accounts are generated, and the processes by which they are 'received' and have differential effect (see, for example, Wetherell et al. 2001). Often, this has been associated with an argument that all language-use

---

[9]Sometimes this has led to attempts to reconceptualise 'truth' in instrumental terms, for example drawing on the pragmatist arguments of James, Dewey, and Rorty. For the background here see Mounce (1997) and De Waal (2005).

is performative, in the sense that it is not simply concerned (or concerned at all) with representing the world, with 'getting the facts straight', but is primarily if not exclusively directed towards performing actions *within* the world. Thus, some commentators have stressed the rhetorical character of all accounts; in other words, even when they *appear* to be concerned solely with description or explanation they are actually aimed at persuading audiences, so that different people will inevitably produce conflicting accounts of the same scene, depending upon their assumptions, interests and purposes.[10] With much the same result, other researchers have noted that accounts often take the form of narratives, and that the same set of events can be narrated in very different ways, leading to divergent versions of what happened.[11] This broad line of argument can be referred to as constructionism.

In the versions outlined above, constructionism still assumes, implicitly, that the accounts generated by researchers accurately correspond to the processes of discursive or narrative construction they depict. However, some writers have drawn more radical conclusions: they take it to follow from the constructed character of any account of the world, and the interested nature of all accounts, that there are no real phenomena independent of accounts: that there is 'nothing outside the text', or that, if there is, human beings can have no access to it, at least in terms of propositional knowledge. This has been motivated both by awareness of the philosophical problems associated with the concepts of reality and truth, and also by the experience of irresolvable disagreements at a practical level. Of particular significance is the fact that reaching complete agreement even about specific factual matters can be far from easy and is sometimes impossible. This is illustrated by the 'Rashomon effect', where witnesses to the same event produce somewhat different, and occasionally substantially conflicting, accounts of what happened (Heider 1988). Persuasive too, no doubt, has been the capacity of this constructionist line of argument to enhance the significance of discourse, *and of its study*, plus the superficially appealing political implication that whatever exists could always have been, and can still be, constructed differently by discursive means – in a cultural climate in which difference is often seen as intrinsically valuable.

In this more radical form, constructionism seems to rule out any relation between accounts and independently existing phenomena to which they might refer. Rather, it suggests that all we have are essentially arbitrary, competing versions of the world that must be judged in aesthetic, ethical, or political terms, not according to their purported representational accuracy. In short, there are only fictions, not facts; and, while some of these will be more appealing, entertaining, or useful than others, we cannot judge them according to their truth.[12] These ideas have dramatic implications for research, in effect they undermine it – suggesting that

---

[10]For examples of work exploring this see Pollner (1987) and Potter (1996).

[11]For an enjoyable historical exploration of narrative variation, tracing the telling and retelling of an eighteenth-century murder story, see Brewer (2004); instructively, Brewer does not adopt a sceptical or relativist position. On narrative analysis more generally see Riessman (2008) and Atkinson and Delamont (2004).

[12]These views are illustrated by many of the chapters in Denzin and Lincoln (2011).

it cannot ever truly represent the world and is actually always, necessarily, geared to 'political' purposes.

While these views highlight, and feed on, some serious philosophical issues about the correspondence theory of truth, and about the whole notion of reference or 'representation', they themselves suffer from problems that are intractable. For example, we could not consistently adopt radical constructionism as a basis for action in everyday life. There, we most definitely *do* treat some knowledge claims as true, in the sense that they document facts, while we dismiss others as false or fanciful; and we could not avoid doing this, since it is essential to basic human activities. As Schutz (1974) showed, the assumption of a reciprocity of perspectives, relating to a single shared reality, is crucial to communication and all coordination of action. Moreover, in putting forward their arguments, and rejecting those of others, radical sceptics themselves necessarily rely upon this assumption: after all, to claim that we can know nothing is itself to make a knowledge claim.

Researchers certainly need to be aware of the fallible nature of all evidence, and must take precautions to try to ensure that their decisions and assumptions, preferences and desires, do not lead them away from discovering the truth. Equally important, they must be prepared to recognise and deal with potential threats to validity, as well as acknowledging that sometimes they simply do not know what is the true answer to a particular question. However, this can be done without implying that no knowledge of any kind is possible, in the conventional sense of that term; that all we can do is to construct entertaining or politically effective fictions. Moreover, as we have indicated, to take this alternative position undermines the very possibility of research: it subverts its distinctive character, turning it into a form of politics, literature or art.

Knowledge as of only instrumental value

The second kind of argument against the traditional view takes an ethical or political form, rather than being primarily epistemological.[13] In other words, it does not question the possibility of producing propositional knowledge about the social world, of the kind aimed at by most social science. Rather, the argument is that such knowledge has no *intrinsic* value; it is only of value if it has desirable practical or political consequences. It is suggested that the findings of research are often trivial or irrelevant from a practical point of view, or (say) have the undesirable effect of reinforcing the socio-political status quo. It is therefore insisted that social inquiry can only be of value if it is *specifically designed* to serve some practical goal or political cause; indeed, that it is politically or ethically unacceptable to carry out research that is not directed towards this goal.

---

[13]However, it is sometimes linked to a methodological argument to the effect that true knowledge is generated through active involvement in the world rather than via contemplation, overturning the ancient Greek privileging of *theoria* over *praxis* (see Lobkowicz 1967, 1977). However, our focus here will be on the specifically political and ethical arguments.

In responding to this line of argument it is not necessary to deny the value that inquiry can have when it forms part of activities directed towards desirable practical or political goals. But we insist that there is also value in specialised social inquiry whose aim is restricted to the production of value-relevant knowledge, and, moreover, that this is the only legitimate institutional goal of both academic and practical research.

There are several points to be made in support of this. First, this second challenge to the traditional view assumes too simple a relationship between gaining and publicising knowledge, on the one hand, and producing desirable practical outcomes, on the other. In pursuing any inquiry, we cannot know what conclusion we will reach, nor can we know what the effect of publicising that conclusion will be: factual knowledge that seems likely to improve the situation may not do so, or could even make it worse, while what does not look as if it has the potential to improve matters may turn out to do so. This means that to direct research towards what it is believed will have desirable practical consequences does not guarantee those consequences, and, acting in this way, other potential practical pay-offs from research findings may be lost. Moreover, if the goal is a political or practical one, why assume that research is the most effective means of achieving it?

On top of this, directing research so as to try to bring about a particular practical or political pay-off greatly increases the danger of bias, since there is no pre-given affinity between the true and the good. Moreover, whatever apparent failings academic research has in terms of seeming irrelevance or lack of impact are offset by its epistemic capabilities: if pursued properly, generally speaking it is less likely to produce false accounts than inquiry subordinated to another activity, however desirable the goals of that activity are (Hammersley and Gomm 2000).

There is also a more fundamental challenge to this second criticism: why should inquiry, and presumably all other activities (including art and literature), be subordinated in value to practical or political goals? To insist on this is a form of instrumentalism which, while it may be very much part of the spirit of the age, should not go unchallenged. There is something to be said for recognising that there are multiple values in human life, some of which are intrinsic rather than instrumental in nature, and one of which is knowledge about the world. While we may, on occasion, feel that pressing political or practical concerns should take priority, and that research ought to be abandoned in favour of these, it is not justified to insist that research is only of value when it serves such purposes. This is to ignore the intrinsic value of coming to understand ourselves and our world.

THE DEMANDS OF THE RESEARCH TASK

The alternative definitions of the goal of research we have been considering seek either to replace the task of producing knowledge with some other goal or to burden researchers with additional goals. In our view, both approaches damage, if they do not completely destroy, the activity.

Nevertheless, scepticism does at least have the virtue of reminding us that producing knowledge is a challenging task. Even the production of accurate *descriptive* information can be very demanding since it is subject to multiple sources of potential error. When it comes to explanatory knowledge – showing why some outcome occurred or what the consequences of a particular action or event were – the difficulties are even greater. Here, especially, it is not just a matter of assessing potential sources of error but also of generating promising explanatory ideas *and* finding ways to test their likely validity. Moreover, the task for the researcher is not simply to try to discover true answers to some set of worthwhile factual questions, which is difficult enough, *but also to generate evidence that is convincing not only to the researcher her- or himself but also to the audience that is to be addressed.*[14]

We can never know with absolute certainty whether or not our conclusions are true (or, for that matter, that they are false), and nor can anyone else. But we can, usually, make reasonable judgments about the likely truth of particular arguments and conclusions, and we do this by assessing whether belief in their truth is justifiable on the basis of the evidence available. In practical terms this requires that researchers try to minimise the chances of error in their findings by monitoring threats to their validity, assessing competing interpretations, and so on. What is involved here is similar to how all of us decide what to believe and what not to believe in everyday life, especially when the truth or falsity of the knowledge claim is consequential for us. At the same time, there are distinctive requirements placed upon research in its pursuit of knowledge. The conclusions produced by research are expected to be more likely to be true than those coming from other sources; if not, what could be the justification for funding research as a specialised occupation, or for expending effort in its pursuit?

In academic research there is an obligation to gear one's claims about what is true and false to an anticipated threshold of acceptance by fellow members of the relevant research community (Hammersley 2011). In other words, in assessing the knowledge claims emerging in a piece of research, the researcher must assess the likely validity of these not just in terms of how cogent he or she personally finds them, though this is an important starting point, but also how convincing they are likely to be to fellow researchers (irrespective of the latter's theoretical orientations, political attitudes, etc.). Of course, how convincing they are judged to be will depend upon how they relate to other knowledge we have and what evidence can be supplied in support of them; and so a major task is to discover whether the evidence likely to be necessary for persuading fellow researchers can be produced.

In the case of practical research – which is concerned with providing specific kinds of information required by some group of policymakers, political activists,

---

[14]Implicit in our position here is that justification is always an audience-relative matter; it cannot take an absolute form. Different types of research have different primary audiences. In the case of academic research, this is fellow researchers in the relevant field, since lay audiences should only be addressed via reviews of all the relevant literature about some particular topic rather than reports of particular studies (MacIntyre 1997; Hammersley 2002: Ch. 7). In the case of practical research it is the policymakers, practitioners, activists, or others for whom the findings are intended to be relevant.

occupational practitioners, etc. – the conclusions must be accompanied by evidence that *should be* convincing to *these* people. What will be convincing to an audience depends, of course, upon their background assumptions; in other words, what they already take to be true, what they are likely to find relevant to their concerns, and so on. This means that the process of inquiry must be tailored, from start to finish, by anticipations of what will and will not be intelligible and convincing to the relevant audience(s); though, of course, people are not always convinced by evidence that *ought to* convince them.[15]

All this implies that researchers have a range of intrinsic obligations. In order to pursue knowledge effectively they must be neither over- nor under-ambitious in the research questions they choose to investigate. They must search and evaluate the existing literature so as not to repeat work that has already been done, or repeat previous mistakes. This involves not only reasonably exhaustive searches but also accurately representing the arguments put forward by others, and evaluating them in ways that are neither under-critical nor over-critical. Only in this way can each project build well on what has gone before, so as to make a genuine addition to collective knowledge. Similarly, the recording and reporting of data must be clear and accurate, and its interpretation carefully attentive to threats against valid inference.[16]

There are also issues about how findings should be put forward in publications. Below a certain threshold of likely validity it would be unacceptable to present the claims as putative knowledge. Above that threshold, the researcher should indicate the appropriate degree of confidence in the likely validity of the claims. This can be done via the words used to describe them. Phrases like 'it has been conclusively demonstrated that', 'it is evident that', 'it would seem to be the case that', and 'it is at least plausible to suggest that' represent an implicit scale, from great confidence to a much lower level of confidence, and should be used with discrimination. It is important neither to exaggerate nor to underplay the likely validity of findings.

The obligations of the researcher also extend beyond the research process itself to include how he or she responds to criticism. There is a distinctive type of dialogue that is at the heart of the process of academic knowledge production, in which critique and defence must be subordinated to a collective commitment to producing sound conclusions (Hammersley 2011: Ch. 7). Much the same ethos must apply when researchers evaluate the quality of research proposals and papers when serving on funding bodies, editorial boards, and as advisers to publishers.

---

[15]It is very important to underscore, though, that the task of research is not to provide persuasive evidence in favour of a knowledge claim: it is to discover whether or not that claim is true, and only if it is judged to be true should the task then become providing evidence that will persuade the relevant audience. In fact, in the case of academic research especially, it is only through trying to provide a case that is likely to be persuasive to colleagues that the appropriate level of likely validity is approximated.

[16]These may seem mundane and obvious matters, but it is our view that weaknesses in all these respects are common in social science today. For examples see Foster et al. (1996) and Hammersley (2000: Ch. 3).

VIRTUES INTRINSIC TO SOCIAL RESEARCH

A rather different way of characterizing the obligations we have just discussed would be to say that they require researchers to develop distinctive virtues, and it is worth elaborating on this idea. In the extract quoted earlier, Shils (1997) presents the work of academics as a profession, so that the virtues associated with it are characteristic of professionalism. Of course, the concepts 'profession' and 'professionalism' are contentious ones. Not only have there been disputes about which occupations are and are not professional, and what this means, but also professionalism has come to be portrayed as little more than an ideology designed to exert illegitimate control over clients and other occupations (Larson 1977; Freidson 1983). Nevertheless, we believe that the notion of professionalism has not lost all value (Hammersley 2011), and that it points to several important virtues that researchers ought to cultivate. We will concentrate on just three of these here: dedication, objectivity, and independence.[17]

Dedication

The word 'dedication' is usefully ambiguous in this context. We speak of 'dedicated computers' when we are referring to machines that are devoted to only one task. In a similar way, as we have seen, researchers should be dedicated to the single task of producing knowledge. In other words, they should not pursue other goals simultaneously *under the auspices of research*: one cannot simultaneously be a researcher as well as a political activist, novelist, poet, artist, or economic entrepreneur (or, for that matter, 'just' an ordinary person).

This sort of 'narrowness' has often been identified as a vice of professionalism, and it may well be undesirable on some occasions from some points of view. But what is involved here is a trade-off: it is a constitutive assumption of professionalism that dedication to a single task, in other words specialization, will bring specific benefits that outweigh any costs, at least in general and in the long run.

The word 'dedication' also implies a high degree of commitment, and it seems to us that research demands this because, like many other professional tasks, it is very difficult to do well. It requires that researchers address research questions of a kind whose answers would make a significant contribution to current, collective knowledge, and that they do this in ways that meet a threshold of likely validity that is higher, as a general standard, than that which is employed by other people in other contexts (Hammersley 2011: Ch. 5). Moreover, the difficulty of the task has important implications for the private lives of researchers. To adapt a concept invented by Lewis

---

[17]In their discussion of 'the modern researcher' in the humanities, Barzun and Graff identified six virtues: accuracy; love of order/orderliness; logic (i.e. careful inference); honesty; self-awareness; and imagination. Furthermore, they mention many others in the course of their discussion, including clarity (Barzun and Graff 1977: 47–50 and *passim*). See also Haack's (2012) list of ten academic virtues and blistering critique of how the present academic environment is sapping them.

Coser (1974), research is 'greedy': it makes potentially unlimited demands upon its practitioners – there is no fixed end point intrinsic to it, and it can always be pursued in a variety of directions. This has implications as regards currently influential cultural themes about the importance of maintaining a work–life balance and about family-friendly employment. It is not that these principles are undesirable, simply that they may frequently be at odds with the sort of commitment required to pursue research well, just as they are with what is necessary in some other professional activities.[18] The general point to be made here, again, is that there is no pre-ordained harmony in which everything that is good is complementary, or even compatible, so that it forms part of a single harmonious whole. Rather, in the modern world at least, ideals are in conflict with one another, and this forces us to make difficult choices that involve compromising some of the things we hold dear.

Dedication also means not 'living off' research (Coser 1965: xvi), not being solely interested in making a living from it, or maximising one's income, status, or power, and so on. This implies a strong belief that the production of knowledge is worth-while for its own sake. Of course, as noted earlier, in becoming researchers, engaging in inquiry, and selecting particular research topics, most of us will be motivated by the hope that the knowledge produced will have beneficial consequences, and this may shape our decisions about which topics to investigate. However, bringing about such consequences should not be the primary concern. As suggested earlier, if it becomes so, then the task of producing knowledge will come to be subordinated to these instrumental goals, and this will increase the chances that what comes to be presented as knowledge is false. This connects with the next virtue we will discuss.

Objectivity

The word 'objectivity' is used in a variety of ways in the methodological literature and beyond, often confusingly (Hammersley 2011: Ch. 4). Viewed against the background of professionalism, it requires that *all, and only*, the considerations relevant to a task are taken into account. Other matters, however significant these may be from the point of view of other roles, or in terms of personal convictions, should be put on one side or downplayed as far as possible. Each of the various roles that we perform in our lives involves not only distinctive goals but also assumptions about the nature and significance of pertinent aspects of the world, why they are how they are, how they *ought to be*, and so on. In other words, in playing any one role we foreground what is taken to be appropriate and necessary to it and background the rest (Hammersley 2002: Ch. 3). While we cannot, and probably should not, *completely* suppress what is relevant to other roles, at the same time the assumptions and preferences associated with these can interfere negatively with how effectively we play

---

[18]Researchers who have made major contributions to their fields have often sacrificed almost everything for their work. For the (far from entirely attractive) example of Pasteur, see Geison (1995). For an illustration of the point in qualitative research, see Atay (2008).

what is our main role on any particular occasion. Objectivity, as a virtue, is concerned with minimising such negative interference.

In the specific case of research, what 'objectivity' means is that in, for example, determining what data to try to collect, and in analysing it and drawing conclusions, the researcher must try to take into account everything required for the effective pursuit of true answers to the research questions, and avoid being influenced by what is irrelevant to this task.[19] One aspect of this, for instance, is that there should be resistance to privileging particular sources of information, whether from people who occupy high or from those in low-status positions (Becker 1967); the reliability of all forms of evidence must be checked where this is open to genuine doubt. Equally important is suspending any tendency for one's own political views or feelings to prevent careful and sustained analysis of the phenomena. Muir (2004: 194) provides an example of the difficulties that may be faced here. He writes: 'Although I thought a good anthropologist should be as tolerant of New Age spirituality as of traditional Aboriginal beliefs, I also struggled to maintain a relativist stance towards practices that seemed, to me, hopelessly silly and politically suspect.' A related aspect of objectivity is a willingness to pursue arguments wherever they lead, irrespective of whether the conclusions have implications that might be judged undesirable in terms of practical values, or whether publishing them may open the researcher up to danger – physical or reputational.[20]

Maintaining objectivity is by no means a straightforward matter because what would and would not be relevant to the task of research in any particular case is rarely clear-cut, and because we are not always aware of having been influenced by irrelevant considerations. All researchers have other identities and roles, which are focused on different goals from research. Moreover, there will often be overlap in areas of concern between research and these other activities. One effect is that researchers may have a tendency to believe that they already know the answers to questions that are, from a research point of view, still uncertain; or they may be too easily persuaded of some things and too resistant to considering or accepting others because of background expectations or preferences associated with other roles and identities (or even as a result of the researcher role itself, since researchers have career interests). In other words, there may be a tendency to opt for or against particular possibilities because of false prior assumptions or pre-existing preferences (for example those associated with evaluative views about particular people, places, situations, etc.); or there may be a temptation to fill in gaps in data in ways that are false or at least speculative, without giving due acknowledgement that this is involved. Similarly, there may be dismissive attitudes towards the likely truth of particular knowledge claims that derive from what are taken to be the latter's political or practical implications and consequences. Moreover, any sense of urgency or disquiet, whether anger over injustice or fear of change, will increase these tendencies. The obligation to be

---

[19] For discussion of failures to do this in studies of religious movements, see Zablocki and Robbins (2001).

[20] This, of course, borders on another virtue, intellectual courage, on which see Montmarquet (1993: 23 and *passim*). See also Macfarlane (2009).

objective demands that we seek, as far as humanly possible, to minimise the negative effects of such factors.

Independence

Given that it is a demanding occupational task, if research is to be done well then researchers must be able to exercise considerable discretion in deciding what the task entails, in any particular case, and how it should be pursued. One requirement for this is the capacity for independence. This is the third virtue we will discuss, a central component of most definitions of professionalism. In the case of research, what is involved is the obligation of researchers to protect and exercise academic freedom.[21]

There are two important aspects to this. First, it is the responsibility of individuals, associations, and organizations that are committed to the pursuit of research to defend themselves against outside pressures that threaten to subvert the effective pursuit of inquiry. The second aspect of academic freedom is the exercise of independent judgment by each researcher, even in relation to colleagues, notably as regards determining what to study and how to study it. A condition required for this is that relevant occupational associations and organizations are collegial in their mode of governance.

There are good reasons to believe that the chances of sound research conclusions will be maximised by researchers having the discretion to carry out research in the manner that they judge to be best in the circumstances (Polanyi 1962; Hammersley 2002: Ch. 5). The argument here is not that researchers should have absolute or unfettered power to pursue their work, only that if they are to pursue it in a way that is most likely to be effective they must have sufficient power to do this, and be prepared to exercise that power.[22]

There are, of course, many potential external threats to the independence of researchers, and some of these have increased in recent times. One source is funders, especially when these are governmental or commercial organizations who seek to specify what is to be investigated and sometimes also how it is to be studied, and/or try to control the publication of findings, claiming a veto on publication or a right to modify research reports (Wilmott 1980; Pettigrew 1994; Norris 1995). Moreover, today, even funders who are explicitly committed to promoting academic knowledge, such as the Economic and Social Research Council in the UK, are increasingly concerned with serving governmental or commercial interests. As a result, a growing proportion of funding is now provided through invitations requiring researchers to compete for funds to investigate specified topics, as against a responsive funding model where researchers decide which topics are worth investigating and viable.

---

[21]Academic freedom is a contested concept, see Tight (1988), Menand (1998), Fish (2011), and Hammersley (2011: Ch. 8).

[22]Contrary to a common assumption, researchers are often in a weak position, not just as regards gaining the resources needed to do their work but also in relation to many of those with whom they must deal in the course of inquiry, including people in the field.

Gatekeepers – those who control access to particular sites and people – are another potential source of external constraint on the pursuit of research. They will often be concerned with promoting or protecting various interests. They may wish to channel the research in a direction that serves their interests, or to prevent it from damaging those interests, by blocking or restricting access to data, and/or seeking to control what can be published. And, of course, the same may be true of people in the field. In dealing with these pressures, researchers have an obligation to try to gain access to the necessary data, even though this obligation does not necessarily override other considerations, including the legitimacy of gatekeepers' concerns and of any authority they exercise.[23]

A more fundamental threat to the independence of researchers stems from the fact that the form of governance that now operates in many universities, in the UK and elsewhere, is not a collegial one, it is more managerialist in character (Hess 1999; Deem et al. 2007; Tuchman 2009). This has several consequences. One is that universities may fail to protect individual researchers from external pressures, indeed they may simply serve as conduits for these pressures. Private universities have long been subject to pressure from benefactors to curb academic freedom when it threatens the latter's interests or prejudices; and they have not always offered much protection. Even in the case of publicly financed universities, dependence upon powerful outside sources of funding, for example pharmaceutical companies, has sometimes resulted in threats to academic freedom (see Crossen 1994). Of course, there are also often pressures coming from government. In many Western societies in recent years there has been a move towards forms of 'new public management' that seek to ensure that the 'investment' of public funds in research produces an appropriate 'return'. This too has led to infringement upon the autonomy needed by researchers. One example is attempts strategically to manage research within universities, so as to maximise the securing of external research funds. Another is discouragement or prevention of research that is judged likely to damage the reputation of the university or research institute, and thereby reduce its funding streams. Thus, individual researchers may sometimes be obliged to resist the pressures that universities seek to exert on them. And much the same is probably true for those who work in other types of research organisation.

In short, then, 'independence' refers not only to the freedom or discretion that is objectively available to an occupational practitioner, for instance deriving from a particular licence and mandate that has been granted by relevant authorities (Hughes 1958; Jonsen 1990: 11), but also to a distinctive mode of orientation, a virtue, on the part of the agent. There must be a concern with establishing and protecting the freedom that is essential for pursuing inquiry effectively, and also with exercising this autonomy in a responsible fashion *as regards this goal*. The primary

---

[23]It is important to recognise that referring to such external pressures as serving interests does not automatically imply that they are illegitimate. Interests can be legitimate or illegitimate, and judgments about this can differ. The key point we are making here is that researchers have a primary obligation to try to ensure that research can proceed unhindered by external interests, even if they also have a secondary obligation to recognise and take account of legitimate external interests on the part of the people with whom they must deal, and others.

responsibility for which research questions are addressed, for how an investigation is pursued, for what conclusions are drawn, and for how they are reported, lies with the researcher(s) concerned. Moreover, this is not just a matter of resisting demands from others that threaten the effective pursuit of research but also exercising independence in relation to the *influence* of others where this also poses such a threat. While the proscriptions and prescriptions to be found in the methodological literature, and those offered by colleagues and others, should be taken into account, research can never be a matter of simply abiding by rules or guidelines, or following others' advice.

Furthermore, as we have emphasised, the principle of independence involves researchers claiming and maintaining considerable power over the research process. This follows from the fact that 'ought implies can': if it is the responsibility of researchers to pursue knowledge in an effective manner, then they must seek to exercise the power necessary to do this, within appropriate constraints.[24] This runs counter to arguments on the part of some qualitative researchers, often framed in ethical terms, to the effect that it is necessary to carry out research 'with' people rather than do research 'on' them, so that inquiry should be collaborative or participatory (Reason and Bradbury 2008; Kindon et al. 2007; Mertens and Ginsburg 2009).

RELEVANT KNOWLEDGE

In specifying the goal of research earlier we made clear that the task is to pursue not just *any* knowledge but rather to aim at knowledge that has some relevance for human beings, either in general or for a specific audience. This makes clear that the researcher has an obligation to ensure that any investigation not only addresses an issue that is still 'live' but also one that has some importance, direct or at least indirect, in lay terms. There are questions, though, about how this requirement should be interpreted.

What counts as relevant, and what is of *sufficient* relevance, will vary somewhat between types of inquiry. In the case of practical research this must be determined according to the current and prospective needs of relevant audience(s). Even here, though, our argument about the importance of independence indicates that what is involved is not simply a matter of seeking to satisfy the *demands* of the anticipated users. Not only must the intended product be limited to knowledge – rather than, say, supplying needed propaganda – but also we must recognise that there can be discrepancies between what audiences want, what they need, and what can feasibly be produced in terms of reliable knowledge. Here, as elsewhere, it is the task of the researcher to make the best judgments possible.

In the case of academic research, relevance relates to what is required to make a contribution to a body of disciplinary knowledge. Clearly, the responsibility falls on

---

[24]These constraints derive from extrinsic values, which are the main focus of subsequent chapters.

individual researchers or research teams to determine which questions would be of sufficient value to pursue, though their judgments will subsequently be assessed by others in the research community. Many of the topics that academic researchers address will have little obvious value in lay terms. One reason for this is that in order to tackle major issues it is usually necessary to break them down into parts that, in themselves, may be of little direct general interest. This is especially necessary if the high threshold of likely validity that academic research claims is to be reached. In other words, very often in order to discover the answer to one question we must first find answers to others, and the immediate interest of these to most people will often be negligible. A key feature of academic research is that it seeks to build bodies of knowledge that enable important questions to be answered, *taking the time necessary to do this* (Pels 2003).

EXTRINSIC VALUES

We have argued that researchers have an obligation to pursue value-relevant knowl-edge as effectively as possible with a view to producing findings that meet the neces-sary threshold of validity. In addition, they have a responsibility to protect the research enterprise from external and internal pressures or influences that threaten to result in deviation from this course. However, researchers clearly should not do this *at any cost*.

In other words, intrinsic values do not exhaust the value principles that research-ers should take into account in doing their work, any more than doctors, nurses, lawyers, social workers, or teachers should pursue *their* occupational tasks with no regard for values that are extrinsic to those tasks. For instance, a lawyer must not invent evidence so as to win a case in the interests of her or his client (Stolyarova 2011); and a doctor should not illegally trade in body parts so as to preserve the health of a patient (Scheper-Hughes 2000b).

By contrast with the way in which we were able to derive key intrinsic values directly from the nature of the research task, a similar approach is not available for identifying relevant extrinsic values. This is because, to some extent at least, these depend upon the researcher: they arise from the range of values to which any par-ticular researcher is committed as a person, including those central to other roles that he or she plays. However, this is not to say that these values are entirely idiosyncratic. On the contrary, they arise from the general contingencies of human life, as well as reflecting the particular character of the societies and sections of society in which researchers live and work. To some extent, commitment to them will also derive from the interests of the research profession, notably in maintaining an environment in which research can continue to be carried out.

While there can potentially be a very large number of extrinsic value consid-erations that a researcher may feel it necessary to take into account, many of these can be summarised under a relatively small number of headings, ones that have been given considerable attention in the literature on research ethics. In subsequent chapters we will focus on three of these: minimisation of harm, respect for autonomy, and the protection of privacy. We would not claim that the priority given to these values, or how they are interpreted, is universal; indeed, as we will make clear, the emphasis assigned to the second and third stems, to some extent, from Western culture. Furthermore, as we saw in the Introduction, there are other extrinsic values that would also warrant attention.

While important, the relevance of extrinsic values is not straightforward. Each is open to interpretation, and involves a *scale* of potential offences, so that we can ask how severe is the harm caused or threatened, how serious an infringement of autonomy is involved, and so on. While we believe that it is possible to make reasonable judgments about these matters, there will often be scope for disagreement. Furthermore, the implications of different values in particular situations may conflict, so that judgments have to be made about their relative priority in the circumstances.

There is also the problem that researchers rarely deal with one person at a time but rather with many people, plus various agencies and organizations as well, *whose interests in terms of particular values may diverge*. In his research on Romani Gypsies, Levinson (2010) began by making contact with the Traveller Education Service and with schools, but found that this created barriers. In addition, he discovered that he was not investigating a single community but a network of communities characterised by 'rivalries, alliances and antagonisms' (p. 204). Moreover, social relations within these communities were often quite hierarchical, and this shaped his dealings with particular individuals. He comments:

> While opportunities were sought to explore the attitudes of the relatively dis-empowered members of communities, it was not always possible to achieve this. Moreover, there were occasions when such individuals sought to distance themselves from opinions articulated previously upon the discovery that more authoritative group members had expressed conflicting views. (p. 204)

So, in their fieldwork, qualitative researchers will often have to recognise that the interests of the various individuals and organisations with whom they deal can be at odds, even in terms of the same extrinsic value.

Decisions about what to do (sometimes made with the benefit of forethought but often instantaneously) must also take account of what seem to be the facts of the situation faced; in other words they must be prudent. And these facts include the value commitments and value judgments of other people. For instance, in her research on prostitutes in Mexico, Kelly (2004) was guided not only by her feminist principles but also by the ethical judgments made by the prostitutes, the people that they dealt with, and the surrounding society. These factual matters had implications both for how her research goals could best be pursued in the circumstances, and also for the action implications of her own values. For instance, had Kelly believed that it was imperative for her to make her political views and allegiances explicit at all times, she would probably not even have gained access in the first place, and she would also have endangered the carefully constructed fictions by which the prostitutes maintained their lives.

Of significance here is the fact that, in much qualitative research, fieldwork is carried out in settings where there is no established researcher role, so that either an existing role in the field must be taken on or a distinctive role forged out of how participants make sense of the researcher's behaviour. In her research on the wives of Japanese businessmen working in the US, Kurotani (2004: 213) notes the contingencies that can be involved in this:

> A couple of months after I started visiting Kawagoe-san and her friends, they began to talk about how funny it was that I could actually be 'working' while I was doing nothing but 'playing' with them. Then one of the women exclaimed, 'Ah, I understand, Sawa-san is an *asobinin*!' An *asobinin* means literally a person who plays, or a loafer without recognizable and honest means of making a living. They may be gamblers, 'wise guys', or someone rich enough to not need a job. The livelihood of an *asobinin* is play, instead of work. *Asobinins*' marginality also serves as a symbol of resistance against social norms and restrictions, slipping in and out of two social milieus. Thus, the reference to *asobinin* made two moves of signification in one stroke, identifying me as someone who played professionally, and also as someone who defied Japanese social conventions in her professional play.

This feature of qualitative research means that, more than in some other cases, ethical considerations have to be weighed against practical factors. One implication of this is that following *general* ethical, or for that matter **general** methodological, prescriptions or proscriptions is not wise. This point extends even to issues such as whether social researchers must always obey the law. For one thing, whether working in societies to which they belong or those in which they are strangers, researchers may regard some laws as unacceptable, or even as unethical. Aside from this, there can be occasions when methodological or prudential considerations override legal requirements for researchers. For example, members of many communities break some laws routinely, and at the very least a researcher who feels obliged always to report this behaviour will probably not be able to carry out research effectively with these people. The classic advice here, in the context of criminology, is that of Polsky (1969: 138):

> If one is to effectively study adult criminals in their natural setting, he must make the moral decision that in some ways he will break the law himself. He need not be a 'participant' observer and commit the criminal acts under study, yet he has to witness such acts or be taken into confidence about them and not blow the whistle.

Thus, Beckerleg and Hundt (2004) insisted that it was essential for them to witness illegal drug use for the purposes of their study. Furthermore, maintaining the line between knowing about and even witnessing crimes but not participating in them can be hard to maintain. In her study of a working-class community in south-east London, Foster (1990: appendix) faced difficulties in this respect, as did Holdaway (1982: 67–70) in his covert research on the police, where he witnessed illegal actions on the part of fellow officers, and was expected to engage in them himself. And others have found it impossible not to go beyond this, needing to draw distinctions between those crimes in which they are prepared to participate and those they are not (West 1980: 38; Pearson 2009).[25]

What all this means is that while there are extrinsic values that operate as proper constraints on how researchers should pursue their work, these always have to be interpreted in particular contexts. Furthermore, it may sometimes be necessary to downplay these extrinsic values in decisions that are made in the field. Thus, qualitative researchers often have to tolerate attitudes or behaviour that they personally regard as unacceptable (Hammersley 2005), and occasionally must even engage in activities they detest (Mitchell 1991: 107). However, these requirements are not unique to the case of research – they can also arise in other occupations, as for example when a lawyer or doctor is obliged to assist someone of whom they strongly disapprove, or perhaps even to do something which they abhor.

CONCLUSION

In this chapter we have argued that research ethics must be treated as a form of professional ethics that is focused on the role of researcher. The primary obligation of any occupational practitioner is to try to pursue the occupational goal effectively. This led us to draw a distinction between intrinsic and extrinsic values. The intrinsic values are those that actually constitute the goal of research as an activity, or relate to how this goal can best be pursued. We challenged some views about the task of research that are currently influential amongst qualitative researchers: those that deny the possibility of social scientific knowledge, or insist that knowledge is only desirable if tailored to serve practical or political goals. Instead, we argued that the only operative goal of research should be to produce knowledge, albeit knowledge that has human relevance. And we spelt out some of the obligations that followed from this commitment. We also discussed three moral virtues required by researchers: dedication, objectivity, and independence. Finally, we argued that extrinsic values indicate proper constraints on how the research task should be pursued, but that deciding when these ought to be given emphasis and what they mean in particular situations is a matter of situational judgment.

It is important to emphasise that when we talk about extrinsic values constraining the work of researchers we mean value judgments to which they are themselves committed – not those they do not hold but which are emphasised by others within the contexts in which they carry out their work, whether their home institutions or the fields that they investigate. The phrase 'research ethics' is sometimes used in a loose way to cover all of the ways in which non-epistemic values may become

---

[25]The same issue arises with institutional rules of various kinds. For instance, Burgess (1985: 88) reveals that he did not report school students smoking in the classroom because it was his 'duty to use this material only for the purpose of sociological study rather than to act as an informer for the head'. This was not a view that the headteacher shared.

relevant in the course of research, not just those that stem from commitment on the part of the researcher. However, while others' value judgments will often need to be taken into account by a researcher in making her or his decisions about how to pursue an inquiry, this is not *primarily* a matter of ethics but rather of recognising the facts of the situation in which action must be carried out: it comes under the heading of prudence.

In the chapters that follow we will discuss the nature and implications of what are perhaps the three main extrinsic values relevant to qualitative research: minimisation of harm, respect for autonomy, and the protection of privacy.

3

THE RISK OF HARM

Perhaps the most common, and usually the most important, principle involved in discussions of research ethics concerns harmful consequences that could result from the actions of researchers. Ethics codes and regulatory frameworks often suggest that harm must be avoided; and it is certainly true that researchers would almost always want to avoid their research doing serious harm to anyone. However, the *risk* of harm, *of some kind*, is probably unavoidable, in virtually any activity. Furthermore, what counts as a significant risk of significant harm is a matter of judgment.

As we saw in the Introduction, initial concern about research ethics arose in the context of medicine. Here a central focus has been on the clinical testing of medical interventions, for example of a new drug or surgical technique. These trials often involve the potential for harm. However, most non-experimental social research, especially qualitative work, does not involve interventions of this sort. Of course, the implication is not that the risk of harm does not arise in qualitative research, only that it takes distinctive forms, and involves a different balance of considerations.[1]

The harm that may be risked in making research decisions can vary in both degree and kind. Many social scientists argue that the risks are low in their work, certainly as compared with medical research, and also by comparison with the danger accompanying many other activities, such as mass media journalism. But there are some social scientists who challenge this assessment. For example, Warwick (1982) has argued that

---

[1]In medicine, clinical research generally involves an intervention that has the potential to cure or improve the condition of someone already suffering from an illness, even though it will always involve costs and dangers: see Foster (2001: Ch. 1) for an excellent discussion of the dilemmas that arise in the context of medical research. By contrast, experimental work in social science does not usually involve interventions that offer any direct intended benefit to the subjects of the research, while the harm, if any, that the interventions risk causing is probably less than that of most clinical interventions. In non-experimental research there is no intervention in either of the above senses, even though the researcher will engage in actions that may affect the people being studied in various ways. An exception to this is the case of action research, but this is not within our focus here: see Chapter 2, note 6.

there is *prima facie* evidence of a great many actual and potential harms caused by social research, and has suggested that we cannot know for certain that it has done little harm because there has been hardly any rigorous investigation of the matter.

The spread of ethical regulation, discussed in the Introduction, has sometimes drawn on this high estimate of the dangers of social inquiry.[2] Moreover, the growth of regulation reflects a broader public preoccupation with the risk of harm. Some social theorists have argued that this has become a central organising principle in modern, or postmodern, societies; despite the fact that the basis for, and even possibility of, calculating the risks coming from modern technology are undermined by the sheer scale and pace of innovation (Giddens 1991; Beck 1992, 1999). One consequence of this is the emergence, in many quarters, of increasing risk-aversion (Pieterman 2001; Furedi 2002), which leads to a search for procedures to eliminate dangers. Within large-scale societies today, particularly in the context of global interdependence, unavoidable reliance upon anonymous others – not just individuals but also agencies of various kinds – tends to encourage demands for 'systems' or 'procedures' that will provide protection against the unknown.

This is part of the context within which the rise of ethical regulation, and the centrality of a concern with harm in discussions of research ethics, must be understood. It may therefore be tempting to dismiss the pressure for regulation, and the sort of arguments put forward by Warwick, as constituting a moral panic that both exaggerates the dangers and at the same time makes unreasonable demands for the elimination of all risk. However, this is too hasty a response: there are issues around the risk of harm in qualitative research that need closer attention.

HARM AND BENEFIT

The problem of harm caused by research has typically been approached from a consequentialist point of view, and has usually involved recognising that research may generate benefits as well as harms, with the idea that these need to be weighed against one another.[3] Given this, before examining the issue of harm, we should note some kinds of benefit that can derive from qualitative research.

The most obvious benefit is the value of the knowledge produced, though it is by no means universally accepted that social scientific knowledge is of value, or more specifically that what qualitative work produces is worthwhile. Very often research knowledge is valued for supplying policy- or practice-relevant evidence, and there have been recurrent disputes about what sort of evidence is of value, and what kinds of research method are required to produce it (see Hammersley 2002). We will simply

[2]Though in the UK the ESRC introduced its regulatory framework while simultaneously declaring that 'almost without exception, social science research in the UK has been carried out to high ethical standards' (ESRC 2005: 1).

[3]See, for example, Warwick's (1982) attempt (albeit in our view rather biased) to balance the benefits and costs of Humphreys'' research.

note here that we believe qualitative research can and does produce knowledge that is of use to policymakers, occupational practitioners of various kinds, and others; though, as we made clear in Chapter 2, we do not believe that the knowledge produced by research is *only* of instrumental value.

However, not all knowledge is of equal value. We saw that its value must be judged in terms of relevance to human concerns. Moreover, the value of particular findings can vary in relation to each concern, and we are also likely to rank these concerns differentially according to importance. In short, judgments about the value of what a research project promises to produce, or of what a completed study *has* produced, will frequently vary. Furthermore, the value of some items of knowledge, in some contexts at some times, may even be judged negative. For instance, in her study of lesbian parenthood in Sweden, Ryan-Flood (2010: 194) discovered that some women were pretending to be heterosexual in order to get IVF treatment. She suppressed this finding, until the law changed, for fear that it would alert the authorities to the practice, and prevent lesbians receiving this service.

There are also incidental benefits that may accrue to people from participating in research, or from their contact with researchers. For instance, many participants enjoy being interviewed, and may occasionally find it therapeutic. Thus, Grenz (2010: 55) notes that some of the men she studied, who visited prostitutes, reported that 'talking [to her] helped them gain some clarity about themselves. They found themselves in conflict between living out what they thought of as their desires and the low social value of being a punter, on the one hand, and, on the other hand, their own moral values such as faithfulness' (see also Goodrum and Keys 2007: 254). More generally, Plummer (1995: 34) notes that in the case of life-history interviews: 'for many the telling of a tale comes as a major way of "discovering who one really is"'. Indeed, there may be benefit even when the experience of being interviewed is distressing: when a researcher asks a question that an informant finds upsetting this may nevertheless result in the latter addressing a personal issue that he or she had previously shied away from, and this may (though it need not) be beneficial for the individual concerned and/or for others.

There are similar potential benefits in the case of participant observation. Here, friendships of one sort or another frequently develop, from which participants may derive at least some of the kinds of benefit that arise from friendship in other contexts; indeed, it is not uncommon for some relationships to continue long after the research has been completed (see Whyte 1993a: appendix; Miller and Humphreys 2004).

A third kind of benefit is that during their contacts with people qualitative researchers often provide minor services of one kind or another. Forsythe (1999: 9) reports that when doing fieldwork both in remote rural areas of Scotland and in an urban German community, 'On request, I taught people to drive, baby-sat, played the organ in church, mucked out barns, corrected people's English, did translations, and so on'. And Okely provides a similar list from her research with Gypsy families: 'at the beginning I made myself available for any odd jobs: reading letters, arranging for the rubbish skip to be emptied and placing liquidiser in the elsan lavatories after the sewage lorry's departure'. At one point she also spent evenings talking long into the night with the wife of a Gypsy family who had suffered a bereavement (Okely 1983: 41). In addition, anthropologists working in relatively poor societies have often given basic medical treatment, and many qualitative researchers provide information or advice. Thus, in his research on Algerian businessmen, Peneff (1985) found himself being asked for evaluations of various products from a French point of view, information perceived as of value in attempts to increase exports to the French market.

Of course, what are identified here as benefits can be a mixed blessing. Levinson's (2010: 201) comment, 'I was drawn into a desire to help those with whom I was working, sometimes with little knowledge as to the potential outcomes', captures a common desire on the part of researchers but also sounds a wise note of caution. The incidental benefits for participants arising from research can sometimes turn into harms, or at least into perceived harms. The basic medical treatment offered by an anthropologist may prove to be inadequate or even come to be viewed as having worsened the illness. Similarly, advice offered can turn out to be misleading, or may be resented by those to whom it is given. And assistance may not have the outcome anticipated. Kelly describes how she helped facilitate a meeting with the Director of Public Health for some of the sex workers in the legal brothel she was studying, to enable them to voice their concerns about the medical treatment they were receiving. She reports:

> The meeting did not go as I had hoped: the most articulate and politically informed worker was not present and the workers complained less of the collective problems of service, mistreatment, and administration that they had spoken of to me, and focused more upon an ongoing dispute that some women had been having with Marco, a former male prostitute employed as a janitor, who also ran errands for sex workers. The meeting did not create any great changes for the women and caused the further degeneration of my relationship with [the medical service attached to the brothel]. (Kelly 2004: 11)

There are also services that researchers may provide, or be asked to supply, whose legitimacy is open to question. For example, Coggeshall (2004: 149) reports being asked to smuggle a letter out of prison. Less incidentally, Mitchell (1993: 44) notes how participants may want the research report written in a way that represents their views and/or promotes their cause.

Our discussion here has relied upon a distinction between benefits or harms caused by the research process itself, on the one hand, and those that are incidental to it, on the other. While this distinction has some importance, in the case of qualitative research there is a large grey area at its core. This is because such research frequently involves researchers participating directly with people over relatively long periods of time, so that there is a blurring between what is and is not part of the research. This blurring is illustrated by the case of sexual relationships between researchers and people in the field.[4] While these may occur in a tangential way, there are also examples where the connection to the research is very close. One is Goode's (2002) study of the National Association for the Advancement of Fat Americans

---

[4]There is a small literature dealing with this issue; see for example Kulick and Willson (1995), Markowitz and Ashkenazi (1999).

(NAAFA) in which, rightly or wrongly, he saw having sex with some of the women as more or less essential to the success of the fieldwork. Similarly, in Carrier's (2006) work on male homosexuality in Mexico, his own sexual relations were a key factor. There are difficult judgments to be made, then, about what is a personal matter and what is relevant to the role of the researcher, as regards both potential harm and benefits.

In summary, while it is true that research must be judged according to its likely benefits as well as any harm it might cause, what constitutes a benefit, how beneficial it is, and to whom, are often uncertain and contestable matters. As we shall see, much the same is true of harms.

WHAT IS HARM?

The word 'harm' may seem immediately obvious in meaning, referring to outcomes whose character is easily identifiable. This is not the case. As Feinberg (1984: 32) comments: 'In its bare formulation, without further explanation, the [term] harm [...] is a mere convenient abbreviation for a complicated statement that includes, among other things, moral judgments and value weightings of a variety of kinds.' There are factual assumptions involved too. Warwick (1982: 103) argues:

> Much of the disagreement about the harms of social research stems not from incon-
> clusive data but from quite disparate assumptions about the fragility or durability of
> a typical person, the goods that are sought and the harms that are feared by members
> of society, and the conditions promoting or retarding collective welfare.

It is necessary, then, to examine carefully what is involved in judgments about harm.

Feinberg (1984: 33) defines 'harm' as 'the thwarting, setting back, or defeating of an interest'; and he defines 'interests' as 'those things in which one has a stake', these being 'components of a person's well-being', in the sense that he or she 'flourishes or languishes as [these components] flourish or languish' (p. 34). So, one person harms another by 'setting back, or thwarting', one or more of those things that affect the latter's well-being. As part of this we must recognise that people's interests often conflict, so that an action may benefit some people while harming others. At this point, even more difficult issues arise to do with equity or justice.

Feinberg's definition gives us a reasonably clear, if rather abstract, sense of what 'harm' means. In identifying harms we are engaging in evaluation: judging some actual or potential outcome to be bad for someone. So we must ask: what set of values, one or more, defines the 'interests' damaged in any particular case, and thereby underpins the evaluation of harm? Sometimes, judgments of harm are so straightforward that we are likely to overlook the particular value principles involved, or even the very fact that our judgment is value-dependent. For example, a clinical trial of a drug in which the majority of participants die or suffer serious consequences for their health seems a fairly obvious case of harm. Most of us, most of the time, value life and health very highly, our own and that of other people, without thinking about it. But harm does not relate solely to these values, others can be relevant as well.

We can identify potential threats of harm arising from research as falling into the following categories:

1   Pain, physical injury, and permanent disability.
2   Psychological damage, for instance emotional distress, erosion of self-confidence, stress-related illness, and so on.
3   Material damage of some kind, for example loss of one's freedom through imprisonment, dismissal from one's job, reduction in income or wealth, damage to property, and so on.
4   Damage to reputation or status, or to relations with significant others, for example through the disclosure of information that was previously unknown to some relevant audience.
5   Damage to a project in which people are engaged, to some group or organisation to which they belong, perhaps even to some institution or occupation in which they participate.

The fact that serious harm, of the kinds just listed, *could* be produced by qualitative research does not imply that it is common or is usually very likely. Indeed, it seems to us that in most qualitative work the danger of significant harm of any of these types is low, and that its occurrence has been rare. But this judgment assumes, among other things, that it is possible to assess the seriousness of harms with a reasonable degree of reliability. And this is also required if we are to make defensible decisions, when doing research, about whether risking some potential harm is justifiable, or about whether the behaviour of other researchers in carrying out particular investigations has involved unacceptable levels of likely harm.

ASSESSING DEGREES OF HARM

One issue that arises here concerns the appropriate benchmark in judging harm. Earlier, we noted how social scientists often compare what they see as the low risk of significant harm involved in their work with the much greater danger for patients involved in clinical trials. By contrast with this, Warwick (1982) implicitly compares the effects of social research with a base-line of no harm. Not surprisingly, these two comparisons produce very different results. But which is the most appropriate?

It seems to us that both can be of value, but that neither should be treated as conclusive. Even if social science involves a lower risk of serious harm than clinical research in medicine, it could still carry significant dangers. At the same time, given the differences in level of risk it highlights, this comparison has the virtue of reminding us about the *range* of variation in potential harm that can be involved in research, and in other activities, thereby helping us to gain a sense of proportion – an essential requirement.

Warwick's strategy serves the opposite function: warning us not to be complacent about harm. At the same time, his approach is unsatisfactory on its own because it employs an unrealistic ideal as a benchmark: no risk of harm at all. It seems to us that, instead, we should judge the risks of harm from qualitative research against the sorts of dangers normally operating in the lives of the people being studied. To modify an example that Warwick himself uses: in the case of research on military recruits, concern about the effects of a researcher asking potentially embarrassing questions pales into insignificance by comparison with the other risks of various types of harm to which the recruits are, and will be, subjected. The threat of harm, of various kinds, along with the possibility of benefits, is a universal and recurrent feature of everyday life. Thus, just as we must judge levels of harmful radiation against background levels, so too with ethical dangers we must assess these comparatively in relation to context, not against a utopian ideal. This is because such an ideal would render research, and indeed most other kinds of action, impossible.

Our point here is not that qualitative researchers should feel free to do anything that does not carry a worse threat of danger than those normally operating on people in the context concerned, so that for example in studying a prison they would be justified in trying to coerce inmates into answering questions, given that coercion of many kinds is routine in prisons (Coggeshall 2004). Instead, our argument is that some reasonable judgment has to be made about what is a significant risk of serious harm from research *in the context being investigated*. Comparison with other contexts, and with the ideal of no harm, can be valuable, but they must *not* be used in ways that abstract potential harms from the situations in which they are likely to occur.

It should be clear from our discussion of the nature of harm that there is no means by which its level in particular cases can be objectively measured, in a manner analogous to the measurement of length or temperature. This is particularly obvious where we are comparing different types of harm, but even when we are assessing the level of a single sort of harm it seems unlikely, generally speaking, that there will be a means of measuring it accurately by any standard procedure. To take one example, loss of income *can* sometimes be measured, but this is normally used as a proxy for other things – such as decline in standard of living – which depend upon additional factors – such as need, preference, the cost of goods, and so on – that are less easily measurable. With other types of harm the problems of measurement are even more salient.

However, the fact that measurement is impossible does not mean that we cannot make reasonable assessments of harm and its risk: it is not true that without rigorous measurement we are faced with mere opinions that are all as false or uncertain as one another. Drawing this sort of conclusion is a common error, to be found not just on the part of those who insist that measurement must be possible if we are to know anything with certainty, but also among those who declare that all such judgments are incommensurable or undecidable (see, for instance, Caputo 1993).

In relation to each *type* of harm, we can usually distinguish different *degrees* of severity. It is possible, for instance, to judge *how big* a blow to self-confidence has occurred, *how large* a drop in standard of living has taken place. Generally speaking, a pinprick is less serious than being gouged to the bone, and failure to get promotion is usually less significant than losing one's job. In all these examples, an implicit scale can be assumed even though it is not one that can be rigorously operationalised so as to allow for measurement, nor one where people's judgments will always agree.

Even where we are assessing the relative seriousness of *different kinds* of harm, we can often make reasonable judgments that would be quite widely shared. In the course of his discussion of 'the moral limits of the criminal law', Feinberg (1984: 45–51) provides us with an indication of one basis on which coming to reasonable practical judgments about the seriousness of different harms is possible. He refers to various experiences that temporarily 'distress, offend, or irritate us', which 'come to us, are suffered for a time, and then go, leaving us as a whole and undamaged as we were before' (p. 45). His examples include 'unpleasant sensations (evil smells, grating noises), transitory disappointments and disillusionments, wounded pride, hurt feelings, aroused anger, shocked sensibility, alarm, disgust, frustration, impatient restlessness, acute boredom, irritation, embarrassment, feelings of guilt and shame, physical pain at a readily tolerable level, bodily discomfort, and many more'.

According to Feinberg, for these to count as harms, they would need to have longer-lasting consequences. In fact, we would be inclined to define his examples as harms, but Feinberg's discussion illustrates how it is possible to draw distinctions among harms as regards their severity, in this case between those that are of very brief duration and little consequence, and therefore (Feinberg infers) generally of low significance, and those that are more long-lasting, and so usually more significant, perhaps because they are harmful in themselves, in the sense of generating further harm. Thus, most people would probably regard even a severe sense of embarrassment as less significant than someone losing her home; and with good reason. There will, of course, be many cases where we are more uncertain about what conclusion to draw, and where there would be major disagreements. However, it is important to note that, by contrast with any attempt at scientific measurement of harm, we are not required to produce a general formula, only to make judgments about the seriousness of *particular* harms occurring, or anticipated as possibilities, on *particular* occasions. While there will be cases that seem undecidable, much of the time we will be able to reach reasonably reliable judgments about how serious actual or projected harms are (when judged against the local context), while recognising that there may be disagreement and that this needs to be taken into account.[5]

HARM IN QUALITATIVE RESEARCH

There are features of qualitative research which make it especially difficult to *predict* the occurrence of harm with any precision. One of these is that such research tends to have an open-ended character. Generally speaking, it starts from a broadly defined interest in some topic and/or in a particular type of person or place, rather than with well-defined hypotheses to be tested. As a result, in the early stages at least, data

---

[5]It is perhaps important to note that while the perspective of a person claiming to have suffered harm is important, in assessing whether harm has occurred and how serious it is, her or his claims cannot be accepted at face value. One reason for this is that claims about harm may be motivated by interests, leading to exaggeration or downplaying of the level of harm; and another is that such claims may be unreasonable as well as reasonable.

collection is not highly focused but has an exploratory character. Furthermore, in the case of participant observation studies, and sometimes even in those that are based entirely on interviews, the researcher is working in contexts over which he or she has very limited control. Also, these contexts may themselves be ones in which various kinds of danger of harm operate for those involved – physical, material, or reputational. And, as regards the publication of findings, researchers do not have control over how others may use, and misuse, them. While here, as elsewhere, precautions are possible, there are limits both to the effectiveness of these and to how far it would be desirable to apply them, given potentially deleterious effects, not least on the research.

It is also important to recognise that harm can be seen as resulting from inaction, as well as from action. Moore (2010: 39) provides an example:

> I have never been able to talk openly and accurately about my work on Marakwet, especially with my feminist colleagues, because the moral trauma of female circumcision has opened up an almost unbridgeable gap between us. One question I have been asked repeatedly but still find that I cannot answer honestly is 'how can you justify observing and participating in these rites since this implies to others that you are condoning them?' I rather weakly reply that I cannot imagine understanding anything without seeing it, engaging with it.

This example also illustrates some of the complexities involved in the idea of research causing harm. First, whether female circumcision is harmful is not a matter of complete consensus but involves some intercultural dispute (Shweder 2005). Second, assuming that it *is* harm, the question of whether Moore can be held responsible for causing, or even reinforcing, it is open to doubt. However, it seems likely that the objections of Moore's feminist critics, and her own unease, stem not so much from consequentialist considerations regarding harm but rather from her failure publicly to deplore this practice. Criticism and unease might stem from a sense that it was her *duty* to declare her opposition to the practice and to refuse to observe it, perhaps even to campaign against it. Alternatively, or additionally, they may arise from the idea that she had a sisterly duty of care in relation to the young women concerned.

In the case of participant observation, harm can also arise from established roles that researchers take on in the field. Thus, O'Brian (2010: 127) studied door attendants ('bouncers'), and in the course of this took on the role herself. She reports that, on one occasion, she carried out a search that resulted 'in an 18 year old woman being taken into police custody for possession of a Class A drug'. Commenting on this, she reports: 'I felt as though I had crossed the line and that I was no longer simply researching the field. Playing an active member role meant that on this occasion I was instrumental in criminalising an easy target.' She adds: 'In the name of academic research I was occupying a cultural environment underpinned by moral codes that conflicted with my own and consequently being provoked to think and behave in ways [to which] I was not accustomed' (O'Brian 2010: 117–18).

The risk of harm can also arise from a researcher's commitment to reciprocity – with repaying participants for any time and effort they have given in answering questions, and so on. McKeganey (2001: 1237) emphasises that:

If we are paying a drug user for agreeing to an interview or for filling in a questionnaire we ought not to entertain the notion that the money is being used to buy a ticket to the ballet or for a hearty meal. In most cases the money will be spent on the drugs to which the individual is addicted. As a result there is always the possibility, however slim, that the individual may suffer a fatal overdose as a result of the drugs they have bought with the money provided to them by the researcher. It would be a hard individual who did not feel that they had contributed in a small way to the drug user's death.[6]

Payment is not, of course, the only kind of action on the part of researchers motivated by a commitment to reciprocity: another is the feeding back of data and/or analysis to participants. And this too may not always be beneficial. In her investigation of primary science teacher expertise, Traianou (2007: 215–16) decided to share her initial data analysis with the classroom teacher who was the focus of her study, and with whom she had built up a close relationship. To her surprise, the teacher wrote back complaining that there were 'many mistakes in the analysis that misrepresented what went on' in her lessons, and clearly hurt by the process. Furthermore, the teacher made clear that she was not prepared to continue participating in Traianou's research because 'a classroom teacher is in a very vulnerable position'. It took some time for the teacher to be reassured about the implications of the analysis, and for this breach in relations to be overcome.

The focus in most discussions of harm in social research is on the effects of particular methodological decisions, whether specific and momentary – such as what follow-up question to ask in an interview – or more deliberative and strategic – such as which method of data collection to adopt or what findings to publish. For example, Dodd (2009: 477–8) notes how questions about sexual orientation or gender identity can pose a risk to participants under some circumstances; and, in terms of methods, she suggests that focus groups can pose substantial risks in this respect. Along the same lines, Geros (2008) reports on the difficulties of carrying out research in Syria, in an authoritarian political culture where a great deal of circumspection is required in talking about anything that might be judged 'political', since it could lead to imprisonment and torture.

While there can be no entirely reliable basis for anticipating the risk of harm, some types of study are generally seen as involving heightened risks for participants. Thus, research topics can be more or less 'sensitive' (Renzetti and Lee 1993); particular sorts of data are viewed as involving danger; and some kinds of participant are often believed to be more vulnerable and therefore seen as needing protection.[7] In the next

---

[6]On the ethics of paying participants more generally, see Head (2009).

[7]Categories of vulnerable participants include, most notably, the very young, people suffering from serious illness, those who have intellectual impairments (whether temporary, for example as a result of the effects of alcohol or drugs, or more long-lasting, such as a learning disability or mental illness), and those in marginal positions within society. However, other people can be vulnerable in particular respects under certain conditions, as indicated by Oeye et al. (2007) in the case of psychotherapists and McWilliam and Jones (2005) as with the Traianou example, in that of teachers. On 'researching the vulnerable', see Liamputtong (2007).

section, in order to explore some of these variations, we will examine the use of a form of evidence that is often thought to be particularly problematic in these terms, visual data, and in relation to a category of participant that is generally regarded as especially vulnerable, children.

THE USE OF VISUAL RESEARCH METHODS WITH CHILDREN

Definitions of 'visual methods' vary, but central to this category are taking photographs, filming, and making video recordings; and these are research strategies that raise some distinctive ethical issues (Prosser 2000; Pink 2007a: Ch. 2, 2007b Clark et al. 2010). Photography and filming have long been used by anthropologists, going back at least to Bateson and Mead's (1942) book *Balinese Character: A Photographic Analysis*.[8] But, recently, as a result of cheap, high-quality digital technology, these methods have emerged as popular among qualitative researchers more generally, not least those doing research on children and young people (Thomson 2008). At the same time in society more generally, increased concern and caution has come to surround the use of images of children.

Researchers may use photographs or video-recordings for various purposes, most notably to document children's living or work conditions, and the activities in which they engage. Furthermore, there has been a growing trend for researchers to give children and young people still or video cameras, asking them to produce images of relevant aspects of their environment or lives (for instance, Allan 2007; Heath and Cleaver 2004; Renold et al. 2008). They are also sometimes asked to produce video diaries (see, for example, Holliday 2004b; Gibson et al. 2007; Noyes 2008).

Various ethical concerns arise about the production of images for research purposes. Some relate to the process of data collection itself; for example photography or video-recording may seriously disrupt the situation being studied, distracting participants from their normal concerns, and perhaps thereby opening them up to risk of harm. Additional dangers may arise where participants are invited to produce visual images: doing this may expose them to danger from people who object to being photographed or video-recorded; and/or the photographs or video-recordings could be used to do harm to others, for example through exposing them to embarrassment or ridicule. Children, perhaps even more than adults, operate within local social systems that involve significant inequalities in power and status, involving the potential for bullying of various kinds.

Perhaps even more significant ethical concerns relate to the publication of images. The fear is that these could be misused or will have negative consequences for those pictured, especially children. After all, those pictured are likely to be immediately recognisable to people who already know them, and perhaps will also become identifiable by others. Various strategies are used by researchers to minimise this danger. Flewitt (2005) mentions fuzzying faces so as to protect identities, and the possibility of producing sketches of video stills and photographs that minimise

---

[8]For a history of the use of photographs in anthropology and social science more generally, see Chaplin 1994: Ch. 5.

identifiability. However, these techniques have themselves been challenged on ethical grounds, for instance as 'an example of the "Othering" of young children in research' (Nutbrown 2010: 3). As this author comments: 'that's what the media does with photographs of people accused of crime' (p. 4).

The response of many researchers who use visual data to these risks of harm is to take what precautions against them seem reasonable in the circumstances, and very often also to obtain informed consent from participants, as far as this is possible. Of course, in the case of children, even teenagers, there is an issue about from whom informed consent can and should be obtained. Much recent writing about research on children has stressed their competence, and how this is often underestimated, as well as their right to make decisions about matters that are directly relevant to them (Alderson and Morrow 2011). At the same time, there remain questions about the danger of harm, and adults' role in the protection of children from this. As we shall see in Chapter 4, informed consent is a complex and uncertain process, and a crucial element of it concerns the ability to understand the threat of particular kinds of harm. There are clear potential tensions here between a commitment to minimising the risk of harm and respecting the autonomy of children.[9] Seeking to obtain informed consent may also obstruct the effective pursuit of research in some contexts.

THE ISSUE OF RESPONSIBILITY

It is necessary to emphasise that the occurrence of harm within the context of a piece of qualitative research does not necessarily imply that the researcher is to blame. Assigning responsibility is a separate matter from judging harm. However, it too is an uncertain business, since most outcomes are the product of multiple factors. Furthermore, when assessing responsibility we take account of various additional considerations, such as whether the actor could have reasonably foreseen the outcome, whether or not he or she had any alternative option that was not worse in some important respect, and so on.

We can illustrate what is involved through a hypothetical example:

A researcher is carrying out an investigation within a large organisation. As part of the access negotiations he has agreed that, after six months, he will report his initial findings to members of that organisation. In line with this, at the appropriate time he produces a brief document that is made available across the organisation. In writing this, he indicates some possible *general* conclusions, rather than simply reporting particular events; and is careful to protect confidentiality, not disclosing from whom he obtained specific information, and seeking to preserve the anonymity of the people mentioned in illustrations. In the body of the report,

---

[9]On the complexities of negotiating informed consent in relation to children, see David et al. (2001) and Heath et al. (2007).

some actions and events are reported that could have led to a major problem for the organisation, though in fact this was avoided at the last minute. The day after the report is made available two of the people who were central to his main example are dismissed. They blame the researcher for this, as do some of their friends. The following day, he receives a message from the general manager. She praises his report for its 'great usefulness in allowing an effective appraisal of key parts of our organisation'.

Harm has probably occurred here, at least in the short term for the particular individuals who have lost their jobs; though, of course, it might be argued that their dismissal was beneficial for the organisation as a whole, or for other employees, notably any who gained promotion as a result. The issue we will focus on here, though, is whether the researcher is responsible for whatever harm (or benefit) occurred. This is the view of some of the participants, but are they right? After all, it is not unknown for scapegoats to be sought when untoward and troublesome events arise.

In deciding on responsibility here there are a number of issues. First, we must decide whether what the researcher did was implicated in the causal process that led to the sackings. A requirement for most causal inference is that the effect comes after the cause: had the people been sacked *before* the report was made available, then this event could not have been blamed on it, unless it were suspected that there had been a leak about what the report was going to say. We also tend to assume that if an event follows *closely in time* after an action it is more likely to have been caused by it than if there had been a long delay, though the latter does not rule out a possible causal link. While 'follows closely' is a matter of degree, and open to interpretation, in this case the fact that the sackings took place the next day fits the existence of a causal connection. Of course, we should note that an action occurring closely before an event may still not actually have been the cause: the outcome might have occurred anyway because of some other parallel causal process. For instance, the actions of the two people would have been known to others, and by coincidence information about these may have reached the ears of the general manager at the same time that the report was made available. So, we must ask: did the report supply information that the manager did not previously have, did it confirm strong suspicions that she already held, or did it simply provide a means by which the decision to sack them could be justified? In all of these cases the provision of the report plays a causal role, but a varying one, with the result that its significance, and the researcher's responsibility, may be judged differently.

So, secondly, there is the question of what specific role, if any, the researcher's actions played in bringing about the dismissal of the two people. A basic requirement in establishing a causal relationship is that the candidate cause is of a kind that might reasonably be expected to have produced the outcome. In this case, the researcher provided information that related to the two people who were sacked, and what was reported about them was of a kind that could perhaps be interpreted as a damaging error on their part, and therefore be seen as grounds for dismissal. So there is a credible causal pathway in this case. Furthermore, even though the information the researcher supplied was anonymised, there is the possibility that the people could have been identified by the general manager, and/or others, from the report. At the very least, we can say that if the report had not discussed the activities of the two people concerned, or if it had not been made available within the organisation, its causal role would be much less plausible.

In making such judgments we rely upon what are called counterfactual inferences: judgments about *what would have happened if the suspected cause had not been present*. In other words, would the two people have been dismissed if the research had not been taking place, if the researcher had not produced the report, and/or if he had not made it available to people in the organisation? We can never know the answers to these questions with absolute certainty, of course, but we must make some assessment of likelihood if we are to come to a conclusion.

As already noted, there is never a single factor involved in the production of an outcome, so that we need to assess the role of the researcher's producing his report *against other factors*. One of these is the management style of the general manager, which appears to have favoured decisive and severe action on the basis of quite limited information. Under a different regime, the report might have prompted less serious punishment, or even praise for those who saved the day. Equally important, it might be argued that the two people who were sacked bear some responsibility for this, through the way in which they created or dealt with the organisational problem.

Finally, even if we were to conclude that the researcher's report had been a major factor in bringing about the sackings, this would not, in itself, be sufficient to ascribe responsibility to the researcher for a wrongful harm. For this to follow several other conditions must be met. First, the researcher must have been able to avoid the action that caused the harm. Second, he must have been able reasonably to foresee the outcome. Third, any precautions he took to reduce the risk of the outcome to an acceptable level, such as anonymisation, must have been patently inadequate at the time. Finally, there must be no overriding reason why he should have carried out the action even though he recognised that it could well produce the harm.

As regards the first of these conditions, there is an issue about what it was that the researcher did that caused the outcome: was it producing a report, or was it the particular nature of the report, for example providing illustrations, or perhaps a failure to anonymise effectively? Depending upon which of these is the crucial factor, we might give different answers to the question of whether or not he was responsible. It may be that, having agreed to produce a report, the researcher was virtually bound to do so. In these terms, it might be said that he had no alternative and therefore any harm resulting was not his fault. Of course, it could be asked whether it was wise for him to agree to this requirement in the first place, but we should note that entry to the organisation might not have been possible without this. What this highlights is that any assessment relates to an agent in a particular situation at a particular time, with particular constraints being assumed, including commitments entered into that it would be costly or even unethical to violate. The conclusion we reach may vary depending upon what we treat as having been open to change and what we assume to have been fixed. One of the dangers in looking back on events that happened in the past is that we treat features of the situation as having been more easily open to change than they actually were at the time.

The second issue – of whether the outcome could have been foreseen – relates directly to the question of risk: how likely is it that a reasonable person, in the position of the researcher in this time and place, would have anticipated the harmful outcome? Here, too, there is great danger that we are misled by hindsight, overestimating the degree to which the perceived risk could have been anticipated – after all, we now know that the outcome did actually occur, whereas the researcher, when writing his report, did not know that it would do so. At the same time, in the particular case we are discussing, it might reasonably have been suspected that some of the content of the report would have led to questions about who was involved in the incidents reported, and to action against them if their identity could be discovered.

This leads us directly on to the question of what legitimate confidence the researcher could have in the effectiveness of the steps he took to maintain confidentiality through preserving anonymity. Here again there are dangers from hindsight, but it also needs to be recognised that it is tempting to overestimate the likely effectiveness of anonymisation, especially in the case of a report that is made directly available to the people being studied. In this context, it is frequently possible for others to identify people from descriptions of their actions, because these descriptions themselves narrow down the range of people within the organisation who could be being portrayed.

We have already mentioned one point relevant to the final question, about whether there might have been good reason to carry out the action even though it was recognised that it involved some risk of serious harm. This was that, having agreed to provide a report, the researcher had an obligation to do so even if this involved a danger of causing harm. Here we have a situation approximating to a 'dirty hands' dilemma. However, it is less clear that he had no alternative but to produce a report of a kind that carried the danger concerned.

In looking at how responsibility should be assigned here, we have been engaged in retrospective assessment of an action and outcome that happened in the past. Usually, though, researchers are faced with making prospective judgments about whether particular courses of action are likely to cause harm of particular kinds, and how likely this is. Here all of the considerations discussed apply, in one way or another, but this task is more complex because it is necessary to assess the likelihood of various potential outcomes that are contingent upon ongoing situations, and about which the researcher usually has only very limited information. In the case of our hypothetical example, the researcher had to decide whether or not to produce a report, as promised, and if so *how* to write it, on the basis of an assessment of the chances that the parties described in examples would be identifiable, and of the risk that this would lead to harmful consequences for them.

He also had to decide whether *some* risk of this outcome would be acceptable; and, if so, below what threshold.[10]

What should be clear from this discussion is that assessing whether a particular research decision has produced harm, could have done, or is likely to do so, can be a difficult process that involves balancing various considerations, factual and evaluative, against one another. While there is no simple means of calculation that could be used to make the decision in a way that would short-cut this process, and thereby lead to certainty or consensus, nevertheless such decisions are ones that we all have to make in everyday life on some occasions; and we know that there are better and worse ways of doing this. Fortunately, most of the time the consequences involved are not life-threatening, and do not even involve serious harm, though there can be rare occasions when this is a possibility, and the resulting decisions can be agonising. This is also true of qualitative research.

HARM TO WHOM?

Up to now, we have been concerned with the risk of harm to the people being studied. However, these are not the only ones who can be affected by research. Others include: organisations from which funds were obtained; institutions within which researchers work; colleagues in those institutions; journals or publishers; broader groups or categories of person with whom the researcher has not had direct contact but who might be affected by publication of the findings; and even researchers themselves.

In media reports of research findings, it is not uncommon for the research to be ascribed to the funding body or the employing organisation, rather than (or in addition to) the researchers themselves. Journals and publishers can be implicated in the same fashion. In this way, and others, these bodies can suffer harm as a result of research projects for which they are seen as responsible. In particular, some aspect of how the research was carried out may bring them into public disrepute, or open them up to legal challenge. In practice, this is rare, but an example is the way in which the American Anthropological Association was implicated in the El Dorado controversy, not least because of how it handled the case (Fluehr-Lobban 2003a: 87; Borofsky 2005; see the Introduction). Of course, we should note that such organisations may also *gain* from their association with particular research projects and researchers.

---

[10]Needless to say, researchers' retrospective evaluations of the risks involved in their research may not correspond entirely to their earlier prospective evaluations. See, for instance, Humphreys (1975: 230). It may also be necessary to prepare resources to provide to participants should the risk of serious harm arise, either from the research or from other sources. Thus, researchers working with children or young people, who fear the divulgence of abuse, often distribute information about helplines, counselling agencies, and so on. In a different context, Keys offered post-abortion counselling contact information to some of the women she interviewed (Goodrum and Keys 2007: 254).

In addition, there are people who have had no direct contact with the researcher who may be harmed by her or his research, notably through the publication of specific findings. Ditton's (1977: iv) study of bread salesmen, which included an account of how they worked various 'fiddles', not only threatened to reduce the income of the people he studied but also those working in other bakeries as well.[11] Tourigny (1993: 14–17) mentions the equally ambiguous case of research on doctors providing euthanasia to patients with terminal illnesses, where publication of findings could result in their being prosecuted and their work brought to a halt. The feared effect may also operate in a more indirect way, thus Sikes expresses concern that 'findings of research like mine could be used to endorse the agendas of those who may be considered to be engaging in academic debate to justify paedophilic desires and practices […]' (Sikes 2010: 148), thereby potentially harming children.

Finally, engaging in research can cause harm to researchers themselves (see Lee 1995; Lyng 1998; Lee-Treweek and Linkogle 2000). This may arise as a result of risks that they have consciously taken, or of decisions that they did not recognise as carrying any threat. As in other cases, what is involved can vary considerably in severity. Warwick (1982: 118) suggests that: 'researchers may suffer harm ranging from torture or death to mild doubts or regret about their professional activities'. Certainly, in some contexts qualitative researchers may be exposed to the risk of physical harm, whether that of assault (Kelly 2004; Jacobs 2006) or the risk of disease (Lankshear 2000). Warwick also mentions two other relevant types of harm: legal jeopardy, the danger of prosecution and even imprisonment; and the psychological effects arising from engaging in deception and manipulation, both in terms of feelings of guilt and self-doubt but also effects on personal behaviour outside research contexts (see also Homan in Homan and Bulmer 1982: 117). There can be other kinds of emotional cost associated with qualitative research too (Corsino 1987; Muir 2004). For instance, discussing her anthropological study of children in a rural primary school in England, Laerke (2008: 144) reports:

> This particular fieldwork, to paraphrase Ruth Behar, broke my heart (Behar 1996). And while writing has been an exorcism, of sorts, of a fieldwork–identity that literally made me sick, a reconstituted and properly dislodged 'me' has yet to materialize. Ten years on, I am still somehow in the grip of it. Rather than putting an alleviating 'full-stop' to my troubles, writing about Little Midby has produced a gradual sedimentation of two feelings: anger and sadness.

Much qualitative research is done by lone researchers, but it is also sometimes carried out in teams, and here the issue of harm to researchers takes on a further dimension: the leader of a team, or the team as a collectivity, may be seen as having some responsibility for protecting individual members, particularly those who are younger and less experienced, or vulnerable in some other way (Bloor et al. 2010). Equally, of course, it may be colleagues in the research team who are responsible for causing

---

[11]Once again, of course, this example highlights the ambiguities surrounding what counts as harm.

researchers harm, for example by divulging information that damages their reputation or even exposes them to physical danger.

We should also note that particular studies can do harm to whole research communities, for example by bringing them into disrepute, and/or by blocking access for future studies in particular settings. This was the major complaint brought against Lofland and Lejune (1960) over their covert research on Alcoholics Anonymous (see Introduction).

Assessments of harm to people other than those who are the focus of inquiry involve the same sorts of complexity and difficult judgments as those we examined earlier. And, once again, it must not be assumed that these forms of harm are very common. How great the risks are will vary considerably according to the circumstances and trajectories of particular research projects.

CONCLUSION

In this chapter we have examined one of the major principles that has informed a great deal of discussion about research ethics. We argued that there is always *some* potential for harm from qualitative research, and what is required is that researchers make reasonable assessments of the likelihood and severity of particular kinds of harm. We noted that there is a complementary concern with benefits, but that balancing the risk of harm against likely benefits requires some means of assessing the relative seriousness of different harms (and the value of different benefits). We outlined how this is possible despite the absence of any means of measurement. We emphasised that it is essential that the seriousness of actual or potential harms be judged *in context*, while yet recognising that comparison with other situations, and with ideals, can be illuminating.

In the second half of the chapter we explored various ways in which harm might arise in qualitative research, and examined the particular case of visual research in relation to children. We went on to consider the assignment of responsibility for harms, noting that this is a complex and uncertain process. In part what is involved is making a causal assessment of how likely it is that a particular action will result in a particular type of outcome in the circumstances, but there are also issues to do with responsibility and wrongfulness.

Finally, we looked at the issue of *who* might be harmed, noting that harm can arise for others besides those people who are part of the focus of a study. These include funding bodies and other institutions associated with the research, broader categories of people to whom the findings of the research relate, and even researchers themselves.

4

AUTONOMY AND INFORMED CONSENT

A second major ethical principle that frequently informs practical judgments within, and about, qualitative research concerns the need to respect the autonomy of those being studied.[1] The idea that people should be free to decide for themselves what is best for them – in other words, to exercise control over their own lives – is a widely accepted principle in modern Western societies, and elsewhere too. The following statement of this principle captures how it is conventionally understood:

> To respect an autonomous agent is to recognise with due appreciation that person's capacities and perspective, including his or her right to hold certain views, to make certain choices, and to take certain actions based on personal values and beliefs. Such respect has historically been connected to the idea that persons possess an intrinsic value independent of special circumstances that confer value. As expressed in Kantian philosophy, autonomous persons are ends in themselves, determining their own destiny, and are not to be treated merely as means to the ends of others. Thus, the burden of moral justification rests on those who would restrict or prevent a person's exercise of autonomy. (Faden and Beauchamp 1986: 8)

In the context of social research ethics, it is this principle that underpins the common requirement that researchers must obtain informed consent from people before research is carried out, and that participants should be able to withdraw from an investigation at any point.[2] It is sometimes argued that only if research meets these conditions has people's autonomy been respected, *and that this is essential for it to be*

---

[1] Synonyms include 'freedom' and 'personal sovereignty'. On the latter see Miller (2010: 380–1).

[2] On the nature of informed consent and its emergence as a key principle in clinical medicine and in research ethics, see Faden and Beauchamp (1986). For an important re-evaluation of its significance in these contexts, see O'Neill (2002) and Manson and O'Neill (2007). See also Corrigan (2003); Miller and Boulton (2007).

ethical. As we shall see, the principle of autonomy also underpins more radical views to the effect that we should not carry out research *on* people, but only *with* them – in such a way that they are able to exercise control over the decisions involved in the research process.

In the quotation above, Faden and Beauchamp refer to one of the main philosophical sources for this principle: the ethical theory of Kant. However, it can also be derived from utilitarianism, specifically John Stuart Mill's defence of liberty as contributing to what he calls 'the permanent interests of [humanity] as a progressive being' (Mill 1859b: 136). So, autonomy can be recognised as a central ethical principle from both deontological and consequentialist points of view.

While the importance of the principle of autonomy is widely accepted, there are some important issues to be addressed about its character and implications.[3] These include whether it depends upon a conception of the good life that is distinctive to modern Western societies, rather than having wider applicability (MacIntyre 1982: 184); and whether it is a distorted or defective ideal. For example, there have been questions about whether it relies upon an attitude toward social relations that is characteristically male – after all, it is not central to feminist versions of relational ethics, such as the ethics of care (see Chapter 1).

In light of these points, we might ask whether individual freedom is emphasised at the expense of other equally, or more, important principles, such as those centring on obligations deriving from relationships with others or from membership of communities. A further question concerns exactly what the word 'autonomy' *means*, and its implications in the context of research. After considering these matters, we will examine when consent for research is required, from whom, and to do what; as well as the issue of what constitutes *free* consent. Finally, we will explore what is involved in *informing* people about research in order to gain their consent. In this way, we will consider when the principle of informed consent is relevant, the demands it places upon researchers, and some of the practical problems to which it gives rise.[4]

INDIVIDUAL FREEDOM AS A LIBERAL IDEAL

As we saw in Chapter 2, it is a feature of modern discussions of ethics that the focus tends to be the individual person as agent: on rights and duties, on how individuals ought to make ethical decisions or should be treated. Within such a framework it is perhaps not surprising that autonomy would become a key value: after all, such agency presupposes freedom. But is autonomy a universal value, or is preference for it a form of Western and/or masculinist bias? This question is not easy to answer, not least because the term 'autonomy' can have different meanings.

---

[3]Dworkin (1988: 7) describes 'autonomy' as 'a term of art introduced by a theorist in an attempt to make sense of a tangled net of intuitions, conceptual and empirical issues, and normative claims'.

[4]For the argument that consent is not always required and that seeking it is not always desirable, see Spicker (2007).

In the West, the emphasis given to autonomy first arose in demands for freedom of religious belief and expression; often on the pragmatic grounds that toleration of a specific range of beliefs and practices was a requirement for civil peace, given the depth and divisiveness of disputes about them. Later, the principle of autonomy was associated with an insistence that the authority of the state must be restricted to a minimum, and/or that its various elements – a monarch, an elected parliament and government, a judiciary, etc. – should be balanced against one another so as to limit the power of each. Also relevant here was the spread of democracy, enabling people to exercise at least some influence over who would rule them. Finally, there was the emergence of free markets, which allowed people to exercise more choice in the production, exchange, and consumption of goods and services.

Of course, while autonomy (in some respects, and to some degree) is frequently seen as of intrinsic value, commitment to it is also often underpinned by the idea that people know better than anyone else what is in their own interests, this sometimes being referred to as the principle of 'agent-sovereignty' (Arneson 1999). In addition, there is the influential idea that it is through processes in which people independently exercise choice that beneficial outcomes arise for all. One version of this, already mentioned, is Mill's insistence that individual liberty is essential for the progressive improvement of human life (see O'Neill 2002: 32); another example, equally influential but often misunderstood, is Adam Smith's 'hidden hand' of the market (Haakonssen and Winch 2006), which is often taken to imply that the pursuit of self-interest results in the best outcome for all.

Within Western thought there has been a tension between different conceptions of freedom, notably between the 'negative' freedom of the individual from external constraints, especially those coming from the state, and 'positive' freedom, interpreted as the exercise of self-rule, and avoidance of subordination to others.[5] While Western liberalism has typically given most emphasis to the former, in the context of ethics the positive concept of autonomy has been central, as in the philosophy of Kant. Furthermore, it is this interpretation of freedom that is most relevant for research ethics (Beauchamp 2010: 61): the researcher is not usually in a position to subject the people being studied to external constraint, though the issue of negative freedom may arise when we consider the role of persuasion, manipulation, or even coercion in gaining consent for research. Generally speaking, the main concern about autonomy in research ethics has been with whether researchers are infringing people's right to self-determination.

The literature on social research ethics has been strongly shaped by liberal individualism, and associated ideas about the importance of autonomy. But in recent years there have been challenges to this. One source has been feminism, especially the ethics of care (see Chapter 1). Another has been from those writers who are particularly concerned with research on indigenous communities and their cultures

---

[5]Berlin (1969), see also Gray (1995). Etymologically, 'autonomy' is made up of 'self' (autos) and 'rule' (nomos), though it seems originally to have applied to the independence of cities or states rather than that of individuals (Dworkin 1988: 12–13). Some commentators treat what is referred to here as negative and positive freedom as complementary (see, for example, Miller 2010: 380) by contrast with Berlin who believes them to be competing conceptions.

(L. Bishop 2005; Smith 2005; Denzin et al. 2008; Chilisa 2009). They have empha-sised the rights of communities, and of traditional bodies representing their interests, to bar researchers' entry to settings and restrict access to information; or to exercise control over how research is carried out, seeking to ensure that it is done 'in the community's interests'. Such arguments link to a major debate within political philosophy between advocates of liberal individualism and those of a more com-munitarian persuasion, from both the Left and the Right.[6]

It is also worth emphasising that, as we argued in Chapter 2, social researchers can themselves legitimately claim a distinctive form of occupational autonomy, one that is essential if they are to be able to carry out research effectively. And, of course, other occupations make similar claims. The result is that there can be conflicts not just between researchers' appeals for autonomy and the autonomy of individual people or communities but also between both of these and what other occupations and organisations take to be *their* rights. Complex claims and counter-claims can potentially be involved in which each party demands that their autonomy be respected; and they may or may not recognise the legitimacy of others' rights – individual, occupational, and organisational.

THE FALLACY OF FREEDOM-IN-GENERAL

It is not sensible to be for, or against, autonomy *per se*. It only makes sense to be for or against *specific sorts of freedom or autonomy*, or to judge *specific interpretations of them* as more or less important than other values in particular circumstances (Cranston 1953). This reflects the fact that one cannot be free from all constraint, nor would most people believe that anyone should act in a way that is free from all restriction. Generally speaking, when people declare themselves to be in favour of freedom they have in mind the lifting of *specific* restrictions, or of people being allowed or enabled to do something that previously they had been prevented from doing.

There is also a deeper conceptual point. This is that if we think of autonomy as the exercise of choice about what to do, we must recognise that any meaningful choice operates within some specified range of options: it is not a matter of being able to do absolutely anything at all. So, paradoxically, there must always be restric-tions operating, specifying the available options, for any kind of freedom to be exer-cised. A related complication is that in order for people to be free to do something they must have relevant capabilities: these allow options that would not otherwise be available. And an essential higher-level capability for the exercise of autonomy is the capacity to suspend preconceptions and impulses and to reflect on goals, constraints, and strategies.

Yet much discussion of autonomy and freedom, in the context of research ethics and beyond, neglects its specific and relational character. Furthermore, there are

---

[6]See the entry on communitarianism in the Stanford Encyclopedia of Philosophy, available at: http://plato.stanford.edu/entries/communitarianism/ The dispute between liberalism and communitarianism is discussed in Kymlicka (2002).

philosophical arguments that encourage the mistaken idea that there is some general state or property corresponding to these terms. One source can be found in the work of Kant, though his writings also highlight many of the complexities. He argues that in order to preserve any concept of ethics it is essential for human beings to act *as if* they were capable of abstracting themselves from all causal processes and influences, so as to recognise and respond to the ethical demands of Reason. At the same time, he is all too aware that these demands are frequently experienced as constraints by human beings, as duties rather than as inclinations; and he argues that this is because we are, by nature, caught up in a world where our preferences, beliefs, and scope for action are constrained by causal processes. He draws a contrast with a wholly rational, in other words a fully autonomous, agent for whom the ethical requirements flowing from Reason would not be experienced as constraints at all but rather would be entirely natural.[7]

Some later thinkers radicalised Kant's perspective, tending to treat all constraints operating on agents as signalling the imperfection of the world, so that these constraints needed to be eliminated if true autonomy was to prevail (see Pippin 1991 and Ameriks 2000). From this point of view, freedom as an ideal means being unaffected by any causal influences, so that in effect the agent is entirely 'self-moving', in the manner of a god. The background to this ideal, as Kant made clear, is the drawing of a sharp contrast between determinism and free will. Determinism is seen as implying that we are unable to choose what to do because we are part of a causal nexus that controls our behaviour, this making any idea of holding people responsible for their actions senseless. After all, people must already have, or be given, the freedom to determine their own actions if they are to be held responsible for these and their consequences. Similarly, if they are taken to have an obligation to resist pressures to act wrongly – whether from their own desires and interests, from the influence of other people, or even from institutional demands backed by force – they must have the capacity to do this. It is one thing for them to be subject to weakness of will or testing circumstances, quite another for them to be *incapable* of resisting *any* pressures – they cannot be held to account for that.

For some post-Kantians, then, autonomy contrasts with determinism and any constraint is treated as an imposition that must be resisted. In line with this, appeals to obligations, or to restrictions of any other kind, tend to be dismissed as ideological – as reflecting the yet-to-be-overcome imperfection of the world and/or as a form of bad faith (see McBride 1997). Furthermore, this implies it is not just *perceived* constraints that are to be eliminated but even those unperceived ones that shape what we take to be 'thinkable', 'viable', 'worthwhile', and so on.

This overblown concept of autonomy is no more convincing as a philosophical position than the kind of determinism it rejects. Any reasonable interpretation of the principle of autonomy must recognise that the scope for exercising this capacity is always potentially limited by various perceived constraints, and that these can take a variety of forms. Some are material in character, to do with what is physically

---

[7]Kant's views here parallel older religious ideas, in terms of which human beings have one foot in the natural world of animals, and the other in the divine world of God and the angels.

possible. Others relate to excessive costs that would come into play if a particular course of action were adopted, notably as a product of the actions of others, including political authorities. There are also ethical limits on what we should be prepared to do. And while it is possible to resist or get round some constraints, there will usually be severe restrictions on how far this is possible or desirable: for any particular agent in any particular place and time.

More fundamentally, what is a constraint is always *relative to some goal*: nothing is a constraint *per se*. While there is much to be said for reflexivity, for an agent attending to assumptions that he or she makes about what features of the situation faced are fixed *that it would be wise to question*, the idea that we should subject all 'constraints' to reflexive reconstruction is a mirage, not least because it would be a reflexivity that had no ground on which to stand: to question anything we have to take something else for granted.

So, the very meaning of the term 'freedom' implies freedom *from* something in particular and/or freedom *to do* something particular (MacCallum 1972). In other words, the idea of absolute freedom is meaningless because any exercise of freedom requires taking quite a lot as already given: that there is an agent of a particular kind in a particular situation, who has (or should have) some particular desire or goal, in relation to which there are specific options and means of achievement available (as well as obstacles of various kinds in place), and so on. Moreover, as we have made clear, which features of the agent and of the situation are salient, which judged as fixed and which regarded as changeable, will be relative to the particular desire or goal in play, as well as to the other commitments of the actor, over and above the facts of the situation.

WHAT DOES RESPECTING AUTONOMY MEAN IN THE CONTEXT OF SOCIAL RESEARCH?

What specific freedoms does the principle of autonomy require researchers to respect, in relation to the people they study? Sometimes this is interpreted as a right not to be researched (Sagarin 1973). In a limited form, this would mean that people should control whether researchers gather and/or use information that relates to them *as individuals*. Some rights over the control of information of this kind are, of course, enshrined in data protection legislation. However, the arguments for a 'right not to be researched' often extend well beyond this to the notion that people should be able to control whether or not researchers can do research about *some category or group* of persons to which they belong. This idea is enshrined in the phrase 'nothing about us without us', which was originally developed by the disability activist movement (Charlton 2000). Here the implication seems to be that nothing can be written about a particular category or community of people without their agreement. Associated arguments are that only black people should research black people, only women women, or only children children. Similar attempts at restricting who can research whom sometimes arise in relation to researchers writing about indigenous communities, particular religions, or particular occupations. As Skomal

(1993: 26; quoted in Benjamin 1999: 57) notes: 'people everywhere are increasingly anxious to control the information that is being released about themselves', and respect for this concern seems to have underpinned one of the most restrictive research contracts ever agreed, that of Benjamin with the Curaçaoan Jewish community (see Benjamin 1999: 55; Fox 1999: 63, 69 and *passim*).

However, in our view, any global right not to be researched is impossible to defend. Most social science, including qualitative research, is not primarily concerned with documenting the views and behaviour of particular named individuals (by contrast with journalism). Instead, people are treated as representative, in some sense, of broader categories, for example as occupants of particular roles within social institutions or as members of groups of various kinds, rather than being studied in their own right. Their behaviour is taken as exemplifying, or deviating from, particular types of social action, group, institution, or social structure.[8] It would surely be unreasonable to insist that no one should analyse and write about these categories of phenomena, or use publicly available data that relate anonymously to particular individuals associated with them. The idea that any set of people should be able to control what is said or written about them, beyond narrow limits, or to specify who can and cannot analyse data about them, is in breach not only of the licence that social scientists must exercise if they are to do their work, but also of the principle of freedom of speech.

The right not to be researched, as we have discussed it so far, seems to involve a claim to negative freedom, but there is also a more radical, positive version. This insists that people have a right to participate on an equal footing with researchers in the pursuit of any research that relates to their lives, making decisions about what is to be investigated and how, what forms of analysis will be used, how the conclusions will be written up, how the findings will be disseminated, and so on. It is suggested that simply carrying out research *on* people implies disrespect for their autonomy. So, from this point of view, what is required for the principle of autonomy to be respected is that the people being researched become at least equal partners in the research process, a notion that underpins participatory, and some versions of action and practitioner research (see Reason and Bradbury 2008).

In our view, this is both an unrealistic and an unjustifiable ideal. How could everybody be equally involved in the governance of all the many activities that touch their lives? This is at odds with the institutional structures that exist within most if not all past and current societies. And attempts to apply this ideal to inquiry undermine the distinctive ethical responsibilities of researchers, as derived from both intrinsic and extrinsic values.

It is worth noting that this interpretation of what respecting autonomy amounts to is typically advanced in the context of carrying out research about types of people

[8]This is at odds with the way in which some qualitative researchers today think about and portray their work, believing themselves to be studying individuals, as exemplified in some versions of 'case study' (see Stake 1995) and even more obviously in biographical and autobiographical work (Stanley 1995; Roberts 2001; Ellis 2004; Merrill and West 2009). We suggest, however, that even in the case of life-history work the aim in social science should be to treat individuals as exemplifying general types.

for whom the researcher has personal or political sympathy; it is much less likely to arise where researchers are studying people with whom they feel little solidarity, whom they find morally objectionable, or to whom they are politically opposed. Thus, researchers studying rapists, paedophiles, and elite power groups of various sorts rarely suggest that they wish to involve these people as equal partners in the research process; and if they did they would rightly be subjected to widespread criticism. But on what grounds could it be decided that some people are to be given the positive freedom to participate in research while others are to be denied it? In the terms we introduced earlier, there are no such grounds implied by the values intrinsic to research as an activity; and, given this, researchers have no authority to make these judgments. Even more importantly, those intrinsic values place responsibility for effective pursuit of inquiry on the shoulders of the researcher, and this responsibility cannot be passed on to others.

So, in our view, respect for autonomy, in the sense of freedom to make decisions about one's life, does not imply a right not to be researched, whether this is conceived as a negative or a positive freedom. Instead, the principle relates specifically to the data collection process, and to issues about whether people must consent to allowing some particular kind of data to be collected about them or to provide data themselves, and whether they need to be informed that research is taking place, notably where this will involve their being observed. Often these two matters are treated together under the heading of 'informed consent'.[9] However, it is important not to assume that informed consent is always required, or that it should always take the same form. For this reason, we will examine the seeking of consent and the provision of information separately.

CONSENT

The issue of consent arises primarily in the following situations:

1   when researchers are seeking entry to settings to which they do not automatically have access as 'members of the public' or as citizens;
2   when they are trying to obtain documents that are not publicly available;
3   when they want to elicit information or data from people through interviews, questionnaires, diaries, and so on.

There are a number of questions that must be addressed regarding consent. These include: *whether* it is necessary or desirable to seek consent; *from whom* consent should be obtained; *how* consent ought to be secured; *for what* consent is being sought; and what counts as *free* consent? The answers to these questions are likely to differ according to circumstances.

---

[9]For a review of the social science literature on informed consent, see Wiles et al. (2005).

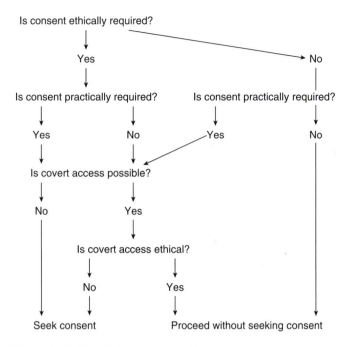

Figure 4.1   Pathways in deciding whether consent should be sought

When is gaining consent necessary or desirable?

We need to begin by recognising that when researchers seek consent they do not always do this because they believe that it is *ethically* required. Gaining consent can be a *practical* necessity if access to relevant data is to be achieved; and this is separate from the question of whether it is needed in order to respect participants' autonomy. These two issues, the ethical and the prudential, need to be distinguished; and, as we shall see, there can be conflicts between them.

Figure 4.1 indicates something of the complexities potentially involved in decisions about whether consent must be obtained. As it makes clear, there may be circumstances where consent is neither practically nor ethically required, while there are others where it may be necessary, in one or both senses. At the same time, both ethical and prudential requirements are defeasible – in other words they are not absolute. Researchers may try to circumvent the practical need to obtain consent by using a covert strategy. For example, in planning research in Syria, Geros (2008: 92–3) decided against seeking the required government permit because of the risk of refusal and the restrictions that would have accompanied any agreement, even though this opened him up to some danger. Equally important, an *ethical* requirement to obtain consent on the basis of the principle of autonomy can be outweighed by other considerations, ethical or methodological. Thus, despite recognising that it could be argued that his fellow 'bouncers', guarding the doors of nightclubs, had a right to know he was a researcher, Calvey (2000) came to the conclusion that a covert strategy was essential.

In order to provide a little more detail about the considerations involved here, let us consider first the case of whether consent is required to carry out *observation*. Some situations are relatively open to view, in the sense that there may be no practical or ethical need to gain consent to enter them. This is most obviously true of what are thought of as public settings, for example streets and parks, but perhaps also shopping centres, train stations, airports, football grounds, theme parks, beaches, public libraries, and so on.

However, there are a couple of qualifications that need to be made here. First, it is important to recognise that within such settings there may be some parts that are *not* open to public access, and therefore not automatically available for observation by researchers. For instance, there are parts of shopping centres and railway stations that are restricted to staff who work there. In relation to these, a practical and/or ethical need to obtain consent may still arise. A second point is that even in the public parts of these settings the researcher may not be free to do everything that is required for the purposes of collecting data. A code of etiquette of some kind will normally operate: for example there may be conventions of inattention, so that researchers are not free to 'stand and stare', and thereby observe; or, at least, not without risking unpleasant consequences.[10] Even in relatively public settings, then, researchers may decide that in practical terms it is necessary, or would be desirable, to negotiate consent, perhaps with a view to reducing the constraints on data collection or protecting themselves from harm. They may also come to the same decision for ethical reasons, believing that people have the right to avoid being observed for research purposes even in these settings.

Of course, what is a public and what is a private setting can be less than fully clear, or even a matter of dispute. For instance, are shopping centres public settings? They are frequently privately owned, and the owners often seek to exercise control over what is done there. On the other hand, access to them is routinely open to the general public; entry to them is not usually controlled by security personnel, even if the latter have a legal right to eject those they judge to be undesirable. Similar issues arise with other settings. For instance, in defending his covert observation of religious services, Homan and Bulmer (1982: 113) pointed to the fact that there was a sign outside the church which said 'All are welcome'. Other settings are less open to the public – music venues, theatres, legal courts, and so on – but they are still in some sense public situations. Humphreys' (1970) research on homosexual encounters in public restrooms or lavatories raises these issues in a peculiarly delicate manner.

In the case of those settings where it is not practically possible for a researcher to gain automatic access, or where there are restrictions, a rather different choice is faced: whether to seek consent or to try to find a covert strategy of entry. The second option is most likely to be considered where the gatekeepers concerned are regarded as illegitimate; where they are expected to block entry, or to grant it only under very restrictive conditions; and/or where it is assumed that gaining permission would

---

[10]Etiquette is not ethics, of course, but the observance of etiquette may become an ethical matter, for example as part of respecting local cultures. And we should recognise that what is acceptable in public settings is culturally variable.

introduce serious error into the research process through changing the behaviour of participants. The question is, though, whether these considerations are sufficient to warrant a covert approach in particular cases.

Covert strategies can take a variety of forms, and each involves somewhat different ethical issues. A researcher may be able to gain entry under the auspices of a role that he or she already plays, for example as a member of the organisation or group being researched. For example, Holdaway (1982) was already a serving police officer and carried out his study of policing covertly in this role; while Armstrong (1998) used his involvement as a Sheffield United supporter to investigate 'hard-core' soccer fans and the violence in which they engaged. A second strategy involves researchers joining an organisation or group, or taking on a new role, specifically to obtain research data. For example, Shaffir (1985) obtained a clerical position in the Hassidic community he wished to study. Finally, researchers may seek to 'pass' as members or role incumbents of some sort when, in fact, they are not. Thus, Lofland and Lejeune's (1960) students infiltrated an open meeting of Alcoholics Anonymous posing as alcoholic newcomers, while Rosenhan (1973) and his accomplices gained admission to mental hospitals by faking auditory hallucinations. However, we should also note that covertness can vary in terms of who does, and does not, know that research is taking place. For example, in their studies in hospitals both Atkinson (1997) and Marzano (2007) were known by the doctors to be carrying out research even though patients did not know this.

There has been much debate around whether covert observation is ever justified, and if so under what conditions (Bulmer 1982; Leo 1996; Herrera 1999). Some commentators argue that it is virtually never legitimate (Shils 1959; Bok 1978; Warwick 1982). Shils writes that:

> It is plainly wrong for an inquirer ostensibly to take up membership in a community with the primary intention of conducting a sociological inquiry there without making it plain that that is what he is doing. His disclosure of his intention might occasionally hamper the research he is conducting, but the degree of injury suffered by his research does not justify the deviation from straightforwardness implied by withholding his true intentions (1959: 434)

Others insist that covert research is a legitimate and necessary strategy in particular research settings (Douglas 1976; Homan 1980a, 1980b; Calvey 2008; Pearson 2009). These discussions have identified a range of considerations that need to be taken into account. However, in our view, any judgment about whether or not covert observation is legitimate must be made in relation to specific cases rather than being formulated either as a general prohibition or even as a global permissive statement. This is because the nature of covert research can vary significantly, and so too can conditions in the field.

Of course, not only ethical but also methodological and practical considerations are involved, and there may be considerations of each type that go in opposite directions. Thus, while methodological justifications are often offered for covert research, for example suggesting that access would not otherwise be possible, there are also methodological arguments against it. For instance, it frequently involves practical constraints on the sort of observation that can be carried out, and even more restrictions on means of recording the data. Also, there is the risk of being discovered and its consequences, which may bring the research to an end prematurely, or have even worse consequences (Scott 1983: 132–3).

Turning to the case of access to documents, while a great many are publicly available, and so accessible to researchers, others will be under the control of some agent, whether an individual, group, or organisation. In these cases, it may seem that, short of theft, consent will need to be sought to gain access. Yet it may be possible to use covert strategies here too. If one already has access, or potential access, to the documents via an existing role, they could be obtained this way. If not, it may be possible to take on a new role specifically for the purposes of doing the research. For example Jeffrey Masson was accused of becoming Projects Director for the Sigmund Freud Archives in order to carry out research on Freud's early ideas (Malcolm 1984; Masson 1984, 1991). Many of the same ethical, methodological, and practical considerations are involved here as with covert observation.

In the case of interviews, covert options will sometimes be available, for example where a researcher hangs around a setting and mingles with people, asking them questions: for instance, standing in a bus or shop queue, travelling on the train, sitting in a bar, and so on. This was Chambliss's (1975) main entry strategy in studying organised crime. Such covert questioning can be carried out in settings that are open to public access or those that are closed but which the researcher has found some covert means of entering. Where interviewing is covert, ethical issues clearly arise, centring on respecting autonomy, as well as protecting privacy, but once again there are also practical and methodological considerations, notably to do with whether interviewing of this sort can provide worthwhile data, or data that could not be obtained otherwise. There will, after all, usually be severe restrictions on how many and what questions can be asked under covert conditions. Generally speaking, for these reasons researchers seek formal consent to carry out interviews.

Consent from whom?

Often in discussions of informed consent it is assumed that it is the people from whom data are to be obtained who must consent. The explicit or implicit model here is the experimental subject or the person being interviewed. Clearly these are people from whom it may well be necessary to obtain consent, but there are others. In particular, consent may be required for practical and/or ethical reasons from gate-keepers who control not only what settings can be observed and what documents accessed but even who can be interviewed.

In such cases, questions arise about whether or not to seek permission, as already noted, but in any case sometimes it will not be entirely clear in either practical or ethical terms exactly *who* must consent. There may be multiple people whose permission could be sought – there are occasionally alternative routes into a setting, or that can be used in gaining access to documents or to interviewees. Similarly, consent may be sought from *some* of those from whom data is being collected but not from everyone. As we saw, much research that is covert in relation to some participants was nevertheless known about by others. For example, Dalton (1964) negotiated access to the branch of the organisation he was studying through its head, but his research role was covert in relation to the people with whom he worked.

In practical terms, *whose* consent is required is a matter of determining who has the power to allow or prevent entry to a setting for the purposes of observation, to allow or block access to documents, or to facilitate or prevent the carrying out of interviews. In relation to relatively public settings, or in very fluid situations, there may be uncertainty about who falls into this category, but most institutions and groups have some internal organisation that differentially distributes, formally and/ or informally, the right to make key decisions, including who can enter institutional or group territory, which parts of the setting outsiders can have access to, how long they can stay, how they are expected to behave, what they can be required to do while they are there, and so on. Also involved here, as we noted, may be rights to access particular documents or even to contact members of the group or organisation to request interviews.

Very often, those who act as gatekeepers do so in the name of members of the group or organisation concerned – claiming to protect or further their interests; and in rather fewer cases they may be appointed through some democratic process, as when the officers of a voluntary association are elected by the membership. However, even in such cases the considerations that inform decisions made by gatekeepers are likely to extend beyond the assumed interests of individual members, and perhaps even beyond what are taken to be the collective interests of the group or organisation itself. For example, in negotiating with Benjamin over his access to their community, the Board of Directors of the Congregation Mikvé Israel-Emanuel 'defined themselves not only as representatives of the living members of their community and the extended family units to which they belong, but also of their deceased ancestors, and of the generations of the "yet unborn" progeny who will follow them' (Fox 1999: 70). Furthermore, those in power within organisations have their own distinctive agendas, by virtue of that position as well as of other interests deriving from their background characteristics. And, even where the decision is made in terms of the interests of an organisation, it may be at odds with how at least some members see their own interests and/or how they view those of the collectivity. This is an aspect of how individual autonomy may be routinely infringed through the operation of many social organisations that researchers investigate.

It is important to recognise that there are often significant cultural differences in views about who can and should give consent for whom to be involved in what. For instance, in many Western societies it is usually assumed that, in principle, adults ought to be treated as free agents in terms of their decisions, even if this is curtailed in particular institutional or group settings. By contrast, in the case of children, and that of adults who have learning disabilities or mental-health problems, there are disputes centring on their capacity to consent in a manner that takes account of their own interests (Farrell 2005; Heath et al. 2007). And this is an area where the ethic of care can come into sharp conflict with valuing people's autonomy: a concern to respect this autonomy may be overridden by an obligation to protect.

In some non-Western cultures, and in some subcultures within Western societies, autonomy is given little weight. The head of a kin group or a community leader may be regarded as having the proper authority to give permission for members of the family or community to participate in research. And once permission has been granted there may be an obligation on those members to cooperate with the researcher. Such cultural differences are important in ethical as well as in practical terms, and can pose difficulties: should the researcher respect the conventions of the established culture or insist that individuals freely consent? This is aside from the question of whether gaining individuals' consent would be feasible.

So, once again, there may be discrepancies between practical and ethical considerations. There could be a practical requirement to obtain consent from one or more agents whom the researcher does not feel ethically obliged to consult, indeed whose authority he or she does not recognise. For example, in studying some inner-city communities it may be necessary to negotiate with local crime gangs, or in traditional rural communities in some parts of the world one may only be able to contact women living there through male elders. Conversely, the researcher may feel ethically obliged to gain consent from people who have no power to prevent observation, to refuse access to relevant documents, or even to decline being interviewed.

Thus, in negotiating access to settings for the purpose of observation, or after they have already entered the setting, researchers may insist, or try to insist, that they require permission from the individual people whom they will be observing, not just from the gatekeeper, even though there is no locally recognised practical requirement for this. However, this may involve complications. First, gaining the agreement of all participants may be difficult or impossible in logistical terms, particularly where there is a large and changing population passing through the site, as in the case of Kelly's study of a youth drop-in centre (Davies and Kelly 1976). Second, in some instances such a move will be regarded by the gatekeeper as an infringement of, or a challenge to, her or his authority; and the result could be detrimental to the research or to participants. A third point is that what is involved here may not be a matter of each individual being allowed to choose whether or not to be observed, but rather of individuals deciding if observation in a particular setting can begin or continue: it may only take refusal by one participant to prevent the whole process of observation, so that others' consent would effectively be annulled. Here, then, potentially, each participant in the setting is being granted the autonomy to infringe that of others, as regards research participation.[11]

How is consent to be obtained?

Another important issue concerns by what means consent is obtained; in other words, what counts, and should count, as consent having been given. Here there are questions about whether there can be implicit as well as explicit consent (Herrera 1999), and

---

[11]Similar problems arise in giving people the right to withdraw from the research at any time. If their withdrawal requires removing any data they have supplied, then where this is observational or group interview data it may well involve removing data relating to other participants as well.

about whether explicit consent can be oral or must take the form of a written contract. The issue of implicit consent points to a dimension rather than a dichotomy,
this ranging from the inference that since people make no objection to the presence
of a researcher or to being asked questions they can be taken to have consented,
through various informal ways of requesting consent, to much more formal procedures up to and including written agreements.

With this issue, as with others, it is essential to recognise that what is appropriate
can vary with circumstances. Aside from the question of whether the people concerned are literate, there is cultural variation in interpretations of oral and written
agreements. For example, insistence on written consent may be regarded as insulting
or threatening by some people, and can have undesirable effects on the research
relationship.[12] For instance, Colic-Peisker (2004: 88), an Australian of Croatian
descent studying a previous generation of migrants, found that:

> the older working-class migrants were generally uneasy about providing their
> signatures [...]. While filling in and signing forms is a common experience for
> most Australians, it is not so in Croatia, where things are more often done on the
> basis of trust, and with common friends as guarantors. By asking my respondents
> to sign a consent form I positioned myself as a cultural outsider, someone coming
> from the 'Australian side'.

Furthermore, while there may be advantages in having a permanent record of what
was agreed, for both sides, it is necessary to remember that, however carefully worded,
any contract can be interpreted in different ways. Its use always requires shared understanding and trust; which may be built, or may change in other ways, over the course
of the research. A written contract cannot be a substitute for trust; at most it is only an
aid to establishing and sustaining it. Any attempt to make it work as a substitute will
not only result in a very lengthy, detailed, and legalistic document, but will also be futile.

Consent for what?

Another important issue concerns to what people are being asked to consent, and to
what they believe they are consenting. In immediate terms consent allows the
researcher access to data, but we should note that there is some scope for variation
and uncertainty even here. There may be agreement for observation to take place,
but observation can take different forms in qualitative research: watching what happens from the sidelines, observing and talking to participants, engaging marginally in
the activities being observed, or participating in those activities in a more central way.
These variations may have very different implications from the point of view of the
person(s) whose consent is being sought.[13] Similar variation arises with interviews:
How long will these be? Where will they take place? What sorts of question will be
asked? How sensitive will be the issues raised? Much the same applies if people are

---

[12]On the issue of written consent forms, see Singer (1980); Bradshaw (2002); Coomber (2002).

[13]For discussions of different types of observation, see Foster (1996).

to be asked to fill in diaries or supply life histories: what is involved in this can vary significantly, for example according to whether a highly structured or more open-ended approach is adopted.

Consent for data *recording* is a separate, but equally important, matter. In some settings, it might be argued that, while access does not in itself require permission from anyone, some sorts of data recording *do*. This is particularly likely in the case of photography and video-recording. And, certainly, where consent *is* practically required in order to gain access it will usually also be necessary to gain permission to use particular recording techniques, perhaps even just to take notes. In his study of New Age appropriation of Aboriginal culture, Muir (2004: 194) reports that the 'spiritual workshops' he observed were highly scripted and timetabled, typically taking the form of lectures: 'cameras were commonly banned and note-taking or conspicuous observation was discouraged. To not fully partake of the experience – to appear to be an observer rather than participant – could be perceived as inappropriate or threatening'. In the case of interviews, it is by no means unknown for informants to agree to being interviewed but to *refuse* permission for electronic recording. In the case of documents, there may be consent to reading and making notes but a refusal to allow photocopying or photography.

These are matters concerning potential *practical* constraints on what consent is being given for, but what about the *ethics* of who can give consent for what? Often, the two sets of considerations will be more or less in line, with the researcher believing that those whose consent must be sought for practical reasons have the right to influence what sort of data collection and recording are to take place. But there can be conflicts here. In public settings, what is involved is not only a question of the licence of researchers but also of the rights of individuals: the right to make video-recordings or to take photographs as well as the right not to be video-recorded or photographed without permission. This is an issue, among many, where there are probably substantial conflicts in view, along with considerable uncertainty, even about what is and is not legal.

The issue of for what consent is being sought extends even beyond data collection and recording procedures. What is being requested, generally speaking, is the right to access and record the data *and to use it for research purposes*. For qualitative researchers, this would normally be taken to include the right to report what was said and done, and to quote relevant extracts in research publications, so long as reasonable efforts are made to protect confidentiality, for instance through anonymisation. Whether this is how participants see it, and what their understanding of 'research purposes' includes, is likely to vary. And there are issues here about how far the responsibility of the researcher to clarify these matters extends.

There is also the question of whether data are to be archived, given that today some funding bodies encourage this or even make it a requirement. Is additional consent required for this? This is often assumed or suggested, but it could be argued that this is not required so long as the form in which the data will be archived provides at least the same level of security as the researcher offered in carrying out the research. However, there are clearly issues here about what is within the legitimate autonomy of researchers, what is under their control, what is their responsibility, and what those who are being asked to give consent have a right to expect (Parry and Mauthner 2004; L. Bishop 2005; Johnson and Bullock 2009; Carusi and Jirotka 2009; Williams et al. 2011).

Very often, people asked to give consent have expectations about what will be the outcome of the research. While some will fear negative effects, others may *assume* that there will be benefits. This is common, for example, on the part of patients asked to consent to health research. Indeed, just as some researchers see the goal of research in political or practical terms, as going beyond the production of knowledge, so too may many participants. They may automatically assume that the research will serve their interests or purposes, or the common good, indeed that it *ought* to do so. They may not consider the possibility that it could be of little, or negative, value, from their point of view. They may assume that the research will be designed to produce what they regard as beneficial outcomes; yet this need not be, and in our view should not be, the case.

There are important questions here about what information a researcher supplies about the research in order to obtain consent from particular people, an issue that will be considered below. Furthermore, in our view, a contract to the effect that people will only agree to data being used if they approve of the analysis or judge it likely to have beneficial effects, as in the case of Benjamin's contract with the Board of the Mikvé Israel-Emanuel congregation (Benjamin 1999; Fox 1999), is unacceptable.[14]

Free consent?

It is generally assumed that consent must be voluntary, and of course this require-ment derives directly from the principle of autonomy. The idea of '*free* consent' refers to the extent to which a person might be, or could feel, under pressure to consent – or, for that matter, to *refuse* consent. But what exactly counts as pressure, and more to the point what constitute illegitimate pressures? For one thing, we should not assume that, when people are faced with the issue of consenting or not consenting to provide access to data, they are operating in a social vacuum as sovereign indi-viduals. It is impossible to extricate the decisions made by individual participants from the organisational and other contexts in which they find themselves, including power structures. Their decisions about whether or not to participate in the research are likely to be shaped by these factors, to some extent at least, one way or the other. For example, Seymour and Ingleton (1999) report that decisions of relatives of ter-minally ill patients to consent to research were shaped by healthcare staff and by relatives' own sense of obligation to these staff.

As we have emphasised throughout this book, people live through playing various roles that engage them in relationships with other people, including some that involve differential influence and power. They make their decisions, at least partly, in light of those relationships. And they may feel that their hand is forced to comply or not comply

---

[14]There are also cases where individual informants have been given control over subsequent use of the data; see for example Walker (1993: 189) and Pink (2004: 394–5).

by someone who is in an institutional position above them, by their peer group, or by consideration for people for whom they have a responsibility. Whether these sorts of constraint are legitimate or illegitimate is a matter of evaluative judgment in particular cases, and may often be one about which there can be reasonable disagreement.

Moreover, it is possible that the researcher, and even the people themselves, will not be aware of the forces that are shaping their decisions. If we take account of unconscious constraints, whether background assumptions or forces generating the circumstances in which people act, it is even more difficult to see how free consent, interpreted as decision-making that is unaffected by any kind of causal process, could ever be achieved. Again, what this highlights is that what is a constraint, or an unacceptable constraint, is a matter of judgment, one that depends upon views about what people ought to be free from and what they should be free to do.

This raises both ethical and practical questions for researchers. One of these is: How far should people's decisions regarding consent simply be accepted in the name of respecting their autonomy? Or can the researcher engage in persuasion, for example where he or she believes that a false factual assumption or value inference is being made? And what modes of argument would be legitimate in these circumstances?

Qualitative researchers by no means always take people's initial reactions at face value. For example:

Finally, got to this guy, pottering about in front of a battered, old caravan, with a mangy-looking dog for company – a cross between a pit-bull and something else not quite so cuddly. Both of them were eyeing me warily as I approached. Soon the dog started barking and straining at the frayed rope which held it. The swarthy, thick-set guy (presumably Smithy), in his mid-fifties, perhaps, half-turned to his dog: 'Stop that racket, you cunt.' Quickly, I gave him the usual patter, what I'm researching and why, all the while taking anxious glances over my shoulder to check how the rope was holding up. [...] Smithy heard me out:

Me: So, would you mind answering a few questions?
            No response.
Me: Well, is there anything you'd like to say?
Smithy: Yes – fuck off.
            Now generally I respect subjects' wishes – what's more this Smithy
            didn't look as if he had a great deal to say. More pertinently, I didn't
            much like the expression on his face – nor that on his dog's either, for
            that matter. But on this occasion, I felt bloody-minded. It had been a
            frustrating day: a long drive, nothing to show. Moreover, I realized that
            I had been set up by the other men, who had sent me there merely to
            get rid of me, whilst also, perhaps, getting their own back on Smithy for
            some past altercation. I persisted.
Me: What I'm hoping is that this research will be of some use in . . .
Smithy: I'm not fucking interested in what you say your work's about. I told you
            to fuck off.
Me: Look, I tell you what. I won't even ask you any questions. Just talk to me
            for five minutes – about whatever you like, then I'll fuck off.

> It seemed to me that his expression softened. And if I wasn't imagining it, so did his dog's. By using his language, not mine, I seemed to have become a person, not someone from an official world. Perhaps, too, I had passed some test of maleness.
>
> Smithy: Buy me a drink, and I'll talk to you.
>
> In the event, Smithy gave me more than an hour of his time and provided some valuable insights. [This] emphasised the need for persistence, and also highlighted a significant aspect of data collection: some of the most interesting material came from those who initially were reluctant to speak to me. In such cases, access was often 'bought' with a pint. In Smithy's case, granting me access to him, gained him access to a local pub, noted for its 'No Travellers' sign in the doorway, and while we were there, he would look up at times to glower challengingly at the barman. (Levinson 2010: 196–7)

Of course, there can also be circumstances in which people too freely consent, making the decision without taking sufficient account of important considerations that they ought to address, for example concerning potential harm. Here, should the researcher refuse to accept the expression of consent at face value, working to ensure that proper consideration of the issues takes place? Or would this itself be disrespectful, an infringement of people's autonomy?

FULLY INFORMED OR MISINFORMED?

If consent must be obtained, whether for practical or for ethical reasons, it will be necessary to supply some information about the research and the researcher.[15] In ethical terms, it might be argued that a crucial element of the exercise of freedom, at least in its 'positive' form, is that people have access to full and accurate information that enables them to know how best to act by their own lights in the circumstances they face. Thus, on a strong interpretation of what the principle of autonomy requires, *not* to provide information that would be pertinent to people's lines of action, to supply false information, or even to allow them to draw false inferences from what they have been told, is unethical. The principle of informed consent may thus be interpreted as demanding that researchers ensure people have the information necessary for them to make sound decisions about whether or not to give their consent, or to continue participating in the research rather than withdrawing from it. But is this possible? Is it always necessary or desirable? And what counts as informing people? Finally, is allowing them to retain misconceptions about the research or the researcher, or even misinforming them in some respects, always wrong?

What qualitative researchers tell people about their work can range from nothing to the provision of lengthy accounts, oral and/or written. Thorne (1980) notes the

---

[15]In certain circumstances even where consent is *not* required researchers may feel it is necessary for ethical reasons to tell people that research is taking place and provide some information about it. This could involve putting up a notice in a public setting or on a website, for instance.

tendency to use what she calls 'partial truths' in initially negotiating access. For example, research topics are often formulated in highly general terms, not indicating the specific area of interest. She reports that 'Lofland (1966) introduced himself to leaders of a religious cult as "a sociologist interested in social and religious movements" – true as far as it went, but the cult leader translated that role into "chronicler of the beginning of the New Age in America," an understanding which Lofland didn't try to correct' (Thorne 1980: 287). The provision of such partial accounts continues to be common today, but there is growing pressure, not least from ethics committees, to provide more comprehensive and detailed accounts. Shils (1980: 429) provides an extreme interpretation of what is required in the case of interviewing:

> Questions ought to be justified by the explanation of what [the] answers will contribute to [...] clarification of the problem being investigated. Naturally, it is not necessary that each particular question should be so explained, but groups or types of questions asked in an interview should be explained in this way. I appreciate the difficulties which stand in the way of observance of this standard, and, in many cases, the interviewed person himself will not care to have the explanation. Often he will not be able to understand the intentions of elaborate pieces of research, and, furthermore, the limited time which the interviewee is willing to grant might be excessively consumed by the explanation. The standard is nonetheless valid and should be adhered to at least as a guiding principle.

The information provided by researchers in seeking consent might need to cover a variety of matters: the purpose of the research, its focus, how the researcher plans to pursue the investigation, the sorts of finding that could result, and potential consequences of carrying out the inquiry or of publishing the findings. There is also the issue of where funding comes from. Thorne (1980: 288) cites the case of Stephenson (1978), whose study of Hungarian refugees was secretly funded by the CIA, and who himself noted that his informants 'would probably "not have been so candid in the interviews," had they known the funding source'. These various kinds of information are of rather different character: as regards how reliable they are likely to be, the meanings they will carry for the people being informed, and the possible methodological and practical consequences of supplying them.

At the start of any research project there will be severe limits on a researcher's knowledge of what the findings are going to be and of what consequences could result from publishing them. With qualitative work there will also often be significant uncertainty about *how* the topic will be investigated, and even about the precise focus of inquiry. This arises from the fact that such research is often exploratory in nature, and tends to have a flexible, iterative character, so that ideas about what is being investigated, and what are the best means of doing this, can change significantly over time. So there are practical limits to the information a qualitative researcher can supply at the start, and the uncertain status of this information must also be recognised.

A second point, hinted at by Shils, is that the researcher has to make an assessment of how much and what sort of information people will tolerate: most will not be very interested in research, not even in particular research projects in which they are involved as participants. So, there is often a severe limit on the amount of information that they want. There are various reasons why people may have little interest in the research, or attach low importance to it. It may not be close to any of their interests, and where participants have other pressing concerns they may not be prepared to spend time gaining an understanding of it. Indeed, in many cases doing this would not be worth their while because the decision will not be a consequential one for them: it will not make much difference to their lives one way or the other. In these circumstances, it might even be asked whether we would be infringing the liberty of people by trying to insist that they become fully informed.

Another set of issues concerns the meaning of 'informed'. There is a limit to what people can understand and take in at any one time, especially before data collection has begun – since at that point they may have little relevant experience. More generally, O'Neill (2002: 44) comments: '[…] full disclosure of information is neither definable nor achievable; and even if it could be provided there is little chance of complete assimilation'. So, what does it mean to say that someone is informed about a research project? Does it mean simply that they have been told about it, or does it also imply that they *understand* what they have been told? And what sense should we give to 'understand' here? Does this mean that they understand the research in the same way as the researcher? In fact, this is very unlikely ever to be possible, not least because they are different people with different background knowledge, concerns and preoccupations, who are pursuing different activities.

In the case of information about the purpose and focus of the research, people may or may not understand and accept the importance of the topic. Barnes writes that it can be difficult to explain to someone living in a village community in the majority world that 'an ethnographer would like to know how he addresses his mother's mother's brother [in order], say, to test Festinger's theory of cognitive dissonance or Dell Hymes' notions of genealogical extension'. Yet, optimistically in our view, he insists that 'a resourceful ethnographer can go at least some way towards conveying the general nature of his [or her] intellectual interest' (Barnes 1977: 11). The potential problem here is not only a cultural gap in frames of reference and what is deemed important, but also that researchers and participants will usually draw on different bodies of knowledge and patterns of background experience. Even if participants recognise the importance of a topic, they are likely to have a different understanding from the researcher of what is and is not currently known about it. They may regard some matters as well-established which, from a research perspective, remain open to genuine uncertainty or doubt. Given this, they could have difficulty seeing the point of some research projects, these being regarded as investigating what is already well known (Gage 1991). What this makes clear is that the information offered will need to be shaped to meet the capacities, interests, and needs of the audience.

Similarly, information about the methods to be used in the research may be less than fully comprehensible if the people concerned have little knowledge about, or interest in, social research methodology. Moreover, even when they *are* interested in research, their knowledge may relate to quite different methods from those that the researcher intends to use: someone only having experience of quantitative methods may find it hard to grasp what qualitative researchers plan to do, and why.[16]

There are also questions about *how* to inform people about the research. This could be done in relatively formal ways, for instance through a public oral presentation to a gathered audience, and/or via the provision of printed information sheets, perhaps as part of gaining written consent. Equally important, though, are more informal accounts to individuals, perhaps provided in response to questions. As this hints, informing people about the research and the researcher is not restricted to giving them information at the beginning of the research process, when negotiating initial access (Lugosi 2006). The researcher will continue to have contact with many people in the field over the course of inquiry, and may supply information at various subsequent points.[17] There are, then, decisions to be made about *when* people should be told *what*. This is not just a product of the open-ended nature of qualitative research, with research plans changing over time, it may also be judged that people will be more interested in and better able to understand some types of information later in the research process than at the beginning, partly as a result of the way that their relationships with the researcher develop.

It must also be remembered that during the course of data-collection researchers will inadvertently 'give off' information about themselves (Goffman 1959), often leading to various interpretations on the part of participants about who they 'really' are. In Okely's (1983: 41) research on a Gypsy group a variety of rumours arose about her: 'that I was a journalist, a police collaborator, a foot-loose heiress, a girl friend of the warden, a drug addict and hippy, or someone on the run from the police'. She reports that she 'discouraged all these images except the last', and comments: 'the fact that I stayed around, that I made friends, lived as they did, and went out to work with them, eventually discredited any rumour that I was a journalist or police collaborator [...]'. How interested people are in such informal information, and how they use it, will vary considerably, but to one degree or another it serves as a complement to explicit information provided about the research and the researcher. Indeed, occasionally participants may put quite a lot of effort into observing and 'sussing out' researchers, in order to work out what they are 'up to'; not least to decide whether they can be trusted, whether they could have something to offer, or if they pose a threat.

Referring to information provided in clinical encounters, O'Neill (2002: 44) remarks: 'Informed consent can be quite superficial, fastening on the actual phrases and descriptions used and need not take on board much that is closely connected to, or even entailed by, those phrases and descriptions.' Much the same is true in the context of qualitative research. As a result, researchers may be faced with situations in which it becomes clear that the people they are dealing with have misunderstood what is proposed, or the nature of the researcher's role, and are acting under an illusion of one sort or another. Here a decision must be made about whether to try to

---

[16]For an illuminating investigation of how participants in a genetic epidemiology study understood what they were told about the research, see Dixon-Woods et al. (2007).

[17]For a classic argument about the developmental rather than contractual character of informed consent in qualitative fieldwork, see Wax (1980). See also Murphy and Dingwall (2007).

correct the misconception, and if so what further information about the research and the researcher should be supplied. But this will not always be judged worthwhile or necessary, as in the case of Birckhead's research on fundamentalist Christian 'serpent-handlers' in the southern United States:

> Although I had explained to the saints in a general way that I was 'studying', I never felt that they fully comprehended what I was actually doing in their midst. But they did create a space for me, making sense of my presence according to their own pragmatic and cosmic purposes. (Birckhead 2004: 98)

Clearly, then, what is involved is not simply a matter of providing or not providing 'all the relevant information'. It is a process that is hedged around with constraints deriving from the situations in which researchers are operating and their particular projects, and by judgments about what is legitimate and viable in the circumstances. Necessarily, some information will be omitted, glossed over, or even downplayed.

Over and above this, there is the question of whether deliberate deception can be justified. In an ideal world the answer would be 'no', but this is not the world in which research must be carried out. So, researchers may feel not only that they need to limit the information they provide, but even that they must aim at giving a misleading impression about the research and/or about themselves *in certain respects*, at least temporarily. But is this legitimate?

In thinking about researchers engaging in deception, we need to consider what is meant by this word. A range of actions can be involved. The clearest case is lying: presenting information as true that one knows to be false, or denying what one knows to be true. Closely related is giving a false impression to people through self-presentation, or through one's actions. A third form is leaving out information that one expects or knows would be of significance for the audience. Fourth, there is failing to correct misconceptions that have arisen accidentally. The final form that deception might take is keeping quiet about opinions, personal characteristics, or experiences that could be viewed negatively by the audience. In practice, it is not easy to distinguish among these various forms, but we have tried to arrange them in what we take to be a descending scale of seriousness: indeed, whether the fifth, fourth, or even the third amount to deception could be disputed. The key point is that there are degrees and kinds of deception, and that the significance of these often depends upon assumptions about who should have been told what, when, and why.

There are methodological reasons why researchers may not want to provide full information, or may even want to deceive people about the nature of their work. The most obvious is that gatekeepers and others could refuse to give their consent if they knew precisely what the focus of inquiry was, thereby blocking an important line of inquiry – for example preventing the production of knowledge about how an organisation exercises control over a field to serve its own interests, or why some group resorts to violence or experiences severe psychological distress. Another methodological consideration concerns the danger that giving participants particular sorts of information will affect their behaviour and thereby possibly render the findings of a study invalid or non-generalisable. This can even result from a benign response on the part of participants. For instance, if a researcher tells teachers that he is interested in students' responses to questions in class this may encourage them to ask more classroom questions than they would normally do, perhaps simply in order to be helpful to the research (Hammersley 1984: 49–50).

Similar issues arise with explaining to people *possible* consequences that could result from a research investigation, since this may generate undue alarm, when in fact the chances of the outcome occurring are very small. The researcher needs to think about how people are likely to assess any potential risk, and this may shape what information is given, and how. This is of particular significance in societies where trust has been undermined and risk-aversion is a dominant cultural tendency (Beck 1992; Furedi 2002).

CONCLUSION

In this chapter we have examined another of the major principles that underpin much thought about, and discussion of, research ethics: the idea that the autonomy of the people studied should be respected. We have shown that this is a contested and complex notion and that it is only meaningful in specific terms – as regards what people should be free *from* and be *able to do*. In relation to qualitative research this principle has sometimes motivated the commitment that people have a right not to be researched. We rejected this, focusing on how the issue of consent arises in gaining access to settings in order to carry out observation, in obtaining access to documents, or in being able to carry out interviews or elicit diaries and life histories.

The principle of autonomy underpins the idea that there should always be informed consent from participants, and we looked at a number of issues here, concerning: when consent is required; from whom consent may be necessary; what form gaining consent should take; what the consent is *for*; what counts as *free* consent; and what it means for people to be '*informed*' about a research project. We emphasised that whether consent is required is both a practical and an ethical matter, but that neither sort of requirement is indefeasible. Equally open to deliberation is what amount, and kinds, of information researchers should provide to gatekeepers and participants, and whether it is legitimate to engage in deception, of various kinds. Whether deception is involved, and whether it is legitimate, must be judged on a case-by-case basis.

What is clear is that informed consent must not be treated as a sacred principle. Whether it is required, what it means, and what is possible and desirable, will vary according to circumstance. Complex and uncertain judgments are likely to be involved. We regard the principle of autonomy as important, but it does not have fixed and standard implications and it is not the only consideration that researchers must take into account. For this reason informed consent does not have the overriding significance often ascribed to it.

5

PRIVACY, CONFIDENTIALITY AND ANONYMITY

We noted in Chapter 2 that there is scope for overlap among the principles we identified as underpinning social research ethics, and the potential overlap is especially great when it comes to the topic of this chapter. The invasion of privacy has sometimes been conceptualised as a form of injury, and on other occasions as an infringement of individuals' autonomous right to protect what is personal to them (Kelman 1977). Indeed, some commentators believe that there is no separate principle here: that, for instance, the requirement to preserve people's privacy can be derived entirely from the need to respect their autonomy (Faden and Beauchamp 1986: 9). This is a debate that has also prevailed within jurisprudence (see Bloustein 1964), but there have long been influential arguments to the effect that the protection of privacy is an independent legal principle (Warren and Brandeis 1890). Furthermore, the topic is often given separate treatment in discussions of research ethics, and we shall do so here.

Closely intertwined under the heading of privacy are issues to do with the control of both territory and information. Each of these aspects is, in turn, somewhat heterogeneous and variable in character. The territory involved is not only physical space, itself of course always socio-culturally constituted and differentiated in significant ways, but also includes the kinds of 'virtual' space that exist on mobile phones, personal and institutional computers, and the Internet. Similarly, the *sorts of information* that are deemed personal or private vary across cultures and contexts, and the boundaries between these and what is public are often subject to disagreement and change, even if in all societies there is recognition that *some* kinds of information should be under the proper control of particular people rather than freely available.

In its legal form, the issue of privacy was originally framed as the protection of individual citizens against intrusions by the state into their lives, and against demands for the disclosure of information. But, of course, being a citizen is not the only role in which issues of privacy can arise; there are many others. Furthermore, once we acknowledge that claims to legitimate control of territory and information are intrinsic to the rights and obligations associated with particular social roles, we can recognise that it is not just individual people who can claim privacy rights but also various kinds of organisation – from commercial firms, through voluntary associations (such as political parties or charities), to governments themselves. Included here are restrictions on the distribution of information under the headings of trade secrets and national security.[1]

The issue of privacy takes on particular significance in research ethics when we recognise the crucial role that publicity plays in the functioning of research. Generally speaking, there is an obligation upon researchers to *publish* their findings, and, increasingly, to make their *data* publicly available too (notably through archiving). In the case of academic research, publicising the findings, and evidence for them, within the research community is a crucial part of the research process: it is what gives the knowledge claims produced their distinctive authority (Hammersley 2011). There is also an obligation to make the well-established findings of research available to wider publics where these might be of use to them. Given this intrinsic commitment to publicity, there is considerable scope for tension and conflict between research and any commitment to maintaining privacy, as we shall see.

PUBLICITY IN MODERN WESTERN SOCIETIES

The valuing of publicity is not restricted to research, however. Increasingly in modern Western societies areas of life that were previously regarded as private have been opened up to public scrutiny, this being made easier by technological developments: printing, photocopying, and electronic reproduction of text; photography; devices that enable sound and video recordings and their transmission; and the Internet (Wacks 2010). Using these technologies, the mass media report on the private lives of public figures, celebrities, and others – frequently documenting their activities without permission, reporting what was said in private, and so on. Private documents, both official and personal, are leaked and widely publicised. Media interviews often delve into intimate aspects of people's lives; and, at the same time, there is a growing desire on the part of some people to publicise their life stories and personal experiences.[2] There are television shows that film most aspects of what people do when living together, and there are documentaries that include personal exposure, dealing for example with embarrassing medical conditions or including confessions

---

[1] A distinction is sometimes drawn between privacy and secrecy, and there may be grounds for doing this (see Bok 1984: 10–11), but there are also important similarities and it is these that we will emphasise here.

[2] This is one aspect of what commentators have referred to as 'the interview society' (Atkinson and Silverman 1997; Gubrium and Holstein 2002: Ch. 1; see also Gay 1995). Bauman (2000: 37) notes the other side of this process, arguing that in modern Western societies the 'private' has come to 'colonise' the 'public'. He reports that '"public issues" which resist reduction [to private experiences] become all but incomprehensible'.

of transgressions of one sort or another, as well as other programmes that provide 'fly-on-wall' reports of events in a variety of settings produced by undercover cameras. The behaviour of ordinary people is now monitored by CCTV cameras in public, and in not so public, places. In all these various ways the private is increasingly being made public.

The United States has been in the vanguard of this move towards greater publicity. Many years ago, Shils (1956: 39) reported that:

> The supreme value and self-constituted task of the journalistic, advertising and mass communication professions, reinforced by tradition, the Constitution, and their own professional interests and the pleasures of professional virtuosity, became the maintenance and furtherance of publicity. No society has ever been so extensively exposed to public scrutiny as the United States in the twentieth century.

He explains that this derives from the fact that:

> American culture is a populistic culture. As such, it seeks publicity as a good in itself. Extremely suspicious of anything which smacks of 'holding back', it appreciates publicity, not merely as a curb on the arrogance of rulers but as a condition in which the members of society are brought into maximum of contact with each other. (p. 41)

While the US was relatively unusual in these respects at the time Shils was writing, subsequently other Western countries have become similar. This is highlighted by the now very dated character of his account of the situation in the UK, which emphasised for example the reserved manners of the population and their deferential attitude towards politicians (1956: 47–57).

Another illustration of the value now given to publicity in Western societies is the preoccupation with biography, and the increasing popularity of the version of this genre whose aim is to expose secrets and lies. Here is Janet Malcolm's diagnosis:

> The organs of publicity that have proliferated in our time are only an extension and a magnification of society's fundamental and incorrigible nosiness. Our business is everybody's business, should anybody wish to make it so. […] In any struggle between the public's inviolable right to be diverted and an individual's wish to be left alone, the public almost always prevails. […] The biographer is portrayed almost as a kind of benefactor. […] The transgressive nature of biography is rarely acknowledged, but it is the only explanation for biography's status as a popular genre. The reader's amazing tolerance […] makes sense only when seen as a kind of collusion between him and the biographer in an excitingly forbidden undertaking: tiptoeing down the corridor together, to stand in front of the bedroom door and try to peep through the keyhole. (Malcolm 1995: 8–9)

In a rather different way, in the sphere of public policy, demands for 'transparent accountability' also reflect a belief not just in the value of publicity but also in the public's *right* to know about how they are being governed. Arguments about the importance of publicity in this respect go back into the nineteenth century (Bok 1984: 112–14). Shils (1956: 23) writes:

> The struggle for constitutional government, for the extension of the franchise, and particularly for the freedom of the press, which was both an instrument and a symbol in the war against government as a private affair of the monarchy and the aristocracy, was directed against privacy in government. Almost as much as the extension of the franchise and constitutional restraint on monarchical absolutism, publicity regarding political and administrative affairs was a fundamental aim of the modern liberal democratic movement.

A central claim here is that people need to be aware of government actions that are being taken that could damage their interests. There is also sometimes the assumption, explicit or implicit, that only if policies are publicly discussed will the assumptions on which they rely be subjected to proper test, so that in this way too publicity improves the quality of governance. Taking a rather different form, the more recent emphasis on a need for 'transparency' on the part of publicly funded bodies has been closely associated with the idea that these organisations must be accountable to taxpayers in economic terms: what is being done must be documented so that they can assess both its costs and its pay-offs.[3]

Besides political and economic rationales, there are also some specifically ethical arguments for the importance of publicity. An example deriving from a deontological position is Kant's requirement that we should not be prepared to act on an assumption, or engage in a course of action, that we are not willing for others to know about (Kant 1795: 125; Caygill 1995: 341). This is echoed in Woodrow Wilson's insistence that 'secrecy means impropriety' (1913: 114, quoted in Bok 1984: 8). Rationales for publicity can also be derived from consequentialist points of view, though here *particular kinds* of publicity are judged in terms of their benefits and costs; and, of course, secrecy may sometimes be justified on the same grounds. A leading utilitarian, Sidgwick (1907, quoted in Bok 1984: 113), noted that 'secrecy may render an action right which would not otherwise be', but insisted that this fact should itself be kept 'comparatively secret' because it could be misused by 'the vulgar'.

If we examine the motives that lie behind the value given to publicity, we find that these can be evaluated in differing ways. For instance, Malcolm refers to 'nosiness', but this could be reformulated as curiosity about others' lives. Indeed, one strand of modernist thought is concerned with understanding human nature and society *as they really are*, as against accepting both idealised pictures and demonisations. In fact, one might see this 'demythologisation' as one of the rationales for social science itself.

Another driver behind the valorisation of publicity is distrust or suspicion of the accounts and motives of others, *especially* those who claim virtue, who insist, for

---

[3]See, for example, McLaughlin et al. (2002), Hood and Peters (2004), Newman and Clarke (2009). Of course, closely associated with such demands and the growth of media designed to serve them, has been the development of machineries for controlling and manipulating information in the public domain, with the result that advertising and 'public relations' have become a multi-million pound businesses.

instance, that they are dedicated to promoting the good, seeking the truth, and so on. This could be dismissed as cynicism, but viewed in a more favourable light it might be regarded as pointing to the need for a properly critical attitude towards others' accounts, especially those from authorities of one sort or another. This attitude of scepticism is closely related to the ideal of democracy, especially in its deliberative mode, but also to assumptions about the conditions under which markets operate best, where people must have accurate information in order to make sound judgments about the goods and services on offer. In both contexts, there is an awareness that interests and motives may lead to distortion of information, in the form of political spin or advertising. Similarly, it is distrust of public professionals, as serving their own interests under a claim to altruism, that has led to calls for the 'transparent accountability' of public services. We might also note that a suspicious attitude of this kind is central to some rationales for social research, especially 'critical' approaches.

DEMANDS FOR PRIVACY

It is perhaps not surprising that, alongside increased public availability of information about many private areas of life, there have also been influential calls for greater protection of privacy (Shils 1956). One of the initial rationales for the promotion of privacy as a principle in US law concerned the activities of the new mass media in the late nineteenth century:

> Instantaneous photographs and newspaper enterprise have invaded the sacred precincts of private and domestic life; and numerous mechanical devices threaten to make good the prediction that 'what is whispered in the closet shall be proclaimed from the house-tops'. (Warren and Brandeis 1890: 195)

Later, the principle of privacy was enshrined in the United Nations Declaration of Human Rights, where Article 12 reads:

> No one shall be subjected to arbitrary interference with his privacy, family, home or correspondence, nor to attacks upon his honour and reputation. Everyone has the right to the protection of the law against such interference or attacks.

Generally speaking, as indicated by Warren and Brandeis's statement, pressure for the protection of privacy has appealed to the sacredness of what Shils refers to as 'the reserved sphere of the individual' (Shils 1980: 435). This appeal originally had religious origins, but in more recent times the emphasis has been on the fact that the individual self is:

> a moral entity capable of entering into relationships of personal love and affection, capable of becoming wise, capable of assuming responsibility for her or his actions and of acting on behalf of a collectivity, be it a family, a civil community, or any other corporate body or aggregate of human beings. (p. 425)

On this basis MacIntyre (1982: 188) argues:

> The study of taboos by anthropologists and of privacy by sociologists show how important it is for a culture that certain areas of personal and social life should be protected. We need sanctuaries, we need to be able to protect ourselves from illegitimate pressure, we need places of confession, and we need to disclose ourselves in different degrees to people to whom we stand in different degrees of relationship.

As Shils points out, this is an idea that became central to influential forms of Western liberalism (Shils 1980: 426), though it seems likely that some notion of individual privacy is a universal feature of human communities; albeit limited, variable, and subject to the contingencies of living conditions (Westin 1967: Ch. 1).

As noted earlier, there are also arguments that there is a need for privacy on the part of organisations. Thus Shils suggests that 'continuous publicity about public institutions' is undesirable, since it 'not only breaks the confidentiality which encourages the imaginativeness and reflectiveness necessary for competent decisions, but also it weakens [...] the respect in which political institutions should, at least tentatively, be held by the citizenry' (Shils 1980: 441). In the case of commercial organisations it is often argued that secrecy is required in order to protect information that gives one firm competitive advantage over others.

Within a society, or even within small communities, what should be private or secret, and what can or must be made public, are often contested matters. While there may be considerable agreement in distinguishing public places, such as parks, from private places, like bedrooms, there are many uncertain cases. Are religious ceremonies public events if they are open for anyone to attend? Is the talk among people in a bar public or private? Similarly, what about mobile-phone conversations carried out in public places, or discussions in online chatrooms?

Of course, disagreements about what is public and what is private, what should and should not be made public, and so on, are not simply matters of principle. Arguments are often put forward and criticised so as to protect or promote interests. For instance, the mass media insist on the importance of openness and publicity in order to facilitate their work, while others, especially those who have much to hide, emphasise the right to privacy. In the course of such disagreements, principles and precedents of various kinds may be stretched in a variety of directions.

More fundamentally, the reason why privacy is open to different interpretations is that the word does not refer to an intrinsic feature of particular types of setting or of specific sorts of information. This is true however obvious it may appear to us that some sorts of setting, or kinds of information, are private, while others are public. In fact, privacy is always about *who* should be allowed or entitled to view what, or to gain information of particular kinds about what. This is often made explicit in the case of traditional societies, where some information is treated as sacred, and therefore as restricted to priests, while other information should only be available to women (for example that involved in the initiation of girls into adulthood, see Moore 2010), and so on. In the case of places and information that are treated as private, some quite minimal and specific sort of audience is regarded as having legitimate access, whereas with what is public there will be little or no restriction on audience. But these are two ends of a spectrum, and much lies in-between.[4]

The conflict we have identified between the drive for publicity and concern to protect privacy may be seen as a distinguishing feature of Western liberal culture. However, there are reasons to believe that, to some degree, it is ubiquitous:

> Any inquiry into the ethics of secrecy must consider the conflicts that we all experience […]: between keeping secrets and revealing them; between wanting to penetrate the secrets of others and to leave them undisturbed; and between responding to what they reveal to us and ignoring or even denying it. These conflicts are rooted in the most basic experience of what it means to live as one human being among others, needing both to hide and to share, both to seek out and to beware of the unknown. (Bok 1984: xvi)

Privacy is, then, a complex and variable notion.[5] This will affect researchers' judgments about what is private and public in the cases they are investigating, and also the judgments of gatekeepers and the people being studied.

PRIVACY AND SECRECY IN QUALITATIVE RESEARCH

The tension between publicity and privacy takes on distinctive forms in particular contexts. In relation to social science, Shils (1980: 427) argues that

> the ethical problems with which we are dealing here arise from the confrontation of autonomy and privacy by a free intellectual curiosity, enriched by awareness of the depth and complexity of the forces that work in us and implemented by the devices of an effort to transform this awareness into a more systematic body of knowledge shared with others.

In some important respects the conflict between the demand for publicity built into the mission of social science and a commitment to respecting privacy is at its sharpest in the case of qualitative research. Even more than their colleagues, many qualitative researchers aim at discovering what is 'really going on' in some type of situation, as opposed to what is claimed officially, or what is generally thought, to happen. This is an especially common orientation when powerful groups or institutions are being investigated, or secretive ones with which the researcher has little sympathy.

---

[4]There is also a temporal dimension here: what was private or secret information in the past may come no longer to be so, for example because of leaks, or because it has lost its earlier significance. It may even be that what was not previously regarded as private or secret comes to be redefined in this way at a later point.

[5]Grimshaw (1982). As Solove (2008), Wacks (2010: 38–44), and others, have argued we use the word to cover a variety of rather different, but often overlapping, concerns. Solove describes it as 'a concept in disarray' (p. 1). See also Pinkard (1982), who argues that it is·an essentially contested concept.

Equally important, and perhaps even more common today, is a commitment to under-standing people's perspectives, attitudes, and feelings *in depth*. In these ways, the intended reach of qualitative inquiry is greater than some other kinds of social research, and this heightens the tension with concerns about privacy.

There is another reason too why qualitative research may represent a greater threat to privacy. This is because the social relations built into most forms of qualitative inquiry extend well beyond those that are characteristic of, say, survey research – where there are relatively fleeting contacts between hired interviewers and respond-ents, or the even more attenuated relationship between the designer of a postal or online questionnaire and those who fill it in. Taking the case of ethnography, there is usually contact with people in a variety of contexts, over weeks, months, or even years. This generates personal relationships, of various kinds, that are integral to how the researcher's role gets defined in the contexts being studied. Even where qualita-tive research relies exclusively on interviews, relations between interviewer and interviewee frequently become personal to at least some degree and in some ways. The key point is that these relationships are not governed solely by a formalised, relatively standardised research role, and that, as a result, the researcher may gain access to data that would not have been possible via that role alone.[6] From some ethical perspectives this is unacceptable, as indicated by Alderson and Morrow's (2011: 6) absurd suggestion that researchers wear a badge when they are 'in role' in the field.

To illustrate the issue, we can use Bok's discussion of Festinger et al.'s (1956) clas-sic study of a small millenarian religious group, who believed they had received messages from aliens about the end of the world. Bok writes:

> Through [covert] means, [the researchers] had gained entry to what members of the sect strove to keep secret. Intending to make their findings public, they had deceived the members into revealing their innermost hopes and fears as they never would have to strangers and least of all to researchers. [...] By every defini-tion of privacy, the investigators had invaded that of their unwitting subjects; and they had done so, not out of any desire to help these men and women, but strictly for the purposes of research. (Bok 1984: 234)

The most important point for Bok is that the research was covert, but even aside from this we can see that through joining the group, and participating in it on an intensive basis, Festinger et al. gained access to situations and information that would have been regarded as private by the people concerned. And this is true of most participant observation studies, whether or not consent is obtained.

Moreover, it is not just that in the course of qualitative research personal relations build up between researcher and researched. In fact, researchers intentionally work at presenting themselves in ways that will encourage trust on the part of the people being studied – there is advice in many textbooks about how to do this (see, for example, Hammersley and Atkinson 2007: Ch. 4). The purpose of this is specifically to facilitate

---

[6]Personal relations in the field can, of course, sometimes work in the opposite direction, blocking off areas and information from access by researchers.

greater access to data. As Hume and Mulcock (2004a: xii) comment: participant observation involves 'forming and maintaining intimate relationships for professional purposes'. This may be taken to indicate that participant observation is inherently unethical. However, it is not just observational studies that involve strategic trust-building; researchers who rely entirely on interviews will also often go to considerable lengths to set people at ease, to 'build rapport', and thereby to encourage the informant to disclose anything that might be relevant to the research. In discussing the problems of interviewing white collar criminals, Dodge and Geis (2006: 80) recommend a 'babe in the woods' approach: pretending ignorance and inviting the informant to '"teach" you, as only he or she would be able to do'. And similar strategies are sometimes employed in the elicitation of life histories and diaries, as well as in the recruitment of participants to take photographs or make videos for research purposes.

It is also sometimes claimed that social scientists have displayed differential attitudes towards the privacy of the various sorts of people they study, reflecting differences in the latter's social status and power; more specifically, that the lives of non-Western communities, of the working classes, of ethnic minority groups, and of children, have often been seen as less private than those of dominant groups. Shils (1980: 423) explains this as resulting from the fact that, 'These subjects possessed no secrets which were sacred to the investigators; they possessed no secrets penetration into which could be expected to arouse discomfiture among the investigators or the circles in which they moved'. This is an important point; and it may well be that even today such discrimination persists. It must be recognised, however, that researchers' practices in relation to the people they study are always qualified by other concerns, and shaped by other factors; not least, the differential power of individuals, groups, and organisations to protect settings and information that they believe are private or that they wish to keep secret. This will, inevitably, introduce some variation in treatment of them by researchers.

It is quite clear, then, that social research in general, and qualitative inquiry in particular, involves at least the potential for invading privacy, even if what is and is not legitimate in this respect is open to disagreement and dispute.

PRIVACY JUDGMENTS IN PRACTICE

There are important questions, then, about whether, how far, and under what conditions the kind of access to settings and to information that qualitative research frequently demands can be justified.[7] We will look here at privacy issues in relation to the selection of topics and the collection of data. Of course, in deciding what topics can and cannot legitimately be investigated, what sorts of data should be sought, and so on, researchers

---

[7]Another potential infringement on privacy is the taking of biological samples from participants. This is rare in qualitative research, but it is worth noting that McKeganey and Barnard (1996) collected samples of saliva from informants in order to assess the level of HIV infection among them. Furthermore, part of the El Dorado controversy concerned Chagnon's collection of DNA samples for Neel's research on population genetics: see Borofsky (2005).

are not just making judgments about privacy, but also about the implications of other ethical principles; and they are always doing this in the context of assessing how best to contribute to the development of knowledge in the fields in which they work.

'Sensitive' topics

It is part of the ethos of science that, in principle, no topics should be ruled out of bounds. As Sikes (2010: 146) comments, for a researcher: 'Avoiding taboo, controversial, and/or sensitive topics solely because they are that [...] can [...] be considered a basic abrogation of ethical and moral responsibility.' However, it is recognised that research questions vary considerably not just in how worthwhile their investigation is, what contribution to collective knowledge they can make, but also in their sensitivity. Renzetti and Lee (1993: ix) characterise sensitive research topics as those that 'deal with behaviour that is intimate, discreditable, or incriminating'; and they list four likely sources of sensitivity, relating to where a topic:

- 'intrudes into the private sphere or delves into some deeply personal experience'
- 'is concerned with deviance and social control'
- 'impinges on the vested interests of powerful persons or the exercise of coercion or domination'
- 'deals with things sacred to those being studied that they do not wish profaned'. (Renzetti and Lee 1993: 6)

The connection with privacy is clear for at least two of these headings; and it is hardly surprising that investigating topics considered to be private, in some sense of that word, will usually render a study 'sensitive', as Goodrum and Keys (2007) note in discussing studies of bereavement and abortion.[8]

However, Renzetti and Lee make the important point that predictions of what will prove to be sensitive inquiries as far as participants are concerned are open to error: 'It is not uncommon [...] for a researcher to approach a topic with caution on the assumption that it is a sensitive one, only to find that those initial fears had been misplaced.' And they add: 'Neither is it unusual for the sensitive nature of an apparently innocuous topic to become manifest once research is under way' (p. 5). Furthermore, they note that judgments of sensitivity, even about the same topic, will vary across audiences.

These authors also recognise that 'the values and beliefs of some groups are threatened in an intrinsic way by research. Some religious groups – fundamentalists, for example – quite literally regard research into their beliefs and activities as anathema' (Renzetti and Lee 1993: 6). MacIntyre (1982: 183) generalises this point, suggesting that 'the fieldworker who tries to understand [an] alien culture in a systematic and unlimited way will, by the very act of trying to understand, be apt to commit an act

---

[8]Interestingly, researching sensitive topics may lead to threats to the privacy of researchers, especially through the activities of the mass media: see Sikes (2008).

of aggression wherever that culture is one which itself sets boundaries to, and imposes taboos upon, acts of cultural understanding'. He continues:

> Modern anthropologists blush at [the crudity of Victorian anthropologists' efforts to expose primitive superstition from the vantage point of civilisation]; what they do not always ask is whether a far less crude, but thereby in some ways more seductive, version of the same attitude is not implicit in the whole enterprise of fieldwork, with its assumption that understanding an alien culture is a good even when that culture does not think that such kinds of understanding are good.

This sort of tension, sometimes formulated in terms of conflicting 'ways of knowing', has for example been at the centre of debates about research on 'indigenous cultures' (see Smith 1999; Walker et al. 2006; Denzin et al. 2008; Chilisa 2009).

Several issues are involved here. There is the ethical question of whether it is legitimate to investigate a particular topic that touches on private matters. And there is another about whether it is acceptable to study a topic that others, perhaps including the people from whom data are to be collected, are likely to regard as private, irrespective of whether the researcher holds this view. This relates to respect for autonomy. But must others' views about what is private be accepted at face value, given that as we noted earlier privacy arguments are frequently used to protect and further various interests? Finally, there is the prudential question of whether or not access to the data can be negotiated without unacceptable costs; and, if not, whether it would be practicable and legitimate to use covert means of investigation. Implicit in MacIntyre's argument, quoted above, is the claim that participants' definitions of privacy and secrecy must be accepted without question – that not to do so constitutes doing a wrong to them. Moreover, elsewhere in the same article he insists that wrongs cannot be counterbalanced by benefits (MacIntyre 1982: 188). We accept neither of these arguments.

So, in our view, assessments of the legitimacy of investigating a particular topic depend not only upon assessments of its sensitivity in relation to privacy, and in other respects, but also on weighing these against the value of the proposed research into this topic. While this is frequently an uncertain matter, reasonable judgments can be made, based on relevant considerations. Moreover, these can be affected by changing socio-cultural circumstances. For instance, the rationale for Coxon's (1996) research on the sexual activity of gay men was perhaps stronger than that for Humphreys' (1975) earlier work on the same topic because of the spread of AIDs in the gay community in the period between the two studies, and the importance of information about the prevalence of risky sexual activities for policies dealing with the pandemic.

Of course, researchers may sometimes be inclined to exaggerate the importance of the topics they investigate, as well as their chances of being able to answer the research questions they address. Bok (1984: 231) also points to the temptation for them to misrecognise their own motives. She suggests that the attraction of investigating private matters for many researchers:

> is not rooted in their desire for knowledge alone, nor only in their hope that it might bring insight and possible benefits. They are also drawn to it by the allure

of secrecy, of boundaries, and of the forbidden. Some take pleasure in dispelling the mystery, in showing it to be 'wholly superficial', in Durkheim's words. Others, on the contrary, want to get to the heart of the secret in order to partake of it, relish its intimacy. Trespassing on what is taboo attracts still others. The extraordinary amount of research into every minute aspect of sexuality or religious belief is simply not explicable on other, strictly scientific grounds.

While Bok seems here to claim extraordinary insight into the private motives of social scientists, she is certainly correct that a mixture of motives will often be involved, perhaps including those she mentions. Furthermore, it could be true that at least some of the decisions about what to investigate made by qualitative researchers today would not survive close scrutiny: that they are open to the charge of reflecting merely personal interests, current intellectual fashions, the demands of career advancement, or intellectual over-ambition.[9]

Decisions about what topics to investigate is an area where a striving for objectivity is important, a virtue identified in Chapter 2 as one that, in appropriate forms, social scientists need to cultivate in themselves. Difficult, and often contentious, judgments are involved here, in which many different sorts of consideration must be taken into account. But, in our view, no one is in a better position to make these judgments than researchers; indeed most other commentators will be in a worse position, as a result of relative ignorance about the field of inquiry and about research methodology. The primary responsibility lies with the researcher to make a decision about whether or not investigating a particular topic is justified, and to defend this decision where necessary.

Of course, these decisions will not be made in a social vacuum. In our everyday lives, we make judgments against the background of what we believe significant others will, or would, think or believe. We are all aware, to one degree or another, that we can make errors, and taking account of others' views can help us to decide whether or not our judgments are sound. Furthermore, these others will often include not only colleagues but also people in the field. Thus, researchers' own judgments about what is and is not private may evolve and change during the course of an investigation.

Research design and data collection

The issue of privacy does not just arise in the selection of topics but also in decisions about how best to carry out an investigation: what types of data to seek, what methods to employ in producing these data, who to approach as potential informants, in which settings to try to carry out observation, what means of data-recording to employ, and

---

[9]In her discussion of this issue, Bok once again singles out for criticism Festinger et al.'s (1956) study of a millenarian group. Yet this study was based upon a quite clear scientific justification, in which naturalistic case study complemented previous experimental work in offering a test of a well-developed and important social psychological theory. Whether such a justification warrants any invasion of privacy, and even more the deception practised on the people concerned by these researchers, is an important question, but in our view much contemporary qualitative research relies on considerably weaker scientific justification than this study.

so on. Returning to the comparison between the work of Humphreys and Coxon, the former's decision to *observe* homosexual activity in public restrooms may be judged to carry different implications, as regards invasion of privacy, from Coxon's use of the diary method, which allowed an open process of recruitment involving informed consent procedures.[10] While Humphreys recognised the private nature of the activity he was observing, he argued that since it happened in a semi-public setting, and that he took considerable precautions to protect participants from harm resulting from the research, a participant-observation approach was justified. As we saw in the Introduction, this study generated considerable controversy, much of it centring around the charge that there had been an invasion of privacy. No similar level of controversy arose with Coxon's work; though this may also reflect the fact that it was done at a later time and (as we noted earlier) in a political climate changed by the AIDS pandemic.

It is worth looking in a little more detail at the differences, in terms of their implications for privacy, between the use of observational strategies and the elicitation of accounts from informants.

Observation

In carrying out observations, qualitative researchers operate in places whose character can vary considerably according to whether they might be judged private or public. Compare, for example, Duneier's (1999) study of sidewalk traders, Tourigney's (2004) visits to derelict buildings that served as 'shooting galleries' where addicts inject themselves (see also Beckerleg and Hundt 2004: 128), and Cahill's (1985) investigations of what goes on in public bathrooms. However, as we saw earlier, the term 'privacy' does not carry a single meaning. We can identify a set of overlapping definitions of what 'private place' could mean:

1   *Private in the sense of being the 'home area' for some group or type of people.* While home areas are often officially marked and widely recognised, they may sometimes be only informally and unilaterally defined. For instance, in urban streets some locations constitute home areas for organised gangs, and passers-by may be well advised to recognise this. Informally defined privacy can also extend to the social space surrounding each person, so that stalking can be interpreted as an invasion of privacy.

2   *Private in the sense that a place is privately not publicly owned.* Of course, there are places that are private in this sense yet also open to the public, as in the case of entertainment venues of various kinds. So, even though a setting may be privately owned, in practical terms a researcher may be able to enter it and carry out research activities there without gaining permission to do so – whether this is legally or ethically acceptable is a separate point.

3   *Private in the sense that there are restrictions exercised on who can and/or who cannot enter a place.* As we have just noted, there are privately owned settings that

---

[10]It is important to recognise that these two researchers were studying rather different populations of gay men, not just in terms of geographical location and time period but perhaps also as regards the kind of sexual activity in which they engaged.

involve few restrictions on entry. By contrast, there are publicly owned places that have severe restrictions on entry, notably government offices and prisons.

4 *Engaging in private activity in a public area can create a temporary private enclave.* An example would be playing cricket, or picnicking, in a park. The occurrence of 'private activity' tends to turn a public place, or parts of it, into a private one, in the sense that people may feel that they must not intrude into the space, and perhaps even that they should avert their eyes from what is going on there, depending upon the nature of the activity.

These four criteria are ones that researchers are likely to use in determining how private some setting or situation is, and whether or not it would be legitimate to observe it. But they will also be used by others, including the people whose activities the researcher wishes to observe. And the fact that there are multiple criteria, and that each is open to interpretation, means that judgments about what is and is not private, or about the degrees to which a situation is private, can be in conflict.

Researchers' judgments about whether or not particular private places can be studied may well be affected by the field relationships that develop around them, or those that they are concerned with cultivating. For example, in studying school students Hudson (2004) was invited by some of them to visit 'the ditch' where they congregated at break-times and dinnertimes, this being an area where private (and, from the school's point of view, illicit) activities took place. However, Hudson felt that she could not accept this invitation because to be seen going to this place by the staff would be interpreted as condoning unacceptable student activities. What this example brings out is that there are identity implications associated with being in or visiting some spaces, and that these can have significant implications for researchers, given that negotiating identities and roles with participants is a major part of their task in the field.[11]

We need to recognise that places, especially those that are quite large in size, are frequently not homogeneous as regards privacy. In particular, in Goffman's (1959) terms there may be front regions and back regions, differentiated relative to intended audience. The privacy status of places can also vary temporally. For example, while people's homes can be taken to be a paradigm case of a private setting, not only do parts of a house vary in degree of privacy, but the same part of a house can change in status depending upon the activity taking place. Thus, Kurotani (2004: 207) found that a good way of spending time with Japanese wives of corporate executives living in the United States was to visit them when they were hosting an 'at home' for their friends. However, she comments that:

my 'field' vanished daily at 6 p.m. sharp. The house where we were gathering had to be turned over to another function, for the tired husband of our hostess would soon return home, expecting a hot meal and a restful evening. It was like one of those dramatic scene changes in *kabuki* theatre, in which a whole set turns upside down and disappears into the basement, to make way for the new set that emerges out of the bottom of the stage. In fifteen minutes or less, all the traces of the

---

[11]For a researcher who took a different approach in a similar setting, see Hey (2002).

daytime gathering were gone, children's toys and books put away, dirty coffee cups washed, the cost of lunch and afternoon sweets squared away, the mothers and children in their cars and on their way home.

In practical terms, then, what is and is not observable, where and when, is often a matter of judgment, and even of trial and error. Furthermore, to some degree, the same is true as regards what it is ethical in privacy terms to observe, where, and when.

Eliciting accounts about private matters

As we noted earlier, it is not just places that can be regarded as private, and for that reason be treated as off-limits to research, but also information. Interview questions, the use of diaries, or the collection of visual data may result in 'disclosure of behaviours or attitudes which would normally be kept private and personal, which might result in offence or lead to social censure or disapproval, and/or which might cause the respondent discomfort to express' (Wellings et al. 2000: 256). Here too judgments about what is private, how private it is, and to what extent it is appropriate to try to elicit information about it, have to be made. And, once again, this must be done against a background where what is public and what is private is by no means always agreed, or straightforward to determine, as well as being a matter of degree.

In eliciting accounts from informants, qualitative researchers collect data of many kinds. Some of this is equivalent in its focus to the products of observation: instead of, or in addition to, a researcher observing situations, informants may be asked to provide data about what goes on in particular places at particular times; for instance, about who participates, in what role, doing what with whom, how frequently, and so on. Here, many of the same issues arise as with observation, even if eliciting accounts about private activities may be judged to be less intrusive than direct observation – if done openly, and through gaining consent.[12] However, in eliciting accounts researchers are usually not solely concerned with gaining access to witness testimony. Questions may be asked about people's past experiences or decisions, about their feelings, or about their personal attitudes and beliefs (political, religious, etc.). And these could well be regarded as private matters.

Various factors will affect whether they are categorised in this way. One concerns who is seen to be asking the questions. We have already noted that researchers can take on a variety of identities for participants in the field, and (once again) there are issues to do with whether benefitting from non-researcher identities, or manipulating them to gain private information, is legitimate (or, rather, when it is and is not). However, it is an intrinsic feature of much qualitative research that it is impossible to act towards people in the field solely as a researcher, or to be treated in this way by them. And what is important here is that different expectations about the transmission and use of information are associated with different identities. These can significantly shape interviewing in qualitative research, including judgments about privacy and its infringement.

---

[12]There are also, of course, methodological considerations relevant here: observations and informants' accounts can differ in the character of the information provided, and in their likely validity.

Closely related is the issue of *why* questions are being asked about a particular sensitive issue, in other words what are the intentions and motives of the researcher. Here the information given to participants about the research may be crucial, and (in line with Shils' recommendation) more specific indications of the purpose of particular questions may sometimes be required from both a practical and an ethical point of view. However, the provision of such information will need to be balanced against the danger of undesirable effects of a methodological or ethical kind.

Also relevant will be *how* questions are asked, for example whether this is done respectfully and politely or in a more confrontational manner, what sort of terminology or whose language is used, and so on. In addition, there may be variation in judgments about privacy arising from *when* questions are asked, both in terms of how an interview is located in the pattern of people's lives, and at what point in the course of an interview sensitive matters are raised. In ordinary life there are times when it will be felt that certain sorts of question should not be asked, even though on other occasions they would be acceptable. For instance, asking women about their views on abortion immediately after they have just had a pregnancy terminated would probably be regarded as more intrusive than similar questions several months later (see Goodrum and Keys 2007: 251–2). Within interviews, sensitive questions will usually be less threatening towards the end than right at the beginning. Finally, *where* an interview is carried out, in whose territory, may also affect the extent to which questions are felt to intrude on privacy, and judgments about whether or not they are legitimate.

At various points in the discussion we have noted that whether informed consent has been obtained can affect judgments about the invasion of privacy. We will consider this in the next section.

INFORMED CONSENT

We discussed the question of consent in the previous chapter, but here we return to it specifically in relation to privacy. Some have argued that consent can be regarded as a kind of 'moral magic' (Hurd 1996; Kleinig 2010), in the sense that gaining it transforms what would have been an unacceptable intrusion of privacy into a legitimate act (Miller and Wertheimer 2010a). It might be suggested, for example, that, had Festinger et al. (1956) or Humphreys (1970) obtained the consent of those they were observing, what they did would either not have been an invasion of privacy or would have been a legitimate invasion. At the very least, it seems to be the case that gaining consent from those who are in a position to authorise access to private territory, or to secret information, can mitigate any offence.

At the same time, we should note that in some respects gaining consent amounts to passing the responsibility for making ethical judgments about privacy from researchers to other people. Obtaining consent may sometimes be necessary or desirable, usually on grounds of respecting autonomy, but it does not rule out the requirement that a researcher must evaluate what would count as an invasion of privacy, and whether this is warranted – not least in terms of whether equivalent data could have been obtained in some other more acceptable way, and whether the study is itself worthwhile. Conversely, there may be occasions when a researcher believes that some invasion of privacy, actual or perceived, is warranted despite the fact that consent cannot be obtained, or even when it is refused.[13]

It is worth comparing our view here with that of Shils (1980). He refers to the interviewer as 'a "foreign body" within the private zone of the individual interviewed' (p. 428), and his view of the social scientist as participant observer was much the same. While he does not argue that the private sphere should be completely protected from research, he insists that any invasion of privacy must be warranted and that there should be protections, notably in the form of obtaining and retaining consent:

> Social scientists, whose disinterested quest for serious knowledge must be acknowledged – even though it frequently does not produce results commensurate with the intention – may claim the privilege of permitted entry into the private sphere. Privacy, like freedom, can be restricted for good reasons, but it is essential in our outlook that the diminution of privacy should be for very good reasons; [and also that] it should be voluntary and retractable. (pp. 430–1).

Emphasising the last point, he continues later:

> although there might be some uncertainty regarding the propriety of entering, by permission, into the private sphere, there seems to me to be no doubt at all about the impropriety of unauthorized entry when the persons are observed in situations which they legitimately regard as private to themselves as individuals, as friends, or as a corporate body. (p. 436)

The problem with this position is that it relies upon an idealised view of contemporary societies (Christie 1976; Douglas 1976; Lundman and McFarlane 1976; Littrell 1993). This is revealed when Shils (1980: 426) writes that: 'No individual lives in isolation, and so his sphere of individuality is open to those with whom he accepts association, regardless of whether the association is prized for its own sake as in friendship or love, or whether it occurs in the pursuit of some other end.' In fact, most people in much of their everyday lives are more or less forced to associate with various others: we do not choose to 'accept association' with those with whom we work, or who live next door to us, except in very indirect and limited ways. Nor do we have even an approximation to complete control over what information we reveal, and must reveal, to others. And power in these various respects is differentially distributed.

The effect of Shils' idealisation is to apply a much stronger constraint on researchers – in the name of respect for privacy – than applies generally in most actual societies, and therefore in many of the settings in which qualitative researchers carry out their work. Equally important, giving primacy to agents' own judgments about when their privacy has been invaded, even while specifying that these judgments must be 'legitimate', effectively allows the misuse of privacy claims to block research in order to serve personal or corporate interests.

---

[13]As we saw in Chapter 3, these points also apply to the issue of harm.

Informed consent is not a 'magic' solution to the problem of invading privacy *only* because, as Shils argues, there are occasions when it would be wrong despite consent having been obtained, but also because even when research is overt participants may forget that it is under way. In the course of participant observation, and also during in-depth interviewing, there is often a tendency for the research role to become submerged in people's perceptions: beneath the personal relations that they develop with the researcher. This results partly from the fact that people are usually more interested in the researcher as a person than in the research itself. In her research on sex workers, Sanders (2006: 210) reports that 'the women were not interested in the academic reasons why I was present in their world. They wanted to know other details from which they could make a judgement about my personality, sexual orientation and history before they decided to disclose information.' Furthermore, in our view there is no general obligation on the part of researchers continually to remind people that research is taking place, even though there may be occasions when this should be done (Thorne 1980). In fact, as we noted earlier, qualitative researchers often work quite hard to bring about this submergence of the researcher role, in order to minimise their own impact and to gain access to data that would not otherwise be available. The key ethical issue is what limits ought to operate on the building of relationships with participants in this way.

In her book *The Journalist and the Murderer*, Malcolm (1991) highlights an extreme case. A writer, Joe McGinniss, having secured a contract to author a book about a murder case, obtained the agreement of the 'murderer', Jeffrey MacDonald, to be present as a participant observer on his defence team. Throughout the course of his work on the book, McGinniss gave the accused the impression that he was on his side, and that he believed in his innocence; whereas, in fact, he did not and would make this plain in his book. Malcolm writes:

> Until close to the publication of *Fatal Vision*, when McGinniss apparently felt he could afford to be a bit cold and careless with MacDonald, he wrote letters assuring MacDonald of his friendship, commiserating with him about his situation, offering him advice about his appeal, requesting information for the book, and fretting about competing writers. (p. 37)

She argues that the problems – leading to the 'murderer' suing the journalist – arose from the fact that the latter: 'participated more fully and more intensely in the culture of his subject than most journalists have occasion to do – how many of us live with a subject for six weeks, accompany him daily to a murder trial, form a business partnership with him, and write to him in prison for three years?' At the same time, she suggests that 'what McGinniss did egregiously, most journalists do more subtly and quietly' (pp. 161–2).

The parallels with qualitative research here are very close, even if researchers do not usually have business contracts with the people they study and, generally speaking, their field relationships are not focused as exclusively on the fortunes of a single person. Certainly, there are questions about how far they should make clear what views and judgments they share and do not share with participants, what their relationship does and does not imply, and so on.

In the next section we will explore some of the issues surrounding privacy as they arise in a distinctive context that is now of great importance: forms of research that employ online data, especially from the Internet.

THE CASE OF ONLINE DATA

Information and communication technologies provide qualitative researchers with new sorts of data, both textual and visual, as well as access to new types of social life, in the form of online communities of various kinds.[14] It is worth drawing a distinction between, on the one hand, the use of online strategies for eliciting information, for example using email or conferencing to carry out interviews or the elicitation of diaries or blogs from participants, and, on the other, using naturally occurring online data for research purposes. The ethical issues associated with the former are similar to those arising with any other kind of interviewing or elicitation process: informed consent will usually need to be sought. The more distinctive ethical issues arise with material that is already available online, and we will focus primarily on this here.

Privacy is a key issue in discussions about the ethics of online qualitative research, though of course other extrinsic values, including minimising harm and respecting autonomy, can also be relevant – these arise, most obviously, where an online user discloses intent to harm her or himself, or others (see Stern 2003, 2009; Sveningsson Elm 2009). Commentators have noted that there is a tendency for the Internet to encourage disclosure of information which, via other media, would be regarded as too personal or private to reveal in public. However, there is considerable variation in the character of what is to be found online, and in its accessibility.

There is also much disagreement among researchers about how online data should be treated. For example, because online social activity is manifested through discourse, there are those who argue that the Internet as a whole should be regarded as 'a site for the cultural production of texts' (Bassett and O'Riordan 2002: 233), perhaps with the implication that what is displayed there is by definition public in character. By contrast, others argue that using online data should be treated as 'human subjects research', with careful attention being paid to what material can reasonably be treated as public, what is more private and so might require informed consent if it is to be accessed, and what perhaps should not be used for the purposes of research at all (see White 2002; Stern 2003; Bassett and O'Riordan 2002). A range of perspectives has been drawn on here. For instance, Capurro and Pingel (2002) employ an ethics of care approach which they treat as a necessary component of the dialogical and relational process that lies at the heart of ethical responsibility. However, they do not see this as a replacement for, but rather as a supplement to, the deontological and consequentialist arguments that are more commonly used (see also Bakardjieva and Feenberg 2001).

---

[14]There is now a considerable literature discussing the ethical issues associated with these new opportunities. See, for example, Hine (2000, 2005); Buchanan (2004); Markham (2005); and Markham and Baym (2009).

In our view, here as elsewhere, a key question is: 'how to balance the needs of the research with those of the research subjects' (Berry 2004: 327; see also Waskul 1996). In relation to privacy, what is required, in part, is for researchers to gain an understanding of others' judgments regarding who can and should have access to which places and what information. But researchers must also make their own assessments about what it is and is not legitimate to use as data, and how. At the same time, they must have a realistic understanding of the perspectives and practices of online participation, rather than simply trying to apply general ethical principles.

While the nature and ethos of the Internet can give rise to the assumption that it is a public domain or sphere in which whatever is available can automatically be treated as open to legitimate use by researchers, there is considerable variation in the character of websites and the material they contain. Judgments about their status as public or private need to be made and are frequently contentious. Part of the reason for this is that, as Allen (1996) has pointed out, different parts of the same site can vary in this respect. Equally important, as with physical locations, there is a range of considerations that might be used to decide what is and is not private, or *how* private it is. One criterion concerns the nature of the material, while another is the intended audience or its degree of accessibility.

Content

A useful question to ask is: does the material on a site relate to sorts of experience, activities or locations that would generally be deemed private? Included under this heading might be detailed discussion of personal experiences or expressions of contentious beliefs, perhaps on the part of identifiable people. It is not uncommon to find participants sharing intimate and/or painful experiences online, for example discussing sexual relationships or serious illnesses. Also under the heading of relatively private content would be live webcam footage or recorded videos of activity within people's homes. Such material lies at one end of a continuum, with official information, adverts, and public statements of various kinds at the other end. Much lies in the middle, including for instance personal information about activities and contacts contained on social networking sites.

As we saw earlier, what is judged private (or sensitive) by the researcher will not necessarily be seen in the same way by the person(s) who produced the material, or by the online community in which it appears. In her study of a Swedish web community, Sveningsson Elm (2009: 82) argued that the users' practices suggested that they did not consider their personal pages – including their photo albums, diaries and profiles – as private. Indeed, they put adverts in the more publicly visited spots of the web community site urging people to visit their personal pages, to watch and comment on their photos and diaries, and to sign their guest books. Sveningsson Elm suggests that these people sought the attention of others and she explains this in terms of a wider inclination among individuals to expose private matters in public space, appealing to Bauman's (2000: 40) idea that, increasingly, 'for the individual, public space is no more than a giant scene on which private worries are projected without ceasing to be private'. By contrast, Hudson and Bruckman (2005: 298) have argued that 'people in public online environments often act as if these environments were private'. In their study of public chatrooms, for example, they show that participants acted as if they had been violated when they were told that they had been studied. In fact, after this disclosure two-thirds of potential participants disappeared from the chatrooms concerned. In practice, it seems likely that attitudes will vary even among those participating in the same site.

Audience and accessibility

A second criterion that we might use in judging whether or not particular material is private is intended audience. However, judging this is by no means a straightforward matter: we may need to try to distinguish between an intended target audience, other people who could also be regarded as legitimate audiences, and those that the creators of the material probably did *not* want accessing it. Furthermore, people who produce online material do not necessarily pay careful attention to audience, or even have a clear idea about who their audience might be; any more than those who produce material offline do. They may also operate with assumptions about who is likely to access what they have put online that are ill-founded. For example, Willett (2009: 286) reports that the girls she studied using the Bebo networking site saw their pages 'as private to their peer group (although they were aware that anyone could access them), and [...] said they would find it strange if adults looked at [them]'. Indeed, they were 'clearly not meant for parents or teachers'.

Nevertheless, while it is often hard to judge *directly* in any particular case who were intended and allowable audiences, this is at least partly indicated by how easily accessible the material is. At one end of the spectrum are websites that are specifically designed for a general, public audience. These include message boards, chatrooms, and many blogs. Then there are sites, or parts of sites, where a visitors' book needs to be signed to gain access, or where membership and registration are required (this includes most web communities, and social networking sites such as Facebook or MySpace). Also included here are those websites that charge fees for access. Finally, at the far end of the spectrum, there are closed websites, email accounts and intranet systems that are password protected and restricted to some types of people, for example those who are members or employees of a specific organisation, or who belong to a particular category of staff within that organisation (see Bakardjieva and Feenberg 2001).[15]

What is involved here is not just a matter of access to whole websites; there may be variations in accessibility across different parts of the same site. Thus some content on publicly open websites is hidden and available only to those who are invited to gain access. In this category we find private rooms within chatrooms, online photo

---

[15]Of course, while accessibility can be treated as a sign of who the material was intended for, there are several reasons for restrictions being placed on access that are nothing to do with privacy. Most obviously, commercial reasons motivate restriction where people are being charged for access.

albums that are restricted, for example to friends and family, or areas within web communities where the sender specifies who is allowed to access the content.

Access strategies

In using material available online, then, researchers must take account of variation in its nature, as regards what it refers to and to what audiences it was intended to be available. In addition, they must decide what can be accessed and used for research purposes without asking permission or even notifying anyone, and what is more private, to what extent this can be used as data, and what precautions must be taken and permissions sought. Even in the case of relatively public content that is immediately accessible, copyright issues may sometimes arise if large amounts of data are to be used in research reports. Equally, this material may be such that, while permission for use is not required, it would be polite to notify relevant people if it is going to be used for research purposes. Beyond this, there may be some easily accessible material where the researcher concludes that consent is nevertheless required, for either practical or ethical reasons.

While some have criticised 'lurking' on the part of researchers (watching what goes on in an online community without openly participating in its activities) there are occasions when this is legitimate in our view (see Sanders 2005: 71). Moreover, gaining consent or even informing participants is not always possible. This is true, for instance, where users write messages in online discussion groups or guest books without signing these, or sign them with pseudonyms. Furthermore, in many Internet environments (e.g. chatrooms) far too many participants are online simultaneously, or they log on and off too rapidly, for informed consent to be obtained. There may also be negative reactions to attempts to obtain permission. Thus, Svenigsson Elm (2001, 2009) explains that she was treated as a 'spammer' and removed from the group when she attempted to follow participants and gain their consent. However, here, as elsewhere, much may depend upon how and when the researcher goes about seeking consent. For example, Lewis (2006) explains that he became a genuine member of an online support group for people with irritable bowel syndrome (IBS) and developed a relationship of trust with his participants as a member of the group before he explained his research purpose. Equally important, if consent is to be sought, the question arises *from whom?* Given that many online communities are bound by norms of trust, respect, and confidentiality (see Elgesem 2001), should the community as a whole give permission or only the individuals whose texts are being used? What happens when some participants agree but others do not?

As is well known, there is a problem with knowing who people are on the Internet: whether how they present themselves there corresponds to who they actually are in terms of personal and social characteristics. This relates to a general issue in the use of online data about how far the analysis should be restricted to online identities, or whether what people present online can only be understood properly if related to background information about their offline lives (Orgad 2009; Sanders 2005), especially given the extent to which these are now interrelated as a result of rapid developments in mobile technology and the emergence of social networking sites. But is it legitimate for researchers to trace participants across websites or to seek to identify their offline identities, and what means are acceptable in doing this? Difficult judgments may be involved here.

CONFIDENTIALITY AND ANONYMITY

Up to now we have concentrated on the ways in which qualitative researchers might invade privacy through the topics they choose to investigate, the contexts they observe, the information they seek or gain from informants, or the content of the material that they decide to use. This does not, however, exhaust the issue of privacy for qualitative inquiry. Equally important is how researchers handle the data that they collect – given that, to varying degrees, some of it will be private, or even secret, in character – and, perhaps above all, how they report and publish their findings.

The precautionary principle that usually operates here is confidentiality. Shils (1980: 431) writes that:

> [...] the particular privacy which an individual suspends by making particular disclosures to another (in this case, the interviewer) must be reinstated by the treatment which the disclosed private information receives. The privacy should be restored by the obliteration of any connection with the person who disclosed it; this means that the interviewer must never disclose the connection to anyone, orally or in writing. The particular confidences must be respected; they must not be transmitted in their particular form and in their relationships to the particular individual to anyone else; they may be introduced into the public sphere only by generalisation and anonymity.

Of course, confidentiality is a principle that is held to govern the behaviour of a number of professions, including lawyers.[16] For example, it requires that any information that a lawyer obtains from her or his client should not be disclosed to others except where this is in the interests of the client, and perhaps also when disclosure has been agreed by the client. The function of this principle is to allow clients to provide all the information that may be necessary in constructing an effective case on their behalf, including that which they might not otherwise provide because it is embarrassing or potentially damaging, possibly opening them up to legal prosecution or to retribution from others. In this way, lawyers frequently acquire information about clients that they are obliged to conceal.

So, confidentiality is itself a form of secrecy: it involves controlling rather than publicising information. Whether or not this is appropriate can be a matter of dispute. After all, as a result of the promise of confidentiality lawyers may obtain knowledge

---

[16] It is also central to transactions between doctors and their patients, dating back to the Hippocratic Oath which reads, in part: 'Whatever, in connection with my professional service, or not in connection with it, I see or hear, in the life of men, which ought not to be spoken of abroad, I will not divulge, as reckoning that all such should be kept secret.'

about past crimes, and perhaps even about future ones, about political and financial corruption, and so on, that many would believe ought to be exposed. In effect they may be shielding someone from prosecution, an activity that for others would constitute a criminal offence. Perhaps not surprisingly, the commitment to confidentiality on the part of lawyers is backed up legally: in many countries they cannot be prosecuted for failing to communicate information they have obtained from clients. So, confidentiality is a guiding principle for lawyers, and an aspect of the licence that they exercise as part of their professional work. They are allowed to put aside what, for others, might be judged to be an ethical or even legal obligation to disclose information that they have received. The justification is that being able to promise confidentiality to their clients enables them to do their work much more effectively than would otherwise be possible.

While social researchers normally commit themselves to maintaining the confidentiality of the data they collect, and often specifically promise this to gatekeepers and others, their situation is significantly different from that of the lawyer in several respects. It is closer, in many ways, to that of journalists.[17] First of all, there is no legal protection should authorities demand access to the data collected, so that social scientists' capacity to maintain confidentiality is less secure than that of lawyers. Indeed, protecting confidentiality can in some circumstances turn out to be quite costly to them, up to and including imprisonment (Nejelski 1976; Scarce 1994, 1999; Leo 1995, 1996; Erikson 1996; Adler and Adler 2002; Israel 2004). For example, Brajuha's study of a restaurant in which he worked was brought to an end by a fire and his field notes were subpoenaed as part of an arson inquiry. While the subsequent lengthy legal battle was resolved, the costs to him were considerable (Brajuha and Hallowell 1986). Equally important, it is not uncommon for researchers themselves, or ethics committees, to insist that there are circumstances where information obtained as confidential should nevertheless be disclosed to third parties; and it is frequently argued that these exceptional circumstances must be made explicit when initially negotiating access to data.

A second important divergence from the case of the lawyer is that no service is usually being provided by either social scientists or journalists to the people via whom they gain access to information.[18] Rather, both these occupations are engaged in the production of a public good — knowledge of various kinds — that will be available to everyone. This clearly changes the function of the promise to maintain confidentiality. In the case of the lawyer, it is offered in return for information that the lawyer can *then use to provide a service for her or his client*, whereas in that of journalists and social

---

[17]This is not, of course, to suggest that journalism and social research are equivalent activities, that they have a comfortable relationship, even less that journalists provide a model of good ethical behaviour. For an illustration of the last two points, see Sikes' (2008) account of her experiences when journalists picked up on an article she had written about sexual relationships between teachers and students. On journalistic ethics more generally see, for example, Belsey and Chadwick (1992), Kieran (1997), Page (1998), Berry (2000).

[18]There are exceptions, for example where journalists or researchers are effectively being used by those who supply them with information for publicity purposes.

scientists confidentiality is offered to protect the privacy of, and minimise the risk of harm to, those from whom information is being obtained, *but the latter will frequently not benefit directly from how that information is used by researchers.*[19]

Also distinctive is that for journalists and social scientists the clash with the impulse to make public is especially sharp, precisely because it is their main task to produce public knowledge: as we saw earlier, it is essential to the very activity of research that the findings will be published, and some of the data presented as evidence. What is involved here, potentially, is a weighing of considerations regarding the rights and interests of those providing access to data, or to whom the data refer, against the value of publishing analyses of it and quoting extracts from it as evidence.

While there are similarities between the social scientist and the journalist in these respects there are also differences. Confidentiality for journalists concerns protecting the identity of their sources, whereas social researchers are usually committed also to protecting the identities of the people, organisations, and places referred to in the data they collect, in research reports. A second difference is that, in the case of the journalist, confidentiality is usually offered to sources in order to protect them from harm, rather than to protect their privacy. In fact, the data supplied and published may very well invade the privacy of others, naming (and, often, shaming) them. For social scientists, however, confidentiality is usually important for reasons of protecting privacy as well as protection from harm.

These differences reflect the fact that, as we noted earlier, while, much qualitative research focuses on individual people and their social interactions at particular times and in particular places, *these are usually treated as exemplars of general social categories or types.* There is a contrast here with both literary biography and journalism where, generally speaking, the people at the centre of the stories *must* be named if the account is to be of interest to the audience.

STRATEGIES FOR MAINTAINING CONFIDENTIALITY

The commitment on the part of qualitative researchers to maintaining confidentiality is manifested in a number of ways. First, when recording data in the field they will normally aim to keep what they record secret, for instance trying to avoid others seeing what they are writing down in field notes, perhaps using code or poor handwriting to do this; not allowing others to listen to or watch electronic recordings made in the field, unless these relate exclusively to the person concerned; and so on.[20] It is also important to note that there are some settings where it may be

---

[19]Of course journalists and social scientists sometimes pay for information. There are also researchers who believe that their work should be designed directly to benefit the people they are studying, see Chapter 2.

[20]There may be departures from this where any invasion of privacy is judged to be minimal, and/or where showing data records is part of the process of data collection itself, for instance playing videos recorded in a setting to participants in order to get their commentaries on what is happening. See, for example, Noyes (2008).

quite difficult to secure the secrecy of field notes and other data records. Coggeshall (2004: 146) reports how, in studying a prison, his field notes were continually at risk of confiscation by guards or of theft by inmates.

The concern with protecting confidentiality also extends to the storage of data: field notes, other documents, audio- and video-recordings, and transcriptions must be kept in a secure manner that makes it difficult for others to access it. This applies both to the physical storage of 'hard copy' as well as to files on computers, servers, or in clouds. There are cases where researchers have not been able to do this; for example in Angrosino's (2004: 20) research in a monastery it was an access requirement that all the recordings and transcripts would be deposited in the monastery's library. Not surprisingly, this affected what informants would tell him, as well as leading to concerns about invasion of privacy and potential harm.

Second, researchers will not usually pass on information about what they have observed, or what an informant has told them, to other people in the field; at least not in a manner that would render the source or the people referred to identifiable. However, maintaining confidentiality in this respect is not always easy: on occasion gatekeepers or people in the field may guess what other informants have said and put this to the researcher, and it may be difficult for the latter not to breach confidentiality simply through her or his reaction, especially when there is no warning that such questions are coming. In the case of observation, participants will sometimes have observed the same scene and events, and they may query the researcher about these. Generally speaking, researchers are very circumspect in their responses to such questions, and rightly so.

While in the field, researchers may also incur obligations to keep the secrets of the people they study, and this can require engaging in active deception. Kelly provides an example from her research on prostitutes in Mexico:

> As my relationships with the sex workers grew deeper and they invited me into their homes, I became responsible for maintaining their secrets, lying to their acquaintances and even to their children about how it was I came to know their mother or where I worked. Such lies produce a sense of alienation, create situations of inauthenticity in daily life, and are incredibly stressful to maintain. (Kelly 2004: 7)

Gatekeepers and others in powerful positions may, sometimes, demand access to the research data; and, as we noted earlier, occasionally researchers can be threatened with legal action to obtain it. In these circumstances, researchers will face difficult decisions, but in our view maintaining confidentiality is an important principle and should not be breached unless there are very good reasons for doing so. Much the same applies to cases where the data disclose some threat to one or more people in the field, or to others, or where they show that a serious offence has been committed. Given researchers' commitment to the values intrinsic to research, the default position here must be to maintain confidentiality, even though there will be extreme circumstances when the right course of action is to disclose the information. There may, in any case, be ways of doing this discreetly: Holmes reports how one of the children she was studying said to her: 'Can I tell you something? I hate my life, I just want to kill myself.' She reported this to the teacher and support was provided for the child, without his being aware that the researcher had intervened (Holmes 1998: 25).[21]

Against this background, any specification within research contracts – oral or written – of circumstances under which the promise of confidentiality will be breached must be considered very carefully. In some fields of research this would prevent access to important data, or render the research impracticable. Furthermore, it is impossible to frame any such specification in ways that would indicate *exactly* when confidentiality would and would not be abandoned; and attempts to do so could be found insulting if they mention types of situation or action that participants find inappropriate to their case, rightly or wrongly. Yet, if such an exemption is formulated in very vague terms it could be interpreted as rescinding the very offer of confidentiality.

Another important area where confidentiality issues arise is that qualitative researchers sometimes offer, or agree to provide, a feedback report during the course of data collection, for a gatekeeper or for the people in the field generally. Indeed, doing this is sometimes a condition of their gaining access in the first place. As we saw in Chapter 3, there is a particular danger here that confidentiality will be breached, since the audience will usually know personally the people from whom the data have been collected as well as those referred to (Tolich 2004). Furthermore, the events reported may be recent, and therefore within memory, which also makes identifying sources and people easier. Given this, careful judgments must be made about whether to offer, or agree, to report back during the course of fieldwork, or even at the end. And, if a report of this kind is to be provided, considerable care will need to be taken if confidentiality is to be preserved.

It sometimes seems to be assumed that reporting back to gatekeepers and participants is a virtue, or that people in the field have a right to hear about the research findings, perhaps even to have access to the data being collected. Such ideas are open to serious question. It is important to remember that what is involved in any reporting back process is not simply individuals being informed but an intervention in a local social system; and this can sometimes have unforeseen, and perhaps quite dramatic, consequences. One reason for this is that gatekeepers and people in the field will not usually approach the data, or the analysis, in the same way as the researcher. Josselson (1996: xiii) notes that 'One inherent and indelible contrast between us and our participants is that, although we interrogate their specificity in quest of what may be generalizable, their interest remains lodged in understanding their own uniqueness'. So, rather than being interested in abstract issues about the character and consequences of social processes, they will usually engage with any report pragmatically and personally, for instance using it to promote goals to which they are committed, seeing it as a threat to their own or others' interests, or being preoccupied with how it portrays them (Bloor 1978). Moreover, sometimes requests for feedback during the course of the fieldwork are implicated in local politics. For example, in his study of an Australian school, Forsey came to recognise that:

---

[21]Wiles et al. (2008a) in their study of how social researchers manage issues of confidentiality report that researchers often feel compelled to break confidentiality when participants are perceived as being at risk but not in cases of involvement in illegal activity.

[the principal's] call for me to present a 'warts and all' picture of the school was not necessarily the straightforward granting of license I had imagined. I sensed that she was also [encouraging] me to identify what needed changing, and to join her in the reform program [...]. (Forsey 2004: 63)

Given this, when she asked him to feed back his findings, implying that this request had come from the staff, he carefully declined the invitation.

The commitment to maintaining confidentiality also requires that data are not shared with academic colleagues, informally or via seminars, *in a way that would allow the easy identification of the people and places to which the data relate*. Extreme caution is generally the proper approach here. Wiles et al. (2008a: 421) report that researchers sometimes accidentally break confidentiality, as when, finding their fieldwork to be emotionally challenging, they 'offload' with someone. In doing this they may provide information to colleagues that ought to have been kept secret.

Of course, the point at which the tension between publicity and privacy arises most sharply is in publishing research reports. Here, qualitative researchers need to quote from the data, and this is another respect in which qualitative inquiry may involve a potentially greater threat to privacy than other kinds of social science. Generally speaking, the reporting of evidence must be done in ways that avoid the sources, and the people and settings referred to, being identifiable. The main means used to preserve confidentiality in this respect is, of course, by rendering people and places anonymous.

ANONYMISATION

Anonymisation is a strategy used to maintain privacy, though it may also serve to protect people from harm – such as public embarrassment, or financial or physical threat. While this strategy is routinely adopted by many qualitative researchers, some have challenged its effectiveness and/or desirability.

There are several ways of anonymising data. The most obvious one is to replace actual names with invented ones.[22] Another is to refer to people solely by the roles that they play: doctor, nurse, patient, relative, and so on. Alternatively, first names without second names, or just initials, may be used; or numbers or letters of the alphabet: Informant 1, Informant 2; Doctor A, Doctor B, etc. Alongside these devices, any personal characteristics of people, or contextual features of places, that could lead to their identification may be omitted from accounts, or even changed in order to provide disguise. In an extreme example, Hopkins (1993) used a fictional composite person to protect the anonymity of her informants (see also Sparkes 1995; Piper and Sikes 2010).

---

[22]There are also issues about how pseudonyms are chosen. Several strategies are possible, for example inventing them in a haphazard manner, taking them from fictional sources, formulating them to capture the character of the people concerned (see, for instance, Beynon 1985), or allowing participants to choose their own.

As this makes clear, there can be a tension between preserving confidentiality through anonymisation and providing a detailed and accurate account of the people and places studied. Whether this is a problem, and how difficult it is to resolve, will vary considerably across research projects, depending upon the nature of the people and settings studied, the topics investigated, and so on. Also significant, however, is the orientation of the researcher. If the research task is viewed as treating people and/or places as exemplars of particular social types, in order to develop and test explanatory arguments, then the tension is likely to be less severe than where the aim is to describe people or places 'in themselves' (Stake 1995). But even if the task of research is limited to producing value-relevant knowledge of generic types, or of relatively large-scale social processes, there will still be potential tension between preserving confidentiality and accurate reporting.

It is also important to remember that anonymity is a matter of degree. In being referred to in research reports, people are not *either* identifiable *or* anonymous. Rather, their identities will be more or less difficult to recognise for different audiences.[23] It is sometimes said that the aim in social science is that the people described would be able to recognise themselves but that no one else should be able to do so (see, for instance, Humphreys 1975: 172). But this is an impossible standard to achieve. Almost all qualitative research reports are likely to fail in either one or other of these respects, and possibly even both. The priority should be to try to ensure that people are not identifiable by audiences who should not have access to any private information conveyed, or who could do them harm by acting on that information. This is very much a matter of practical judgment. One issue concerns who is and is not likely to read the research report. A second is what level of difficulty would be involved for various audiences in identifying the people or places.

The process of anonymising data normally begins at the stage of data recording. One of the main ways of protecting against breaches of confidentiality through people illegitimately gaining access to the data is to substitute pseudonyms in the course of writing up field notes, in transcribing recordings, and in labelling the data for storage purposes; with any key to the pseudonyms being kept separate from the data.[24] The same pseudonyms will generally be used in subsequent research reports.

Needless to say, preserving anonymity of sources, and of the people and places referred to in the data, will not always be easy or successful. In some cases they may be immediately recognisable by a wide audience; and in more cases they will be identifiable by people in the local setting, or be discoverable by those who have the necessary expertise and sufficient motivation. Preserving anonymity is especially difficult where people and/or places are very distinctive, such as people who play prominent roles in small recognisable communities, as in the case of Vidich and Bensman's (1958, 1964) study of Springdale, those who lead organisations whose features make them hard to disguise, or those who have celebrity status. In studies of

---

[23]This is even true with visual data, for example where faces are blanked out (see Chapter 3) items of clothing, posture, and indications of location may still enable identification.

[24]Any signed consent forms should also be kept separate from the data, as Thorne (1980: 285) points out these can threaten the preservation of anonymity.

politicians, sometimes the very point of the analysis is to study particular well-known events or policies and the roles which they played in them, so that keeping them anonymous is impossible (see Ball 1994). In such cases, it may be necessary to negotiate over what can and cannot be revealed in published reports; though in this process the researcher must be prepared robustly to champion the needs of research.

Anonymisation is an issue that has been given considerable attention in the case of online research. One question here is whether efforts should be made to disguise the websites from which particular data were drawn, and indeed whether this is possible given the power of search engines. Another concerns whether to use pseudonyms where people have given their own names. Many online users treat the Internet as a forum that enables them to spread their ideas, so that they may not want to be anonymous. But whether or not researchers should collude with this requires careful consideration, as does the threat of participants unwittingly opening themselves up to the risk of harm.

As already noted, even when the sources, people or places referred to would not be identifiable by a *general* audience, there may be significant audiences, not least those directly involved in the setting or field investigated, who would be able to identify at least some of them fairly easily despite the use of pseudonyms. In the past, anthropologists and many other social scientists routinely assumed that the people they studied would never read the research reports they wrote: because they were working in non-literate societies and/or because the research would be published in a different language and in a context that was culturally remote from the communities studied. This has changed to some extent as a result of spreading literacy, increasingly global communication networks, and the rise of English as an international language (Brettell 1993). While it is still the case that relatively few people are aware of and read the academic articles and books published within most social science disciplines, researchers increasingly feel obliged (in our view on questionable grounds) to provide copies of research reports to at least some of those studied. In addition, there is always the possibility that the mass media will follow up research that they take to be newsworthy, seeking to identify and publish the names of the people and places involved (Morgan 1972; Brettell 1993: 16–20; Greenberg 1993).

In the case of Scheper-Hughes' study of an Irish village, which was identified by a newspaper, some of her informants complained that her book had been written in a way that was accessible to them: 'Why couldn't you have left it as a dusty dissertation on a library shelf that no-one would read, or a scholarly book that only the "experts" would read?' (Scheper-Hughes 2001: xvii; see also Scheper-Hughes 2000a and Messenger 1989). This is a comment that goes directly against current pressures on researchers to disseminate their findings widely, and against ideas about a public sociology or anthropology (see, for example, Burawoy 2005). However, it is in line with the belief that academic research reports ought to be directed solely towards an academic audience, and that only reviews of multiple studies should be aimed at wider publics (Hammersley 2011). While this restriction would not prevent interventions by the media, it would reduce the danger. Of course, even without the activities of the media, it is always possible that attempts to preserve anonymity will fail. This can happen through contingent events; for example the people involved may disclose their own or others' identities, intentionally or inadvertently, and this could subsequently become public knowledge.

Aside from the practical difficulties associated with anonymisation, there have also been questions about whether it is a legitimate strategy for researchers to adopt (Richardson 1973: 45; Nespor 2000; Grinyer 2002; Walford 2002, 2005, 2008). One argument here is that if researchers cannot absolutely guarantee that anonymity will be preserved, and confidentiality thereby protected, then they should not promise it. Another is that replacing the names of people, and especially of places, with pseudonyms can lead to inaccuracy: it may prevent readers from using background knowledge they already have to understand what is reported. This danger is even more obvious where the details of people and places studied are actually changed to protect anonymity, or where fictions are employed. Furthermore, in providing minimal, and perhaps inaccurate, information the researcher may encourage misidentification or stereotyping. The dilemma here is that the more information is provided, even about pseudonymised places or people, and the more accurate this is, the more likely they will be identifiable, at least to some audiences.

Another reason why anonymisation has been questioned is that participants sometimes *want* to be named in research reports, and/or wish their organisation and community to be identifiable (see Grinyer 2002; Wiles et al. 2008a). For instance, Janovicek (2006: 163) refers to the case of Mennonites who 'saw their participation as a witness to the work of God in their lives', and requested that 'tapes and transcripts be donated to the church conference archives under their real names as a "legacy for their descendants" […]'. In a study of a critical care unit in a hospital Seymour found that a senior nurse was disappointed that 'her unit' would not be named since she believed that the research would provide positive publicity and thereby benefit staff morale and patient care (Seymour and Ingleton 1999: 71). It might be argued that research participants have a right to be named, that researchers should agree to any such request, and that refusing amounts to an infringement of their autonomy, or a failure to respect their religious ideals, legitimate interests, and so on. Alongside this it is occasionally insisted that informants *own* the data that they have supplied and that their link with it should not be broken (Walker 1993; Lincoln and Guba 1989: 236: Benjamin 1999; Simons 2009); or even that they ought to be viewed as authors of the data, so that they have a right to be named as sources.[25]

Some of these issues are raised in an illuminating way by Grinyer's research on families with a child suffering from cancer. She and her colleagues came to question their use of pseudonyms, and, asking the informants, they found that most wanted their own and their children's real names to be used. What was being researched here was, of course, a very sensitive situation, especially since many of the children had

---

[25]This relates to a broader issue about the extent to which, through their research reports, qualitative researchers represent the people they study in a political not just an epistemic sense; an issue that has been especially salient in anthropology, and has been heightened more generally through the influence of constructionism, with its claim that research 'changes the world, creates reality, and writes culture' (Markham 2006: 37). See Clifford and Marcus (1986).

died by the time the research report was being written. But the issue is more general: Scheper-Hughes came to have similar doubts about anonymisation as a result of the negative reaction to her research in an Irish village:

> Anonymity makes us unmindful that we owe our anthropological subjects the same degree of courtesy, empathy, and friendship in writing as we generally extended to them face-to-face where they are not our 'subjects' but our companions [...]. Sacrificing anonymity means we may have to write less poignant, more circumspect ethnographies, a high price for any writer to pay. But our version of the Hippocratic Oath – to do no harm, in so far as possible, to our informants – would seem to demand this. (Scheper-Hughes 2000a: 128)

There is some truth in these arguments against anonymisation, and they certainly highlight the tension between the character of the personal relations developed by qualitative researchers in the field and the kind of orientation they must adopt as writers. However, the problems can easily be overplayed (Kelly 2009). Much of the time, anonymisation *has* been successful in protecting the identities of people and places. And while there will be occasions when it is unlikely to succeed, this fact does not count against its use generally. Much the same is true about the danger of its misleading readers: this will be a problem in some cases, but not in most. Furthermore, the idea that people have a right to be named, if they wish, that they own the data, or are authors of it, misconceives the nature of research in our view. The aim is not to speak on behalf of, to give voice to, or even to portray the lives of particular people, but rather to answer research questions. Moreover, all data are co-constructed, and developed into evidence by researchers. Even in the case of data from interviews or documents these are not simply the personal expressions of informants. Finally, those who ask to be named will not always recognise the dangers involved. And naming some people may increase the likelihood that *others* can be identified, thereby potentially infringing *their* privacy and perhaps also exposing them to the danger of various harms.

There are a couple of other, rather different, arguments against anonymisation. First, there are those who complain that disguising people's identities protects them from responsibility for their actions when they should be held responsible. Thus, Colvard (1967: 345) writes:

> When a scholar puts his own name on a published paper he assumes some moral and political as well as professional responsibility, at least for that penultimate act itself – perhaps even for some of its uncertain consequences. But when he removes individual informants' names from his findings [...], he is, in effect, if not excusing at least shielding them from individual accountability for the acts analyzed.

A recent case where this issue arose concerned a researcher investigating 'intergenerational sexualities' who guaranteed anonymity to the paedophiles he interviewed (Mega 2002; Yuill 2004). The assumption behind Colvard's argument, and one of the grounds underpinning criticism of Yuill, seems to be that it is the task of researchers to hold those they study to account. In our view, this expectation is incompatible with the specific task of the researcher, and with the licence that is required to pursue this (see Chapter 2).

A rather different argument is put forward by Walford (2002: 100):

> Perhaps the idea of anonymity allows researchers to write their books and articles with less concern for absolute accuracy and to base their arguments on evidence which may not be as strong as desirable. If named [sites] and people are being discussed the need for very strong evidence before claims are made becomes obvious. At the extreme, writers could be sued for libel in a way that is difficult to do where names are not used. Researchers are able to hide poor evidence behind the pseudonyms without those researched being able to make a challenge.

It is certainly true, in our view, that much qualitative research has a weak evidential base and presents findings that are contestable. And it is important that, in assessing the strength of the evidence for their claims, researchers imagine how those whom they have studied might challenge the truth of their accounts. However, Walford seems to assume that the people concerned would be primarily interested in accuracy, so that they would not object to what is true but displeasing or disadvantageous to them. This is unlikely (Becker 1964b). Messenger (1989: 125) reports the post-publication comment of one participant in his study that 'everything [Messenger] says is true, but he had a right not to say it!' Furthermore, if people and places were named, researchers would often feel it necessary to omit or even modify relevant evidence in a substantial way in order to protect participants, as Scheper-Hughes hints in the quote earlier.[26]

In our view confidentiality as regards data is an important ethical principle in qualitative research, and anonymisation is a useful strategy in achieving it. To abandon that strategy would make some research impossible and damage the quality of much of the rest. Of course, sometimes it will not be appropriate, and there is a range of considerations that need to be taken into account in deciding about this, including the nature of the participants and the researcher's relations with them.

CONCLUSION

In this chapter we have explored another important value principle that properly acts as a constraint upon qualitative research: the protection of privacy. We sketched the background against which this issue arises; in particular the endemic tension within human societies between pressure for publicity and the protection of privacy, a tension that is heightened within liberal, social-democratic states. We also explored the complexities surrounding which places and sorts of information are to be treated as

---

[26] It should be noted that Walford's argument is stronger where the researcher sees the task as to critically evaluate what is described or explained, or to challenge orthodox assumptions about it.

private, how private they are, and whether or when it is legitimate for researchers to investigate them. We argued that what is involved most fundamentally is the question of who should (and should not) have access to various sorts of information, and what licences ought to be recognised as legitimating acquisition of it.

A commitment to the preservation of privacy has implications for what topics researchers can investigate, the types of setting or site in which they can carry out observations, and their asking particular sorts of question in interviews or in eliciting documents. We looked at the issues surrounding the investigation of sensitive topics, and also emphasised that *how* a topic is studied can be as important, as far as privacy is concerned, as the topic itself. With reference to data collection strategies, we argued that qualitative inquiry is more vulnerable to the charge of invading privacy than other kinds of social research because it often aims to find out 'what's really going on' and/or to explore people's perspectives in detail; and because it does this through first-hand contact, in ways that involve the development, indeed the cultivation, of personal relationships. We also explored the somewhat different ways in which the issue of privacy arises in researchers' use of online data, and the problems that this generates. Obtaining informed consent has sometimes been presented as absolving researchers from any charge of invading privacy, but we argued that it does not do this, and that seeking it is not always required or desirable.

Equally central to privacy is how researchers deal with the data they collect, as regards storing it, reporting back to people in the field, and writing research reports. The key requirement here is confidentiality. We noted that in the context of research this refers not just to protecting the sources from whom one has derived information, but also protecting people referred to in the data, and in the descriptions and explanations published in research reports. Anonymisation is the major strategy employed for achieving this protection, though we noted that it will not always be successful, and that there has been some debate about its legitimacy. We argued that it is an important and necessary strategy in most qualitative research, even though there are cases where it cannot or should not be relied upon.

CONCLUSION: CHALLENGING MORALISM

Ethical considerations have long been given attention by social scientists. But, as we saw in the Introduction, they have acquired increased salience in recent years, especially for qualitative researchers. Our aim in this book has been to outline a coherent and defensible perspective on the ethics of qualitative inquiry, and to explore its practical implications. However, the position we have developed is at odds not only with the assumptions built into the rise of ethical regulation but also with the views of many qualitative researchers today.

We will begin by providing a résumé of the main elements of our position.

A BRIEF SUMMARY

In Chapter 1 we saw that the term 'ethics' is used in a variety of ways. It is important to be as clear as possible about what sorts of consideration come under this heading, and about the contrast with other relevant categories, such as 'political' and 'prudential'. Equally necessary is to be aware of the range of different types of argument that can be used in thinking about ethical issues. There has been a tendency in many discussions of research ethics to rely upon just one or two of these, thereby losing important perspectives. For this reason in Chapter 1 we outlined a series of philosophical approaches, from those that are primarily concerned with 'good intentions', and with duties or rights, through those that emphasise the *consequences* of actions, to those which focus on virtues, relate ethics back to primordial forms of social relationship, insist that all ethical judgments are relational or situational, or question the epistemological (and even the ethical) status of morality.

In Chapter 2 we argued that research ethics must be viewed as a form of occupational ethics, where the central commitment is the effective pursuit of the occupational task. This is a very different orientation from most discussions of research ethics, in which the focus is primarily upon how the people studied should be treated, this often being interpreted in terms of universalistic or personalistic standards. We argued that the sole operational task of research is the production of knowledge; albeit knowledge that is of human relevance, contributing to a discipline (academic research) or supplying information required by policymakers, practitioners, citizens or consumers (practical research). So, the aim is to produce conclusions that reach a relatively high threshold in terms of likely validity, and that make a worthwhile contribution to collective knowledge.

We rejected competing views of the task of qualitative research that either deny the possibility or desirability of social scientific knowledge (as conventionally understood) or insist that research must be specifically directed at achieving practical or political goals. In our view, qualitative researchers cannot legitimately escape the responsibility to treat the pursuit of knowledge as their exclusive goal. Of course, they may have a variety of practical and political motives for engaging in research, or for carrying out particular projects, including bringing about social improvement or change. But while these are legitimate *motives* for engaging in research, they cannot substitute for its *institutionalised goal*. Turning these motives into goals is likely to increase the danger of error in the findings, thereby undermining the capacity of research to produce reliable knowledge. It also tends to result in value conclusions, evaluations and/or recommendations, being put forward as if they could be validated solely by research. More fundamentally, it amounts to pursuing quite a different activity under the guise of research.

The idea that research ethics is a form of occupational ethics led us to distinguish between intrinsic and extrinsic values relevant to the research process. Intrinsic values constitute, or derive from, the research task itself; and the central one here is truth. So, the primary responsibility of the researcher is to try to ensure that he or she produces sound knowledge, and does not put forward false claims. The concept of truth is often rejected today and we examined some of the arguments against it. We then briefly considered some of the obligations that follow from this primary commitment. These relate to: the setting of research questions; the treatment of research literatures; the collection, interpretation and publication of data; and responses to criticism. Related obligations apply in the various ancillary roles that researchers play within the research community, for example in refereeing proposals for funding bodies or papers for journals, or in mediating the reception of research findings in the public sphere. Arising out of this discussion, we highlighted a number of essential virtues on the part of researchers: dedication, objectivity, and independence.

While pursuing knowledge is the primary responsibility of researchers, we do not suggest that they can adopt *any* means that promise to be effective. There is a range of extrinsic values that can serve as proper restraints on the pursuit of research. We focused our discussion on the three that have been given most attention in the research ethics literature: minimisation of harm, respect for the autonomy of participants, and the preservation of privacy. We showed that each of these principles is open to somewhat different readings, and that in part this reflects the fact that they involve judgments about matters of degree: how likely is harm, how serious is the sort of harm threatened, how significant are the infringements of autonomy or

privacy involved, and so on. Even more fundamentally, the meaning of these principles resides entirely in how they are applied to particular circumstances: they are no
more than generalised statements about what would be judged appropriate in paradigm cases. Some actual cases will be relatively close to a paradigm, but most will be
more marginal, so that it will be harder to know how to judge them in terms of the
value-principle concerned. The implication of this is that such principles can only
serve as guides for action, not as injunctions or rules.

It is also necessary to remember that there can be conflicts among value principles.
These occur not just between the intrinsic and the extrinsic values, though it is
essential to recognise this type of conflict, but also *among* the various extrinsic values.
For example, seeking to avoid or minimise harm will not always be compatible with
fully respecting people's autonomy or privacy. There is no pre-ordained consonance
among values, nor any hope that harmony can be permanently established. As a
result, judgments frequently have to be made about the relative priority of different
value principles in particular situations.

Equally important, there is considerable scope for conflict between researchers'
value commitments, intrinsic and extrinsic, and the practical constraints that they
face in the course of their work: in dealing with funding bodies, university authorities, ethics committees, colleagues, gatekeepers, as well as people in the field. In
research, as in other activities, some adaptation has to be made to the situations
encountered, including to others' value-commitments and interests, these placing
limits upon action. Furthermore, it is characteristic of qualitative research that the
contexts in which it is carried out can vary greatly in character – homes, streets,
organisations of many kinds, virtual spaces produced by digital technologies, and so
on. What these usually share in common, though, is that they are not under the
control of the researcher, so that in qualitative inquiry there are severe demands to
adapt to circumstances; varying somewhat according to the particular methods of
data collection and recording used.

All this means that, in carrying out qualitative research, it will be necessary continually to weigh a whole variety of considerations against one another, among
which the researcher's own extrinsic value commitments are only one component.
While on some occasions these considerations will rule out some research strategy
completely, or perhaps even a whole project, such values will often have to be compromised. *Ethical judgment is primarily about which compromises are and are not legitimate
in the relevant context.*

Given their character, such judgments are almost always open to reasonable disagreement. In addition, it is easy to reach naïve or simplistic evaluations of what
researchers have done or plan to do, positive or negative, if the full range of relevant
considerations is not taken into account, if it is forgotten that the researcher's primary
responsibility is to pursue knowledge effectively, and/or if relevant information
about the situation faced is not available or is not given sufficient attention.

It may seem from our discussion here that we regard qualitative research as an
extremely complex and problematic activity. It is certainly true that doing it well is
difficult. Yet we do not believe that most of the time it is seriously problematic
in ethical terms, by comparison with some other activities, such as medical research or

journalism. In particular, it does not usually entail a direct threat of serious harm. In fact, we regard the ethical issues that arise in qualitative social research as, generally speaking, no more severe than those that face most of us in many ordinary, everyday situations (see Reiss 1979: 69). In any activity it is always possible to raise questions about its value, about what is and is not justified, who is responsible for what, and so on. And, sometimes, it is important to shake off any complacency and reflect on issues that would otherwise be largely taken for granted. However, some balance is required here: without some brake on this kind of ethical reflexivity, no work will get done. This is as true in research as it is more generally.

MORALISM

As we noted earlier, our position here challenges some currently influential views about research ethics, including among qualitative researchers. A useful label for what we oppose is 'moralism', a term that has been defined as 'the vice of overdoing morality' (Coady 2005: 101).[1]

Perhaps the most obvious expression of moralism is the claim that qualitative research is, or should be, *essentially* ethical. For example, Clegg and Slife (2009: 36) argue that it is 'an inherently ethical enterprise' while Mertens and Ginsberg (2009: 2) insist that 'ethics is foundational to the *telos* of the research enterprise'. In one sense this claim is true – we have argued that social research is founded upon certain intrinsic value-commitments, centring on the goal of producing knowledge. However, this is far from what these authors have in mind. The values that they see as central to qualitative research are of an extrinsic kind, in our terms.

In the context of research ethics, moralism can take two forms:

1   The belief that other values than truth should be treated as *integral to the goal of research*, so that researchers must direct their work towards, for example, promoting justice, emancipating or giving voice to marginalised groups, or serving practical activities of various kinds, such as the promotion of health or education.

2   The requirement that *in the course of carrying out their work* researchers must seek to 'realise' one or more extrinsic values, that they should adhere to 'the highest ethical standards' as regards, for instance, avoidance of harm, protection of privacy, respect for autonomy, equity, care, or some other non-epistemic value.

It is not uncommon to find these two kinds of moralism combined, leading to the demand, for instance, that research both be aimed at producing findings that increase social justice *and* be carried out in ways that exemplify this value. However, we will discuss these two forms of moralism separately.

---

[1]There is a parallel between moralism and the religious enthusiasm that the philosopher John Locke and others objected to in the seventeenth century, as part of their defence of political liberalism (Locke 1975: Ch. 19).

Redefining the goal of qualitative research

We addressed the first kind of moralism in Chapter 2, so we will deal with it fairly briefly here. It gives priority to values that, while they may be of great importance from other points of view, are external to the task of research.

It is a feature of all specialised occupations that they involve the adoption of a relatively narrow perspective, focusing on a particular task and what is directly relevant to it, thereby downplaying other matters that are important from other angles. It is precisely from this narrowness that increased gains in tackling the specific task arise. While it is important to recognise that this specialisation also involves losses, it should not be assumed that the gains are available otherwise. Thus, research as a specialised activity maximises the chances of producing sound knowledge. While it should always be practised in ways that are constrained by extrinsic values, this is quite different from treating those values as constituting the goal of the occupation.[2]

In these terms, then, the common claim that a major function of qualitative research is to 'give voice' to marginalised groups involves a fundamental misconception. The task of any research project is to answer a set of factual questions. While this may well involve drawing data from people whose views are rarely heard or listened to, it will also usually be necessary to *interpret* these views; and, where they are being used as a source of information about the world, to *evaluate* their likely validity. In addition, it will almost always be essential to draw data from other people who are *not* regarded as marginalised or oppressed, and who may even be viewed as oppressors (Becker 1967); furthermore, it is important that the validity of their accounts is not simply dismissed (Hammersley 1998).

Also ruled out is any argument to the effect that research must be directed towards benefitting the people studied, an idea that underpins the notion of participatory inquiry. For example, in the field of childhood studies it is often insisted that research should not be carried out *on* children but always *for* and *with* them, treating them as having a right to participate in research decision-making (Alderson and Morrow 2011). Similar views are to be found, as regards other sorts of research participant, among feminists (Mies 1983; Fonow and Cook 1991) and disability researchers (Oliver 1992; Barnes 2009), and in relation to research about 'indigenous' communities (Smith 1999). In our view, these arguments involve a violation of the distinctive character of research: a failure to recognise that it is a specialised activity whose distinctive and exclusive goal is the production of

---

[2]There are some legitimate ways in which extrinsic values can play a positive role in occupational activities. For instance, a lawyer can specialise in providing legal services for the poor, doctors can focus on those in most serious need. And there is also some room for this kind of selectivity on the part of qualitative researchers. Practical research can be designed to provide information required by particular interest groups, for instance a charity or political organisation. And, while this sort of targeting is not possible in academic work, where the aim is to contribute to a body of disciplinary knowledge designed to serve as a general resource, academic researchers *can* legitimately select topics for investigation in terms of perceived importance.

knowledge.[3] In other words, they undermine the very concept of research as a professional occupation. In particular, advocacy of participatory inquiry amounts to an attempt to erase the researcher's distinctive role, and the responsibilities and licence intrinsically associated with it

Realising values within the research process

The second kind of moralism we identified is not concerned with the *goal* of research but rather with the *means* by which it is pursued. Here the requirement is that researchers seek fully to exemplify some set of extrinsic values (one or more) in how they carry out their work; or, alternatively, there is the more generalised demand that they abide by 'the highest ethical standards', a phrase that is common in statements underpinning ethical regulation.

Examples of this second kind of moralism would include the idea that obedience to the criminal law by researchers is *always* required, and that all infringements by others must be reported. Another example is the treatment of informed consent as a human right (Homan 2001; Alderson and Morrow 2011). In our view, these kinds of ethical absolutism amount to an unrealistic constraint on inquiry. The insistence that the law must always be obeyed would make some kinds of research very difficult if not impossible. This is most obviously true in the field of criminology, but the problem extends beyond that area, since deviance of one kind or another is a feature in many settings. Similarly, while in some circumstances seeking informed consent will be both desirable and feasible, there are others where it is not. It may be, for example, that disguised observation is judged necessary to carry out research effectively and that this can be justified, for example on the grounds that serious harm is very unlikely and that what is being observed is not an especially private form of activity. Or it could be that obtaining informed consent is simply not feasible; as in the case of studying an online site where there is a high turnover of participants.

While qualitative research is properly constrained by extrinsic values, what these values mean, and what weight should be given to them in any particular situation, must be shaped by what is required if the production of knowledge is to be pursued effectively. For these reasons, extrinsic values will sometimes need to be compromised. What can reasonably be expected of qualitative researchers is not adherence to the highest standards, only that their behaviour is *adequate* in terms of extrinsic values, *taking account of the constraints operating in the situations concerned*.

Some time ago, in the context of anthropology, Appell (1978: xi) claimed that 'it is one of the paradoxes of the social sciences that their moral stance has not been higher than [that of] the surrounding topography'. This seems to imply that

---

[3]Fish (2008) provides a typically bullish defence of the traditional role of the scholar, encapsulated in the title of his book: *Save the World on Your Own Time* (see also Fish 1995). Thus, he insists that academic researchers 'do not try to do anyone else's job' and 'do not let anyone else do their job'. This echoes a similar sentiment expressed many years ago by Polsky (1969: 140), who suggested that if someone wants to engage in social work, or for that matter police work, that is their privilege, but that they should not do so in the name of social science.

social scientists have a responsibility to be uniquely ethical; an idea that can be traced back to questionable nineteenth- and early twentieth-century ideas about the role of the intellectual (Hammersley 2011: Ch. 2), and perhaps beyond this to ancient views about the philosophical life. A similar notion infuses much discussion of qualitative research today (see, for instance, Mertens and Ginsberg 2009). But it is important to remember that social scientists are members of a profession operating *within* societies, and that all they can distinctively claim is a high commitment to a specific goal and the values associated with this, not some general ethical superiority. Contrary to what Appell claims, there is no 'paradox' here.

A label that could be applied to our position is 'Machiavellianism' (Hammersley and Traianou 2011), a term that carries an evaluative load that, like 'moralism', is ambiguous if not downright negative. However, contrary to what is sometimes assumed, Machiavelli did not propose that rulers, and other political agents, should pursue evil ends. Rather, he argued that they will often have to use means that are regarded as morally questionable, such as deception, and even sometimes those that are abhorrent, like war, *in order effectively to pursue ends that are good.*[4] According to Strauss (1987: 84), Machiavelli was the first of the early modern political philosophers, whose ethical thinking starts not from 'how people ought to live', in the manner of the ancients, but rather from 'how people actually live'. In Max Weber's terms, Machiavelli rejected an 'ethics of ultimate ends' in favour of an 'ethic of responsibility' (see Weber 1946; Bruun 2007: 250–9).

The fundamental problem with the second kind of moralism, then, is that it is premised upon an unrealistic view of human nature and society. Conflicting ideals and interests, and struggle over these, are endemic in social life; and, as a result, the use of coercion, manipulation and deception is widespread. Given this, such moralism is not a viable basis for carrying out any activity, including qualitative inquiry (Douglas 1976; Duster et al. 1979; Littrell 1993). If researchers are to get their work done *in the world as it is*, and produce reliable knowledge, they will often have to engage in actions that fall short of 'the highest standards'.

Another way of trying to capture the point we are making is the idea that researchers must claim a certain moral licence if they are to pursue their task effectively. This is also true of many other occupational roles, notably but not exclusively those labelled professions (see Chapter 2). For example, it is the task of the doctor to try to secure or preserve the health of patients, not to save their souls or to serve the interests of a kin-group or a nation-state. Moreover, in pursuing this narrowly specified task it may be necessary to use means that, from the point of view of some extrinsic values, are undesirable. For example, doctors and other medical personnel will often find it necessary to cause embarrassment or pain, and perhaps also to turn a blind eye to legal as well as moral offences (drug use, for instance). Similarly, the task of lawyers is not to aim directly at achieving justice; instead they are obliged to be partisan on behalf of their clients, and to operate in terms of the existing law, downplaying some aspects of a case in favour of others with a view to serving the

---

[4]The ends he had in mind were not universalistic ones but those specific to a particular political community. In this sense he was a communitarian rather than a liberal universalist. On Machiavelli see Skinner (2000). See also Parrish (2007).

client best. Furthermore, in pursuing their work they can demand answers from witnesses to highly intrusive questions *in public*, and challenge their honesty in order to undermine the persuasiveness of unfavourable evidence.[5]

So, in serving their goals, occupations may be allowed to breach some moral rules that would normally apply. If, by contrast, it is insisted that these rules are always fully enforced, that 'high standards' are adhered to in terms of *applying extrinsic values*, then the scope for exercising the discretion needed to pursue specialised occupations, and thereby to achieve the benefits they offer, will be reduced considerably.

So, what sorts of licence can and should qualitative researchers claim? For one thing, in collecting data they may find it necessary to tolerate, and risk being seen as condoning, behaviour that they believe (and that others would believe) is wrong – up to and including acts that are illegal (Hammersley 2005).[6] Also involved here is tolerating the expression of beliefs that one finds offensive or disturbing (Huff 1999). If the researcher is not able to be tolerant in this way, then access to much data may be blocked, or made relatively inaccessible, in many fields of inquiry. Similarly, it may sometimes be necessary to deceive people, at least passively (for instance through not correcting misapprehensions), if the data required are to be obtained. This is most obviously true in the case of groups and organisations that seek to exercise considerable power over their members and over their external environment: from political and business elites, through state and commercial agencies of various kinds, to exclusive religious or political groups. Such deception may also be necessary where individuals or groups have a hostile attitude towards science or social research (see, for instance, Homan 1980b). A further example is that it may be necessary to ask questions whose implications could be taken to be politically questionable, say sexist or racist.[7] Equally important, researchers may need to entertain lines of argument whose potential implications could be viewed as objectionable, distressing, or repulsive by lay audiences, and perhaps even by the researcher her or himself. Any insistence that researchers be 'authentic', in the sense of *fully* living up to their own personal values, or to those of others, would put very serious obstacles in the way of pursuing social research, often ones that simply make it impossible to do well.[8]

---

[5]Where a researcher takes on a participant role in the field they may also have to exercise moral licence distinctive to *that* role. O'Brian (2010: 119) reports that she had to perform 'the routine tasks of door security work, including vetting customers at point of entry and managing violent and disorderly customers inside venues. I was also required to undertake the gender specific tasks performed by female bouncers such as searching female bodies, monitoring female toilets and performing first-aid tasks.'

[6]We should perhaps reiterate that our argument is not that all immoral or illegal acts must be tolerated, only that researchers must have the leeway to tolerate some such acts where they judge this to be necessary and defensible in doing their work.

[7]Our position here contrasts with that of Troyna and Carrington (1989).

[8]Note that the costs of moralism are often obscured because the task of establishing the likely validity of research conclusions is underestimated. In some areas, this is possible because most if not all researchers in a field are committed to the same extrinsic values, and are conditioned to believe conclusions that they take to be in line with those values.

Of course, in the case of professions like medicine and law the moral licence claimed is justified by appeal to the benefits produced (both for particular individuals and for the wider society), whereas with qualitative inquiry it might be argued that there are no equivalent benefits, or at least that the benefit is much less. Thus, for academic research at least, there is no client group, and the knowledge it produces is sometimes seen as trivial. However, the balance between the level and kinds of 'moral deviance' involved in the work of different occupations, and the benefits they generate, is a matter of judgment; and one about which there will often be disagreement. For our part, we believe that the minimal moral licence required to pursue qualitative research *is* justified by the potential benefit it can bring in terms of knowledge and understanding of the social world.

THE PROBLEM OF BEING 'TOO ETHICAL'

What lies at the heart of moralism of all kinds is the assumption that it is *impossible* to be 'too ethical' (see Louden 1988; Leiter 2001). And, closely associated with this is an unrestrained form of ethical reflexivity which generates the conclusion that social research involves a high risk of severe ethical dangers for the people studied, so that rigorous precautions must be taken to protect them; or that in order for research to be worthwhile, and therefore ethically justifiable, it must aim at more than the 'mere' production of knowledge. Also involved, very often, is the assumption that research could be framed by value judgments that everyone would or should accept, and whose implications for particular situations are quite clear and determinate. However, none of these assumptions is sound. While it is essential that researchers continually adopt a reflexive stance towards their work – as regards ethical, methodological, and other issues – as we noted earlier there are significant limits to how much and what kinds of reflexivity they should exercise, in the sense of what they should treat as open to question.

As we noted in Chapter 5, the other profession to which qualitative research approximates most closely in character is investigative journalism. And the position that we have adopted in this book is similar to the attitude of Janet Malcolm towards the ethics of her profession. Journalists, she suggests, face a 'moral impasse'. In a famous opening sentence she declares, with exaggeration, that 'every journalist who is not too stupid or too full of himself to notice what is going on knows that what he does is morally indefensible' (1991: 3). However, she does not take this as grounds for abandoning the occupation, or for adopting a highly moralistic stance. Rather, her concern is to highlight the difficulties and unavoidable ethical dilemmas involved in investigative journalism. She elaborates on the problem as follows:

> Unlike other relationships that have a purpose beyond themselves and are clearly delineated as such (dentist–patient, lawyer–client, teacher–student), the writer–subject relationship seems to depend for its life on a kind of fuzziness and murkiness,

if not utter covertness, of purpose. If everybody put his cards on the table, the game would be over. The journalist must do his work in a kind of deliberately induced state of moral anarchy.

She describes this as a 'baffling and unfortunate occupational hazard' (Malcolm 1991: 142–3). And we believe that much the same can be said about qualitative research, though researchers are rarely faced with the same level of ethical difficulties as the journalist, largely because they are usually able to anonymise the people and places being referred to, whereas journalists cannot.

It is perhaps necessary to repeat again that our argument is not that the pursuit of research should be unconstrained by extrinsic values. Some restraint of this kind is essential: researchers should not feel free to pursue their research goals irrespective of all other considerations or costs. The issue is the *degree* to which, and *ways in which*, extrinsic values should shape the actions of the researcher; and, equally important, who is to make decisions about this. There is no general answer to the question of how much weight should be given to a particular extrinsic value; this must be decided on a case-by-case basis. However, what we *can* say is that it is individual researchers or research teams who must decide in particular cases what is and is not acceptable, in the light of both intrinsic and other extrinsic values. Such decisions should not be made by funding bodies, gatekeepers, ethics committees, governments, or anyone else. Others can, of course, express views about the decisions that research-ers have made, and take action on the basis of these; but researchers are not obliged to treat their complaints or their actions as legitimate, even if they must nevertheless face the consequences.

However, this commitment to the autonomy of the researcher is rather more dif-ficult to live up to now than it was in the past. One reason for this is the rise of ethical regulation, to which we now return.

THE PROBLEM OF ETHICAL REGULATION

For most of the twentieth century, social scientists operated in relatively independ-ent ways. Of course, their activities were subject to criminal and civil law within the countries where they lived and worked, and they were also constrained by the power of individuals and organisations who control access to funds and to data. However, they were not exposed to ethical regulation. Even when professional codes were developed by research associations, these were almost always retrospec-tive and advisory in character. By contrast, today, in many societies, there is ethical regulation that involves prospective control of what research can be funded or will be allowed, and the locus of control has moved away from research communities to universities or other institutions, these operating increasingly in a managerial rather than a collegial fashion. As a result, regulation is exercised, generally speak-ing, not by people who are engaged in the relevant kind of research, but often by those from other disciplines as well as by lay 'representatives'. Furthermore, over time, the grip of this regulation on research, in terms of what is to be assessed and through what procedures, has been widened and tightened.[9] In effect, ethics committees not only judge whether a proposed research project is ethical, but also whether it is worthwhile, and whether the methods adopted are likely to produce valid conclusions.

In our view, this kind of ethical regulation is itself unethical and extremely damaging (Hammersley 2006, 2010a and b). It assumes forms of moral expertise, and levels of methodological knowledge and practical experience, that no ethics committee could ever have. Furthermore, it seriously infringes the professional autonomy of researchers, to the detriment of the pursuit of research. In practical terms, it threatens to prevent particular sorts of investigation, and tends to distort others, thereby reducing the quality of the knowledge that social science can provide. And this threat is especially great in the case of qualitative inquiry, as a result of its 'emergent' form of research design and the fact that it takes place in 'natural' settings. Finally, ethical regulation has a tendency to reduce the concept of ethical behaviour to the following of procedures, or even to obtaining agreement from ethics committees; as well as encouraging surreptitious deviation on the part of researchers (Melrose 2011).

So, we believe that there are major problems with the level and type of 'ethical' regulation that now operates in many Western societies. By its very nature research is a situated practice. It cannot be governed effectively by code or committee, nor are attempts to do this desirable. It follows from our argument about the professional character of research, and the priority of commitment to its intrinsic values, that all social researchers have an ethical responsibility to resist ethical regulation insofar as it impinges upon effective pursuit of their work. At the same time, of course, the situational character of practical decision-making implies that to what extent they should do this on particular occasions, and *how* they should do it, will vary according to circumstances. Prudential considerations must also be involved. It is important, though, not to allow these to redefine our ethical commitments.

CONCLUSION

In this book, we have challenged those conceptions of research ethics that treat it as the following of procedures designed to protect and respect the rights and interests of those from whom data are collected. We have also criticised the view, common among qualitative researchers today, that research should be aimed at realising ethical or political values. Instead, we see research as devoted to a specialised occupational task, namely the production of knowledge; even though values extrinsic to that goal – minimising harm, respecting autonomy, protecting privacy and others – can and should act as constraints on how this goal is pursued.

---

[9]For the situation in the UK, see Stanley and Wise (2010), and other contributions within the same issue.

We insisted that commitment to extrinsic values must not be given excessive weight, that a certain licence is necessary if research is to be pursued effectively. Equally important, we stressed the situational character of all ethical judgments, since the idea that these are a matter of 'applying' a set of principles, or realising some ideal, fails to recognise the plurality of principles involved, the fact that the meaning of these principles is always determined in context, and that ethical and political values are only one sort of consideration that should be taken into account. Furthermore, each researcher or research team is responsible for making these judgments; no one can take over that responsibility, and no one should be allowed to infringe it.

It is also essential to remember that in the social situations in which researchers carry out qualitative studies they will usually have very limited power and resources, yet they must nevertheless try to produce conclusions that reach a relatively high threshold in terms of likely validity, and that make a worthwhile contribution to collective knowledge. While some commentators have suggested that researchers have great power in relation to those they study, and that they should empower participants in order to balance this, we have argued that researchers need to be able to exercise power if they are to pursue research effectively; and also, for that matter, to live up to their responsibilities in terms of extrinsic values. At the same time, we have insisted that the ethical issues qualitative research raises in terms of extrinsic values are, generally speaking, much less serious than in the case of both medical research and investigative journalism, and are close to what is common most of the time in everyday life.

It should be said that we see the requirements laid upon researchers by the values that are *intrinsic* to research as much more demanding than is generally recognised. Indeed, our primary objection to moralism is that it colludes with many other factors that are increasingly undermining effective practical commitment to the task of research, and the virtues that are required for this (Hammersley 2011; Haack 2012). Adherence to, and the protection of, those values is a primary responsibility of all researchers.

We began this book by suggesting that research ethics is a controversial topic. We are confident that we have proved our point. Indeed, there will be some who regard the position we have taken here as unethical, but this charge relies upon the sorts of moralism that we have rejected; indeed, upon views that *we* regard as unethical. This illustrates the fundamental disagreements that are involved.

REFERENCES

AAA (1971) 'Principles of professional responsibility', American Anthropological Association. Available at: www.aaanet.org/stmts/ethstmnt.htm (accessed 1.7.11).

Adler, M. and Posner, E. (eds) (2001) *Cost–Benefit Analysis*, Chicago, University of Chicago Press.

Adler, P. A. and Adler, P. (2002) 'Do university lawyers and the police define research values?', in van den Hoonard, W. (ed.), *Walking the Tightrope: Ethical issue for qualitative researchers* (pp. 34–42), Toronto, University of Toronto Press.

Akeroyd, A. (1988) 'Ethnography, personal data, and computers: the implications of data protection legislation for qualitative social research', in Burgess, R. (ed.), *Studies in Qualitative Methodology, Volume 1 Conducting qualitative research*, Greenwich, CT, JAI Press.

Alderson, P. (2000) 'Children as researchers: the effects of participation rights on research methodology', in Christensen, P. and James, A. (eds), *Research with Children: perspectives and practices*, London, Falmer.

Alderson, P. and Morrow, V. (2011) *The Ethics of Research with Children and Young People*, London, Sage.

Allan, A. (2007) 'Using photographic diaries to research the gender and academic identities of young girls', in Troman, G., Jeffrey, B. and Walford, G. (eds), *Methodological Issues and Practices in Ethnography*, Amsterdam, Elsevier.

Allen, C. (1996) 'What's wrong with the "Golden Rule"? Conundrums of conducting ethical research in cyberspace', *The Information Society*, 12, 175–87.

Ameriks, K. (2000) *Kant and the Fate of Autonomy*, Cambridge, Cambridge University Press.

Angrosino, M. (2004) 'Secrecy and disclosure in a monastery', in Hume and Mulcock (eds).

Anscombe, G. E. M. (1958) 'Modern moral philosophy', *Philosophy*, 33, 124, 1–19.

AoIRO (2011) *Ethics Guide*, available at: www.aoir.org/reports/ethics.pdf

Appell, G. (1978) *Ethical Dilemmas in Anthropological Inquiry*, Waltham, MA: Crossroads Press.

Aristotle (1976) *Nichomachean Ethics*, London, Penguin.

Armbruster, H. and Laerke, A. (eds) (2008) *Taking Sides: Ethics, politics, and fieldwork in anthropology*, New York, Berghahn.

Armstrong, G. (1998) *Football Hooligans: Knowing the score*, Oxford, Berg.

Arneson, R. (1999) 'Human flourishing versus desire satisfaction', *Social Philosophy and Policy*, 16, 113–43.

Asad, T. (ed.) (1973) *Anthropology and the Colonial Encounter*, New York, Humanities Press.

Atay, T. (2008) 'Arriving in nowhere land: studying an Islamic Sufi order in London', in Armbruster and Laerke (eds).

Atkinson, P. (1997) *The Clinical Experience: The construction and reconstruction of medical reality*, second edition, Aldershot: Ashgate.

Atkinson, P. and Delamont, S. (eds) (2004) *Narrative Methods*, four volumes, London, Sage.

Atkinson, P. and Silverman, D. (1997) 'Kundera's immortality: The interview society and the invention of the self', *Qualitative Inquiry*, 3, 304–25.

Bailey, R. (2009) 'Well-being, happiness and education', *British Journal of Sociology of Education*, 30, 6, 795–802.

Bakardjieva, M. and Feenberg, A. (2001) 'Involving the virtual subject', *Ethics and Information Technology*, 2, 233–240.

Ball, S. (1994) 'Political interviews and the politics of interviewing', in Walford, G. (ed.), *Researching the Powerful in Education*, London, UCL Press.

Banton, M. (1965) *Roles: An introduction to the study of social relations*, New York, Basic Books.

Barbour, R. (1979) 'The ethics of covert research', *Network*, newsletter of the British Sociological Association, September, p. 9.

Barnes, C. (2009) 'An ethical agenda in disability research: rhetoric or reality?', in Mertens and Ginsberg (eds).

Barnes, J. (1977) *The Ethics of Inquiry in Social Science*, Delhi, Oxford University Press.

Barnes, J. (1979) *Who Should Know What? Social Science, Privacy and Ethics*, Harmondsworth, Penguin.

Barzun, J. and Graff, H. (1977) *The Modern Researcher*, third edition, New York, Harcourt, Brace, Jovanovich.

Bassett, E. and O'Riordan, K. (2002) 'Ethics of internet research: contesting the human subjects model', *Journal of Ethics and Information Technology*, 4, 233–47.

Bateson, G. and Mead, M. (1942) *Balinese Character: A photographic analysis*, New York, New York Academy of Sciences.

Bauman, Z. (2000) *Liquid Modernity*, Cambridge, Polity.

Beauchamp, T. (2010) 'Autonomy and consent', in Miller, F. and Wertheimer, A. (eds), *The Ethics of Consent: Theory and Practice*, New York: Oxford University Press.

Beauchamp, T., Faden, R., Wallace, R. and Walters, L. (eds) (1982) *Ethical Issues in Social Science Research*, Baltimore, MD, Johns Hopkins University Press.

Beck, U. (1992) *Risk Society: Towards a new modernity*, London, Sage.

Beck, U. (1999) *World Risk Society*, Cambridge, Polity.

Becker, H. S. (1964a) 'Against the Code of Ethics', *American Sociological Review*, 29, 3, 409–10.

Becker, H. S. (1964b) 'Problems in the publication of field studies', in Vidich et al. (eds).

Becker, H. S. (1967) 'Whose side are we on?', *Social Problems*, 14, 239–47.

Beckerleg, S. and Hundt, G. (2004) 'Reflections on fieldwork among Kenyan heroin users', in Hume and Mulcock (eds).

Behar, R. (1996) *The Vulnerable Observer*, Boston, MA, Beacon Press.

Bell, E. and Bronfenbrenner, U. (1959) '"Freedom and responsibility in research": a comment', *Human Organization*, 18, 2, 49–50.

Bell, S. (2002) 'Sexualizing research: response to Erich Goode', *Qualitative Sociology*, 25, 4, 535–9.

Belsey, A. and Chadwick, R. (eds) (1992) *Ethical Issues in Journalism and the Media*, London, Routledge.

Benjamin, A. (1999) 'Contract and covenant in Curaçao: reciprocal relationships in scholarly research', in King et al. (eds).

Bentham, J. (1789 [1907]) *An Introduction to the Principles of Morals and Legislation*, Oxford University Press.

Bentham, J. (1830) *The Rationale of Reward*, London, Robert Heward.

Berlin, I. (1969) 'Two concepts of liberty', in *Four Essays on Liberty*, Oxford, Oxford University Press.

Berry, D. (ed.) (2000) *Ethics and Media Culture*, Oxford, Focal Press.

Berry, D. (2004) 'Internet research: privacy, ethics and alienation: an open source approach', *Internet Research: Electronic Networking Applications and Policy*, 14, 4, 323–32.

Beynon, J. (1985) *Initial Encounters in a Secondary School*, London, Falmer Press.

Biddle, B. J. (1979) *Role Theory – Expectations, Identities, and Behaviors*. New York: Academic Press.

Biddle, B. J. and Thomas, E. J. (eds) (1966) *Role Theory: Concepts and research*. New York: John Wiley & Sons.

Birckhead, J. (2004) '"And I can't feel at home in this world anymore": fieldwork in two settings', in Hume and Mulcock (eds).

Bishop, L. (2005) 'Protecting respondents and enabling data sharing: reply to Parry and Mauthner', *Sociology*, 39, 2, 333–36.

Bishop, R. (2005) 'Freeing ourselves from neocolonial domination in research: a Kaupapa Maori approach to creating knowledge', in Denzin and Lincoln (eds).

Bloor, M. (1978) 'On the analysis of observational data: a discussion of the worth and uses of inductive techniques and respondent validation', *Sociology*, 12, 3, 545–52.

Bloor, M., Fincham, B. and Sampson, H. (2010) 'Unprepared for the worst: risks of harm for qualitative researchers', *Methodological Innovations Online*, 5, 1, 45–55.

Bloustein, E. (1964) 'Privacy as an aspect of human dignity', *New York University Law Review*, 39, 962–1007.

Boelen, W. (1992) '"Street corner society": Cornerville Revisited', *Journal of Contemporary Ethnography*, 21, 11–51.

Bok, S. (1978) *Lying: Moral choice in public and private life*, Hassocks, Sussex, Harvester Press.

Bok, S. (1984) *Secrets: Concealment and revelation*, Oxford, Oxford University Press.

Borofsky, R. (2005) *Yanomami: The fierce controversy and what we can learn from it*, Berkeley, CA, University of California Press.

Bourgois, P. (2007) 'Confronting the ethics of ethnography: lessons from fieldwork in Central America', in Robben, A. and Sluka, J. (eds), *Ethnographic Fieldwork: An anthropological reader*, Oxford, Blackwell.

Bowden, P. (1997) *Caring: Gender-sensitive ethics*, London, Routledge.

Bradshaw, M. (2002) 'Contracts with research participants', *Building Research Capacity*, Issue 4, 4–6, available at: www.tlrp.org/rcbn/capacity/Journal/issue4.pdf

Brajuha, M. and Hallowell, L. (1986) 'Legal intrusion and the politics of fieldwork: "The impact of the Brajuha case"', *Urban Life*, 14, 4, 454–78.

Brettell, C. (ed.) (1993) *When They Read What We Write: The politics of ethnography*, Westport, CT, Bergin and Garvey.

Brewer, J. (2004) *Sentimental Murder*, London, HarperCollins.

Bridges, D. (2003) *Fiction Written Under Oath? Essays in Philosophy and Educational Research*, Dordrecht, Kluwer.

Bronfenbrenner, U. (1952) 'Principles of professional ethics: Cornell studies in social growth', *The American Psychologist*, 7, 452–5.

Bruun, H. H. (2007) *Science, Values and Politics in Max Weber's Methodology*, Aldershot, Ashgate.

Brydon-Miller, M. (2009) 'Covenantal ethics and action research: exploring a common foundation for social research', in Mertens and Ginsberg (eds).

Buber, M. (1958) *I and Thou*, second edition, New York, Scribner

Buchanan, E. (ed.) (2004) *Readings in Virtual Research Ethics: Issues and controversies*, Hershey, PA: Idea Group.

Bulmer, M. (ed.) (1982) *Social Research Ethics: an examination of the merits of covert participant observation*, London, Macmillan.

Burawoy, M. (2005) 'For public sociology', *American Sociological Review*, 70, 1, 4–28.

Burgess, R. (1985) 'The whole truth? Some ethical problems of research in a comprehensive school', in Burgess, R. (ed.), *Field Methods in the Study of Education*, London, Falmer Press.

Cahill, S. E. (1985) 'Meanwhile backstage: public bathrooms and the interaction order', *Urban Life,* 14, 33–58.

Calvey, D. (2000) 'Getting on the door and staying there: a covert participant observational study of bouncers', in Lee-Treweek and Linkogle (eds).

Calvey, D. (2008) 'The art and politics of covert research: doing "situated ethics" in the field', *Sociology*, 42, 5, 905–918.

Cannella, G. and Lincoln, Y. (2007) 'Predatory vs dialogic ethics: constructing an illusion or ethical practice as the core of research methods', *Qualitative Inquiry*, 13, 3, 315–35.

Caplan, P. (ed.) (2003) *The Ethics of Anthropology: Debates and Dilemmas*, London, Routledge.

Capurro, R. and Pingel, C. (2002) 'Ethical issues of online communication research', available at: www.nyu.edu/projects/nissenbaum/ethics_capurro.html (accessed 22.7.11).

Caputo, J. (1993) *Against Ethics: Contribution to a poetics of obligation with constant reference to deconstruction*, Bloomington, IN, Indiana University Press.

Caputo, J. (2000) 'The end of ethics', in LaFollette, H. (ed.), *The Blackwell Guide to Ethical Theory*, Oxford, Blackwell.

Carrier, J. (2006) 'Fieldwork on urban male homosexuality in Mexico', in Hobbs and Wright (eds).

Carusi, A. and Jirotka, M. (2009) 'From data archive to ethical labyrinth', *Qualitative Research*, 9, 3, 285–98.

Cave, E. and Holm, S. (2003) 'Milgram and Tuskegee – paradigm research projects in bioethics', *Health Care Analysis*, 11, 1, 27–40.

Caygill, H. (1995) *A Kant Dictionary*, Oxford, Blackwell.

Chambliss, W. (1975) 'On the paucity of original research on organized crime', *American Sociologist*, 10, 36–9.

Chaplin, E. (1994) *Sociology and Visual Representation*, London, Routledge.

Charlton, J. (2000) *Nothing About Us Without Us: Disability, oppression and empowerment*, Berkeley, CA, University of California Press.

Chilisa, B. (2009) 'Indigenous African-centered ethics', in Mertens and Ginsberg (eds).

Christians, C. (2002) 'Introduction to the Issue', *Qualitative Inquiry*, 8, 4, 407–10.

Christians, C. (2005) 'Ethics and politics in qualitative research', in Denzin and Lincoln (eds).

Christie, R. (1976) 'Comment on conflict methodology', *Sociological Quarterly*, 1, 7, 513–19.

Cicero (1991) *On Duties*, Cambridge, Cambridge University Press.

Clark, A., Prosser, J. and Wiles, R. (2010) 'Ethical issues in image-based research', *Arts and Health*, 2, 1, 81–93.

Clarke, S. (1987) 'Anti-theory in ethics', *American Philosophical Quarterly*, 24, 3, 237–44.

Clegg, J. and Slife, B. (2009) 'Research ethics in the postmodern context', in Mertens and Ginsberg (eds).

Clifford, J. and Marcus, G. (eds) (1986) *Writing Culture: The poetics and politics of ethnography*, Berkeley, CA, University of California Press.

Coady, C. A. J. (2005) 'Preface', *Journal of Applied Philosophy*, 22, 2, 101–4.

Coggeshall, J. (2004) 'Closed doors: ethical issues in prison ethnography', in Hume and Mulcock (eds).

Colic-Peisker, V. (2004) 'Doing ethnography in "one's own ethnic community"', in Hume and Mulcock (eds).

Colvard, R. (1967) 'Interaction and identification in reporting field research', in Sjoberg (ed.).

Coomber, R. (2002) 'Signing your life away? Why Research Ethics Committees (REC) shouldn't always require written confirmation that participants in research have been informed of the aims of a study and their rights – the case of criminal populations', *Sociological Research Online* 7, 1. Available at: www.socresonline.org.uk/7/1/coomber.html

Corrigan, O. (2003) 'Empty ethics', *Sociology of Health and Illness*, 25, 3, 768–92.

Corsino, L. (1987) 'Fieldworker blues: emotional stress and research underinvolvement in fieldwork settings', *Social Science Journal*, 24, 3, 275–85.

Corti, L., Day, A. and Backhouse, G. (2000) 'Confidentiality and Informed Consent: Issues for Consideration in the Preservation of and Provision of Access to Qualitative Data Archives', *Forum Qualitative Sozialforschung/Forum: Qualitative Social Research* 1, 3. Available at: www.qualitative-research.net/fqs-texte/3-00/3-00cortietal-e.htm/

Coser, L. (1965) *Men of Ideas*, New York, Free Press.

Coser, L. (1974) *Greedy Institutions: Patterns of undivided commitment*, New York, Free Press.

Coxon, A. (1996) *Between the Sheets: Sexual diaries and gay men's sex in the era of AIDS*, London, Cassell.

Cranston, M. (1953) *Freedom: A new analysis*, London, Longmans Green.

Crisp, R. and Slote, M. (eds) (1997) *Virtue Ethics*, Oxford, Oxford University Press.

Crossen, C. (1994) *Tainted Truth: The manipulation of fact in America*, New York, Simon & Schuster.

Crowder, G. (2002) *Liberalism and Value Pluralism*, London, Continuum.

Cunningham, R. (1970) *Situationism and the New Morality*, New York, Appleton-Century-Crofts.

Dalton, M. (1964) 'Preconceptions and methods in men who manage', in Hammond, P. (ed.), *Sociologists at Work*, New York, Basic Books.

Dancy, J. (1992) 'Caring about justice', *Philosophy*, 67, 447–66.

Dancy, J. (2004) *Ethics Without Principles*, Oxford, Oxford University Press.

David, M., Edwards, R. and Aldred, P. (2001) 'Children and school-based research: "informed consent" or "educated consent"', *British Educational Research Journal*, 27, 3, 347–65.

Davidson, A. (1994) 'Ethics as ascetics: Foucault, the history of ethics, and ancient thought', in Gutting, G. (ed.), *The Cambridge Companion to Foucault*, Cambridge, Cambridge University Press.

Davies, M. and Kelly, E. (1976) 'The social worker, the client, and the social anthropologist', *British Journal of Social Work*, 6, 2, 158–65.

Davis, F. (1961) 'Comment on "Initial interaction of newcomers in Alcoholics Anonymous"', *Social Problems*, 8, 4, 364–5. Reprinted in Filstead (ed.) (1970).

Deem, R., Hillyard, S. and Reed, M. (2007) *Knowledge, Higher Education, and the New Managerialism*, Oxford, Oxford University Press.

d'Entrèves, A. (1994) *Natural Law: An Introduction to Legal Philosophy*, New Brunswick, NJ, Transaction. (First published in 1951.)

Denzin, N. (1968) 'On the ethics of disguised observation', *Social Problems*, 15, 4, 502–4. Reprinted in Bulmer (ed.) (1982).

Denzin, N. (1992) 'Whose Cornerville is it anyway?', *Journal of Contemporary Ethnography*, 21, 120–32.

Denzin, N. and Lincoln, Y. (eds) (2005) *Handbook of Qualitative Research*, third edition, Thousand Oaks, CA, Sage.

Denzin, N. and Lincoln, Y. (eds) (2011) *Handbook of Qualitative Research*, fourth edition, Thousand Oaks, CA, Sage.

Denzin, N., Lincoln, Y. and Smith, L. (eds) (2008) *Handbook of Critical and Indigenous Methodologies*, Los Angeles, Sage.

De Waal, C. (2005) *On Pragmatism*, Belmont, CA, Wadsworth.

Diener, E. and Crandall, R. (1978) *Ethics in Social and Behavioral Research*, Chicago, University of Chicago Press.

Dingwall, R. (1977) '"Atrocity stories" and professional relationships', *Work and Occupations*, 4, 4, 371–96.

Dingwall, R. (1980) 'Ethics and ethnography', *Sociological Review*, 28, 871–91.

Ditton, J. (1977) *Part-time Crime*, London, Macmillan.

Dixon-Woods, M. and Ashcroft, R. (2008) 'Regulation and the social licence medical research', *Medical Health Care and Philosophy*, 11, 381–91.

Dixon-Woods, M., Ashcroft, R., Jackson, C., Tobin, M., Kivits, J., Burton, P. and Samani, N. (2007) 'Beyond "misunderstanding": written information and decisions about taking part in a genetic epidemiology study', *Social Science and Medicine*, 65, 2212–22.

Dockrell, W. B. (1990) 'Ethical considerations in research', in Keeves, J. P. (ed.), *Educational Research, Methodology and Measurement: An international handbook*, Oxford, Pergamon.

Dodd, S.-J. (2009) 'LGBTQ: protecting vulnerable subjects in *all* studies', in Mertens and Ginsberg (eds).

Dodge, M. and Geis, G. (2006) 'Fieldwork with the elite: interviewing white-collar criminals', in Hobbs and Wright (eds).

Douglas, J. D. (1976) *Investigative Social Research*, Beverly Hills, CA, Sage.

Douglas, J. D. (1979) 'Living morality versus bureaucratic fiat', in Klockars, C. and O'Connor, F. (eds), *Deviance and Decency: The ethics of research with human subjects*, Beverly Hills, CA, Sage.

Duneier, M. (1999) *Sidewalk*, New York, Farrar, Straus & Giroux.

Duster, T., Matza, D. and Wellman, D. (1979) 'Fieldwork and the protection of human subjects', *American Sociologist*, 14, 136–42.

Dworkin, G. (1988) *The Theory and Practice of Autonomy*, Cambridge, Cambridge University Press.

Economic and Social Research Council (2005) *Research Ethics Framework*, Swindon, ESRC. Available at: www.esrcsocietytoday.ac.uk/ESRCInfoCentre/Images/ESRC_Re_Ethics_Frame_tcm6-11291.pdf (accessed 19.8.10).

Economic and Social Research Council (2010) *Framework for Research Ethics*, Swindon, ESRC. Available at: www.esrcsocietytoday.ac.uk/esrcinfocentre/opportunities/research_ethics_framework/ (accessed 19.8.10).

Elgesem, D. (2001) 'What is so special about the ethical issues in online research?', available at: www.nyu.edu/projects/nissenbaum/ethics_elg_full.html (accessed 22.7.11).

Ellis, C. (2004) *The Ethnographic I*, Walnut Creek, CA, Altamira Press.

Ellis, C. (2007) 'Telling secrets, revealing lives: relational ethics in research with intimate Others', *Qualitative Inquiry*, 13, 1, 3–29.

Emmet, D. (1966) *Rules, Roles and Relations*, London, Macmillan.

Erdos, D. (2011a) 'Stuck in the thicket? Social research under the first data protection principle', *International Journal of Law and Information Technology*, 19, 2, 133–52.

Erdos, D. (2011b) 'Systematically handicapped? Social research in the data protection framework', *International Journal of Law and Information Technology*, 20, 2, 83–101.

Erikson, K. (1967) 'A comment on disguised observation in sociology', *Social Problems*, 14, 4, 366–73.

Erikson, K. (1996) 'A response to Leo', *American Sociologist*, 27, 1, 129–30.

Faden, R. and Beauchamp, T. (1986) *A History and Theory of Informed Consent*, New York, Oxford University Press.

Farrell, A. (ed.) (2005) *Ethical Research with Children*, Maidenhead, Open University Press.

Faubion, J. (2003) 'Toward an anthropology of ethics: Foucault and the pedagogies of autopoiesis', in Wyschogrod, E. and McKenny, G. (eds), *The Ethical*, Oxford, Blackwell.

Feinberg, J. (1984) *Harm to Others*, New York, Oxford University Press.

Ferrara, A. (1998) *Reflective Authenticity*, London, Routledge.

Festinger, L., Riecken, H. and Schachter, S. (1956) *When Prophecy Fails*, Minneapolis, MN: University of Minnesota Press.

Filstead, W. (ed.) (1970) *Qualitative Methodology: Firsthand involvement in the social world*, Chicago, Markham.

Finch, J. (1984) '"It's great to have someone to talk to": the ethics and politics of interviewing women', in Roberts, H. and Bell, C. (eds), *Social Researching: Politics, Problems, Practice*, London, Routledge & Kegan Paul.

Fish, S. (1995) *Professional Correctness: Literary studies and political change*, Oxford, Oxford University Press.

Fish, S. (1999) *The Trouble with Principle*, Cambridge, MA, Harvard University Press.

Fish, S. (2008) *Save the World on Your Own Time*, Oxford, Oxford University Press.

Fish, S. (2011) 'Sex, the Koch brothers and academic freedom', *New York Times*, 16 May, available at: http://opinionator.blogs.nytimes.com/2011/05/16/sex-the-koch-brothers-and-academic-freedom/#more-92873 (accessed 31.5.11).

Fisher, A. and Kirchin, S. (eds) (2006) *Arguing about Metaethics*, London, Routledge.

Fletcher, J. (1966) *Situation Ethics*, Philadelphia, PA, Westminster Press.

Flewitt, R. (2005) 'Conducting research with young children: some ethical considerations', *Early Child Development and Care,* 175, 6: 553–65.

Fluehr-Lobban, C. (2003a) 'Darkness in El Dorado: research ethics, then and now', in Fluehr-Lobban (ed.).

Fluehr-Lobban, C. (ed.) (2003b) *Ethics and the Profession of Anthropology*, second edition, Walnut Creek, CA, Altamira.

Fluehr-Lobban, C. (2008) 'Anthropology and ethics in America's declining imperial age', *Anthropology Today*, 24, 18–22.

Fonow, M. and Cook, J. (eds) (1991) *Beyond Methodology: Feminist scholarship as lived research*, Bloomington, IN, Indiana University Press.

Foot, P. (1978) *Virtues and Vices*, Berkeley, CA, University of California Press.

Forsey, M. (2004) 'He's not a spy; he's one of us', in Hume and Mulcock (eds).

Forsythe, D. (1999) 'Ethics and politics of studying up in technoscience', *Anthropology of Work Review*, 20, 1, 6–11.

Foster, C. (2001) *The Ethics of Medical Research on Humans*, Cambridge, Cambridge University Press.

Foster, J. (1990) *Villains: Crime and community in the inner city*, London, Routledge.

Foster, P. (1996) *Observing Schools: A methodological guide*, London, Sage.

Foster, P., Gomm, R. and Hammersley, M. (1996) *Constructing Educational Inequality*, London, Falmer.

Foucault, M. (1984a) *The History of Sexuality Volume 2: The use of pleasure*, Paris, Gallimard; English translation London, Viking, 1986.

Foucault, M. (1984b) *The History of Sexuality Volume 3: The care of the self*, Paris, Gallimard, English translation London, Viking, 1986.

Foucault, M. (1990) 'An aesthetics of existence', in Kritzman, L. (ed.) *Michel Foucault: Politics, Philosophy, Culture; Interviews and other writings 1977–84*, London, Routledge. (First published in French 1984.)

Fox, R. (1999) 'Contract and covenant in ethnographic research', in King et al. (eds).

Freidson, E. (1964) 'Against the code of ethics', *American Sociological Review*, 29, 3, 410.

Freidson, E. (1983) 'The theory of the professions: the state of the art', in R. Dingwall and P. Lewis (eds), *The Sociology of the Professions*, London, Macmillan.

Furedi, F. (2002) *Culture of Fear*, second edition, London, Continuum.

Gage, N. (1991) 'The obviousness of social and educational research results', *Educational Researcher*, 20, 1, 10–16.

Galliher, J. (1973) 'The protection of human subjects: a re-examination of the professional code of ethics', *American Sociologist*, 8, 93–100.

Galliher, J., Brekhus, W. and Keys, D. (2004) *Laud Humphreys: Prophet of homosexuality and sociology*, Madison, WI, University of Wisconsin Press.

Gay, P. (1995) *The Naked Heart*, London, HarperCollins.

Geertz, C. (2001) 'Life among the anthros', *New York Review of Books*, 8 February.

Geison, G. L. (1995) *The Private Science of Louis Pasteur*, Princeton, NJ, Princeton University Press.

Geros, P. (2008) 'Doing fieldwork within fear and silences', in Armbruster and Laerke (eds).

Gibson, B., Young, N., Upshur, R. and McKeever, P. (2007) 'Men on the margin: a Bourdieusian examination of living into adulthood with muscular dystrophy', *Social Science and Medicine*, 65, 3, 505–17.

Giddens, A. (1991) *Modernity and Self Identity*, Cambridge, Polity.

Gilligan, C. (1982) *In a Different Voice: Psychological theory and women's development*, Cambridge, MA, Harvard University Press.

Gjessing, G. (1968) 'The social responsibility of the social scientist', *Current Anthropology*, 9, 5, 397–402.

Goffman, E. (1959) *Presentation of Self in Everyday Life*, Garden City, NY, Doubleday/Anchor.

Goode, E. (1999) 'Sex with informants as deviant behavior', *Deviant Behavior*, 20, 301–24.

Goode, E. (2002) 'Sexual involvement and social research in a fat civil rights organization', *Qualitative Sociology*, 25, 4, 501–34.

Goodrum, S. and Keys, J. (2007) 'Reflections on two studies of emotionally sensitive topics: bereavement from murder and abortion', *International Journal of Social Research Methodology*, 10, 4, 249–58.

Gray, J. (1995) *Berlin*, London, Fontana.

Greenberg, O. (1993) 'When they read what the papers say we wrote', in Brettell (ed.).

Grenz, S. (2010) 'The desire to talk and sex/gender-related silences in interviews with male heterosexual clients of prostitutes', in Ryan-Flood and Gill (eds).

Grimshaw, A. (1982) 'Whose privacy? What harm?', *Sociological Methods and Research*, 11, 2, 233–47.

Grinyer, A. (2002) 'The anonymity of research participants: assumptions, ethics and practicalities', *Social Research Update*, 36, available at http://sru.soc.surrey.ac.uk/ SRU36.html (retrieved 1.7.11).

Gubrium, J. and Holstein, J. (eds) (2002) *Handbook of Interview Research*, Thousand Oaks, CA, Sage.

Guignon, C. (2004) *On Being Authentic*, London, Routledge.

Gunzenhauser, M. (2006) 'Theorizing a relational turn for qualitative research', *Qualitative Inquiry*, 12, 3, 621–47.

Haack, S. (2009) *Evidence and Inquiry: Towards a reconstruction of epistemology*, second edition, Amherst, NY, Prometheus. (First edition published in 1993 by Blackwell.)

Haack, S. (2012) 'Out of step: academic ethics in a preposterous environment', in *Putting Philosophy to Work*, second edition, Amherst, NY, Prometheus.

Haakonssen, K. and Winch, D. (2006) 'The legacy of Adam Smith', in Haakonssen, K. (ed.), *The Cambridge Companion to Adam Smith*, Cambridge, Cambridge University Press.

Haggerty, K. (2004) 'Ethics creep: governing social science research in the name of ethics', *Qualitative Sociology*, 27, 4, 391–414.

Hall, B., Gillett, A. and Tandon, R. (eds) (1982) *Creating Knowledge: A monopoly?*, New Delhi, Society for Participatory Research in Asia.

Hammersley, M. (1984) 'The researcher exposed: a natural history', in Burgess, R. G. (ed.), *The Research Process in Educational Settings*, Falmer Press (pp. 39–67).

Hammersley, M. (1992) *What's Wrong with Ethnography*, London, Routledge.

Hammersley, M. (1995) *The Politics of Social Research*, London, Sage.

Hammersley, M. (1998) 'Partisanship and credibility: the case of anti-racist educational research', in Connolly, P. and Troyna, B. (eds), *Researching 'Race' in Educational Settings*, Buckingham, Open University Press.

Hammersley, M. (1999) 'Reflections on the current state of qualitative research', *Research Intelligence*, newsletter of the British Educational Research Association, 70, December.

Hammersley, M. (2000) *Taking Sides in Social Research: Essays on partisanship and bias*, London, Routledge.

Hammersley, M. (2002) *Educational Research, Policymaking and Practice*, London, Paul Chapman/Sage.

Hammersley, M. (2003) 'Can and should educational research be educative?', *Oxford Review of Education*, 29, 1, 3–25.

Hammersley, M. (2004a) 'Action research: a contradiction in terms?', *Oxford Review of Education*, 30, 2, 165–81.

Hammersley, M. (2004b) 'Get real! A defence of realism', in Piper, H. and Stronach, I. (eds), *Educational Research: Difference and diversity*, Aldershot, Ashgate.

Hammersley, M. (2005) 'Ethnography, toleration and authenticity: ethical reflections on fieldwork, analysis and writing', in Troman, G. Jeffrey, B. and Walford, G. (eds), *Methodological Issues and Practices in Ethnography*, Amsterdam, Elsevier.

Hammersley, M. (2006) 'Are ethics committees ethical?', *Qualitative Researcher*, 2, Spring, available at: www.cardiff.ac.uk/socsi/qualiti/QR_Issue2_06.pdf

Hammersley, M. (2010a) 'Against the ethicists: on the evils of ethical regulation', *International Journal of Social Research Methodology*, 12, 3, 211–25.

Hammersley, M. (2010b) Creeping ethical regulation and the strangling of research', *Sociological Research Online* 15, 4, 6, available at: www.socresonline.org.uk/15/4/16.html

Hammersley, M. (2011) *Methodology, Who Needs It?*, London, Sage.

Hammersley, M. and Atkinson, P. (2007) *Ethnography: Principles in practice*, London, Routledge.

Hammersley, M. and Gomm, R. (2000) 'Bias in social research', in Hammersley 2000.

Hammersley, M. and Traianou, A. (2011) 'Moralism and research ethics: a Machiavellian perspective', *International Journal of Social Research Methodology*, 14, 5, 379–90 (first published on: 5 April 2011 (iFirst)).

Head, E. (2009) 'The ethics and implications of paying participants in qualitative research', *International Journal of Social Research Methodology*, 12, 4, 335–44.

Heath, S. and Cleaver, E. (2004) 'Mapping the spatial in shared household life: a missed opportunity?', in Knowles, C. and Sweetman, P. (eds), *Picturing the Social Landscape: Visual Methods and the Sociological Imagination*, London, Routledge.

Heath, S., Charles, V., Crow, G. and Wiles, R. (2007) 'Informed consent, gatekeepers and go-betweens: negotiating consent in child- and youth-oriented institutions', *British Educational Research Journal*, 33, 3, 403–17.

Heider, K. (1988) 'The Rashomon effect: when ethnographers disagree', *American Anthropologist*, 90, 1, 73–81.

Held, V. (1993) *Feminist Morality: Transforming culture, society, and politics*, Chicago, Chicago University Press.

Held, V. (2006) *The Ethics of Care*, New York, Oxford University Press.

Herrera, C. (1999) 'Two arguments for "covert methods" in social research', *British Journal of Sociology*, 50, 2, 331–43.

Hess, D. (1999) 'The autonomy question and the changing conditions of social scientific work', *Anthropology of Work Review*, 20, 1, 27–34.

Hey, V. (2002) '"Not as nice as she was supposed to be": schoolgirls' friendships', in Taylor, S. (ed.), *Ethnographic Research*, London, Sage.

Hill, K. (n.d.) 'A statement on Patrick Tierney's book *Darkness in El Dorado*', available at: www.psych.ucsb.edu/research/cep/eldorado/kimhill.html (accessed 2.1.12).

Hine, C. (2000) *Virtual Ethnography*, London, Sage.

Hine, C. (ed.) (2005) *Virtual Methods*, Oxford, Berg.

Hobbs, D. and Wright, R. (eds) (2006) *The SAGE Handbook of Field Research*, London, Sage.

Holdaway, S. (1982) '"An inside job": a case study of covert research on the police', in Bulmer (ed.).

Holliday, R. (2004a) 'Reflecting the self', in Knowles, C. and Sweetman, P. (eds), *Picturing the Social Landscape: Visual methods and the sociological imagination*, London, Routledge.

Holliday, R. (2004b) 'Filming the closet: the role of video diaries in researching sexualities', *American Behavioral Scientist*, 47, 12, 1597–616.

Holmes, R. M. (1998) *Fieldwork with Children*, London, Sage.

Homan, R. (1978) 'Interpersonal communication in Pentecostal meetings', *Sociological Review*, 26, 499–518.

Homan, R. (1980a) 'The ethics of covert research: Homan defends his methods', *Network*, newsletter of the British Sociological Association, January, p. 4.

Homan, R. (1980b) 'The ethics of covert methods', *British Journal of Sociology*, 31, 46–59.

Homan, R. (1991) *The Ethics of Social Research*, London, Longman.

Homan, R. (2001) 'The principle of assumed consent: the ethics of gatekeeping', *Journal of Philosophy of Education*, 35, 3, 329–43.

Homan, R. and Bulmer, M. (1982) 'On the merits of covert methods: a dialogue', in Bulmer (ed.).

Hood, C. and Peters, G. (2004) 'The middle aging of new public management: into the age of paradox?', *Journal of Public Administration and Theory*, 14, 267–82.

Hooker, B. and Little, M. (eds) (2000) *Moral Particularism*, Oxford, Oxford University Press.

Hopkins, M. (1993) 'Is anonymity possible? Writing about refugees in the United States', in Brettell (ed.)

Hopper, C. (1999) 'A comment on Erich Goode's confession', *Deviant Behavior*, 20, 331–3.

Horowitz, I. L. (1967) *The Rise and Fall of Project Camelot*, Cambridge, MA, MIT Press.

Horowitz, I. (2004) 'Laud Humphreys: a pioneer in the practice of fugitive social science', in *Tributes: Personal reflections on a century of social research*, New Brunswick, NJ, Transaction.

Hudson, C. (2004) 'Reducing inequalities in field relations: who gets the power?', in Jeffrey, B. and Walford, G. (eds), *Ethnographies of Educational and Cultural Conflicts*, Amsterdam, Elsevier.

Hudson, J. M. and Bruckman, A. (2005) 'Using empirical data to reason about internet research ethics', in Gellersen, H. et al. (eds), *European Conference on Computer-Supported Cooperative Work: Proceedings of the ninth European conference on computer-supported cooperative work*, Paris, pp. 287–306.

Huff, D. (1999) 'Dialogue across the divides: "Moments of rapport" and power in feminist interviews with anti-feminist women', *Sociology*, 33, 4, 687–703.

Hughes, E. (1958) *Men and their Work*, Glencoe, IL, Free Press.

Huizer, G. and Mannheim, B. (eds) (1979) *The Politics of Anthropology*, The Hague, Mouton.

Hume, L. and Mulcock, J. (2004a) 'Introduction', in Hume and Mulcock (eds).

Hume, L. and Mulcock, J. (eds) (2004b) *Anthropologists in the Field: Cases in participant observation*, New York, Columbia University Press.

Humphreys, L. (1970) *Tearoom Trade*, London, Duckworth.

Humphreys, L. (1975) *Tearoom Trade: Impersonal sex in public places*, second edition, Chicago, Aldine.

Hurd, H. (1996) 'The moral magic of consent', *Legal Theory*, 2, 121–46.

Hymes, D. (ed.) (1972) *Reinventing Anthropology*. New York, Pantheon.

Iphofen, R. (2009) *Ethical Decision Making in Research*, London, Palgrave Macmillan.

Irwin, T. (2000) 'Ethics as an inexact science: Aristotle's ambitions for moral theory', in Hooker, B. and Little, M. (eds) *Moral Particularism*, Oxford, Oxford University Press.

Israel, M. (2004) 'Strictly confidential? Integrity and disclosure of criminological and socio-legal research', *British Journal of Criminology*, 44, 5, 715–40.

Israel, M. and Hay, I. (2006) *Research Ethics for Social Scientists: Between ethical conduct and regulatory compliance*, London: Sage.

Jacobs, B. (2006) 'The case for dangerous fieldwork', in Hobbs and Wright (eds).

Jaggar, M. A. (2000) 'Feminist ethics', in LaFollette, H. (ed.), *The Blackwell Guide to Ethical Theory*, Oxford, Blackwell Publishers.

Janovicek, N. (2006) 'Oral history and ethical practice', *Journal of Academic Ethics*, 4, 157–74.

Johnson, D. and Bullock, M. (2009) 'The ethics of data archiving: issues from four perspectives', in Mertens and Ginsberg (eds).

Jones, M. and Stanley, G. (2010) 'Collaborative action research: a democratic under-taking or a web of collusion and compliance?', *International Journal of Research and Method in Education*, 33, 2, 151–63.

Jonsen, A. (1990) *The New Medicine and the Old Ethics*, Cambridge, MA, Harvard University Press.

Jonsen, A. and Toulmin, S. (1988) *The Abuse of Casuistry: A history of moral reasoning*, Berkeley, CA, University of California Press.

Kant, I. (1785) *Grundlegung zur Metaphysik der Sitten (MdS)*. (English translation in Paton 1948; alternative English translation available at: www.earlymoderntexts.com/pdf/kantgw.pdf.)

Kant, I. (1795) *Perpetual Peace*, English translation in Reiss, H. (ed.), *Kant: Political Writings*, Cambridge, Cambridge University Press, 1991.

Kellett, M. (2010) *Rethinking Children and Research: Attitudes in Contemporary Society*, London, Continuum.

Kelly, A. (2009) 'In defence of anonymity: rejoining the criticism', *British Educational Research Journal*, 35, 3, 431–45.

Kelly, P. (2004) 'Awkward Intimacies' in Hume and Mulcock (eds).

Kelman, H. (1977) 'Privacy and research with human beings', *Journal of Social Issues*, 33, 3, 169–95.

Kieran, M. (1997) *Media Ethics: A philosophical approach*, Westport, CT, Praeger.

Kimmel, A. (1996) *Ethical Issues in Behavioral Research*, Cambridge, MA, Blackwell.

Kindon, S., Pain, R. and Kesby, M. (eds) (2007) *Participatory Action Research: Approaches and methods*, London, Routledge.

Kleinig, J. (2010) 'The nature of consent', in Miller and Wertheimer (eds).

Kulick, D. and Willson, M. (eds) (1995) *Taboo, Sex, Identity, and Erotic Subjectivity in Anthropological Fieldwork*, London, Routledge.

Kurotani, S. (2004) 'Multi-sited trans-national ethnography and the shifting construction of fieldwork', in Hume and Mulcock (eds).

Kymlicka, W. (2002) *Contemporary Political Philosophy*, Oxford, Oxford University Press.

Ladd, J. (1991) 'The quest for a code of professional ethics: an intellectual and moral confusion', in Johnson, D. (ed.), *Ethical Issues in Engineering*, Englewood Cliffs, NJ, Prentice Hall.

Laerke, A. (2008) 'Confessions of a downbeat anthropologist', in Armbruster and Laerke (eds).

Lankshear, G. (2000) 'Bacteria and babies', in Lee-Treweek and Linkogle (eds).

Larmore, C. (1987) *Patterns of Moral Complexity*, Cambridge, Cambridge University Press.

Larmore, C. (1996) *The Morals of Modernity*, Cambridge, Cambridge University Press.

Larson, M. S. (1977) *The Rise of Professionalism: A sociological analysis*, Berkeley, CA, University of California Press.

Layard, R. and Glaister, S. (eds) (1994) 'Introduction', in *Cost–Benefit Analysis*, second edition, Cambridge, Cambridge University Press.

Lee, R. (1995) *Dangerous Fieldwork*, Thousand Oaks, CA, Sage.

Lee-Treweek, G. and Linkogle, S. (eds) (2000) *Danger in the Field: Risk and ethics in social research*, London, Routledge.

Leiter, B. (2001) 'Nietzsche and the morality critics', in Richardson, J. and Leiter, B. (eds), *Nietzsche*, Oxford, Oxford University Press.

Leiter, B. (2002) *Nietzsche on Morality*, London, Routledge.

Leo, R. A. (1995) 'Trial and Tribulations: Courts, ethnography and the need for evidentiary privilege for academic researchers', *American Sociologist*, 26, 1, 113–34.

Leo, R. A. (1996) 'The ethics of deceptive research roles reconsidered: A response to Kai Erikson', *American Sociologist*, 27, 1, 122–28.

Levinas, E. (1999) *Totality and Infinity*, Pittsburgh, PA, Duquesne University Press. (First published in French in 1961.)

Levinson, M. (2010) 'Accountability to research participants: unresolved dilemmas and unravelling ethics', *Ethnography and Education*, 5, 2, 193–207.

Le Voi, M. (2006) 'Doing the right thing', in Potter, S. (ed.), *Doing Postgraduate Research*, second edition, London, Sage.

Lewis, J. (2006) 'Making order out of a contested disorder: the utilisation of online support groups in social science research', *Qualitative Researcher*, 3, 2006, 4–7.

Liamputtong, P. (2007) *Researching the Vulnerable*, London, Sage.

Lincoln, Y. and Guba, E. (1989) *Naturalistic Inquiry*, Beverly Hills, CA, Sage.

Little, M. (2000) 'Moral generalities revisited', in Hooker and Little (eds).

Littrell, B. (1993) 'Bureaucratic secrets and adversarial methods of social research', in Vaughan, T., Sjoberg, G. and Reynolds, L. (eds), *A Critique of Contemporary American Sociology*, Dix Hills, NY, General Hall.

Lobkowicz, N. (1967) *Theory and Practice*, Notre Dame, IN, Notre Dame University Press.

Lobkowicz, N. (1977) 'On the history of theory and praxis', in Ball, T. (ed.), *Political Theory and Praxis*, Minneapolis, MN, University of Minnesota Press.

Locke, J. (1975) *An Essay concerning Human Understanding*, edited by Nidditch, P. H., Oxford, Oxford University Press. (First published 1689.)

Lofland, J. (1961) 'Reply to Davis', *Social Problems*, 8, 4, 365–7. (Reprinted in Filstead (ed.) (1970).)

Lofland, J. (1966) *Doomsday Cult*, Englewood Cliffs, NJ, Prentice-Hall.

Lofland, J. and Lejeune, R. (1960) 'Initial interaction of newcomers in alcoholics anonymous: a field experiment in class symbols and socialization', *Social Problems*, 8, 102–11.

Lofland, J. and Lofland, L. (1969) *Deviance and Identity*, Englewood Cliffs, NJ, Prentice-Hall.

Louden, R. (1988) 'Can we be too moral?', *Ethics*, 98, 361–80.

Louden, R. (2007) 'The critique of the morality system', in Thomas, A. (ed.), *Bernard Williams*, Cambridge, Cambridge University Press.

Lugosi, P. (2006) 'Between overt and covert research: concealment and disclosure in an ethnographic study of commercial hospitality', *Qualitative Inquiry*, 12, 3, 541–61.

Lundman, R. and McFarlane, P. (1976) 'Conflict methodology: an introduction and preliminary assessment', *Sociological Quarterly*, 17, 503–12.

Lutz, C. (2008) 'Selling our independence? The perils of Pentagon funding for anthropology', *Anthropology Today*, 24, 5, 1–3.

Lyng, S. (1998) 'Dangerous methods: risk taking and the research process', in Farrell, J. and Hamm, M. (eds), *Ethnography at the Edge*, Boston, MA, Northeastern University Press.

MacCallum, G. (1972) 'Negative and positive freedom', in Laslett, P., Runciman, W. and Skinner, Q. (eds), *Philosophy, Politics and Society*, fourth series, Oxford, Blackwell.

Macfarlane, B. (2009) *Researching with Integrity: The ethics of academic enquiry*, London, Routledge.

MacIntyre, A. (1982) 'Risk, harm, and benefit assessments as instruments of moral evaluation', in Beauchamp et al. (eds).

MacIntyre, A. (1993) 'Ethical dilemmas: notes from outside the field', *American Anthropological Association Newsletter*, October.

MacIntyre, D. (1997) 'The profession of educational research', *British Educational Research Journal*, 23, 2, 127–40.

Mackie, J. L. (1977) *Ethics: Inventing right and wrong*, Harmondsworth, Penguin.

Malcolm, J. (1984) *In the Freud Archives*, London, Flamingo.

Malcolm, J. (1991) *The Journalist and the Murderer*, London, Bloomsbury.

Malcolm, J. (1995) *The Silent Woman*, New York, Vintage.

Manning, P. (2002) 'Fatethics: Response to Erich Goode', *Qualitative Sociology*, 25, 4, 541–7.

Manson, J. and O'Neill, O. (2007) *Rethinking Informed Consent in Bioethics*, Cambridge, Cambridge University Press.

Markham, A. (2005) 'The methods, politics and ethics of internet ethnography', in Denzin and Lincoln (eds).

Markham, A. (2006) 'Ethic as method, method as ethic: A case for reflexivity in qualitative ICT research', *Journal of Information Ethics*, 15, 2, 37–54.

Markham, A. and Baym, N. (eds) (2009) *Internet Inquiry: Conversations about method*, Thousand Oaks, CA, Sage.

Markowitz, F. and Ashkenazi, M. (eds) (1999) *Sex, Sexuality and the Anthropologist*, Urbana, IL, University of Illinois Press.

Marzano, M. (2007) 'Informed consent, deception and research freedom in qualitative research', *Qualitative Inquiry*, 13, 3, 417–36.

Masson, J. (1984) *The Assault on Truth: Freud's Suppression of the Seduction Theory*, New York, Farrar Straus & Giroux.

Masson, J. (1991) *Final Analysis*, New York, HarperCollins.

Mauthner, M., Birch, M., Jessop, J. and Miller, T. (eds) (2002) *Ethics in Qualitative Research*, London, Sage.

McBride, W. (ed.) (1997) *Existentialist Ethics*, New York, Garland.

McKeganey, N. (2001) 'To pay or not to pay: respondents' motivation for participating in research', *Addiction*, 96, 1237–8.

McKeganey, N. and Barnard, M. (1996) *Sex Work on the Streets*, Buckingham, Open University Press.

McLaughlin, K., Osborne, S.P. and Ferlie, E. (eds) (2002) *The New Public Management: Current trends and future prospects*, London, Routledge.

McNamee, M. (2001) 'The guilt of whistling-blowing: Conflicts in action research and educational ethnography', *Journal of Philosophy of Education*, 35, 423–41.

McWilliam, E. and Jones, A. (2005) 'An unprotected species? On teachers as risky subjects', *British Educational Research Journal*, 31, 3, 109–20.

Meagher, G. and Parton, N. (2004) 'Modernising social work and the ethics of care', *Social Work and Society*, 2, 1, available at: www.socwork.de

Mega, M. (2002) 'PhD researcher gave anonymity to child abusers', *Times Higher Education Supplement*, 9 August.

Melrose, M. (2011) 'Regulating social research', *Sociological Research Online*, 16, 2, 14, available at: www.socresonline.org.uk/16/2/14.html

Menand, L. (ed.) (1998) *The Future of Academic Freedom*, Chicago, University of Chicago Press.

Merrill, B. and West, L. (2009) *Using Biographical Methods in Social Research*, London, Sage.

Mertens, D. and Ginsberg, P. (eds) (2009) *Handbook of Research Ethics*, Thousand Oaks, CA, Sage.

Meskell, L. and Pels, P. (eds) (2005) *Embedding Ethics*, Oxford, Berg.

Messenger, J. (1989) *Inis Beag Revisited: The anthropologist as observant participator*, Salem, WI, Sheffield Publishing.

Mies, M. (1983) 'Towards a methodology for feminist research', in Bowles, G. and Duelli-Klein, R. (eds), *Theories of Women's Studies*, London, Routledge & Kegan Paul.

Mill, J. S. (1859a) 'Bentham', in *Dissertations and Discussions*, Vol. I, London, Parker.

Mill, J. S. (1859b) *On Liberty*, Cambridge, Cambridge University Press, 1989.

Miller, B. and Humphreys, L. (2004) 'Keeping in touch: maintaining contacts with stigmatized subjects', in Pole, C. (ed.), *Fieldwork*, four volumes, London, Sage.

Miller, F. (2010) 'Consent to clinical research', in Miller and Wertheimer (eds).

Miller, F. and Wertheimer, A. (2010a) 'Preface to a theory of consent transactions: beyond valid consent', in Miller and Wertheimer (eds).

Miller, F. and Wertheimer, A. (eds) (2010b) *The Ethics of Consent: Theory and practice*, Oxford, Oxford University Press.

Miller, M. (1996) 'Ethics and understanding through interrelationship: I and Thou in dialogue', in Josselson (ed.).

Miller, M. (2007) 'Ethics and action research', in Reason and Bradbury (eds).

Miller, R. (1996) *Casuistry and Modern Ethics*, Chicago, University of Chicago Press.

Miller, T. and Boulton, M. (2007) 'Changing constructions of informed consent', *Social Science and Medicine*, 65, 2199–211.

Mills, C. W. (1959) *The Sociological Imagination*, New York, Oxford.

Mills, D. (2003) '"Like a horse in blinkers": a political history of anthropology's research ethics', in Caplan, P. (ed.), *The Ethics of Anthropology: debates and dilemmas*, London, Routledge.

Mitchell, R. (1991) 'Secrecy and disclosure in fieldwork', in Shaffir, W. and Stebbins, R. (eds), *Experiencing Fieldwork*, Newbury Park, CA, Sage.

Mitchell, R. (1993) *Secrecy and Fieldwork*, Newbury Park, CA, Sage.

Montefiore, A. (ed.) (1975) *Neutrality and Impartiality: The university and political commitment*, Cambridge, Cambridge University Press.

Montmarquet, J. (1993) *Epistemic Virtue and Doxastic Responsibility*, Lanham, MD, Rowman & Littlefield.

Moore, H. (2010) 'Forms of knowing and un-knowing: secrets about society, sexuality and God in Northern Kenya', in Ryan-Flood and Gill (eds).

Morgan, D. (1972) 'The British Association scandal', *Sociological Review*, 20, 2, 185–206.

Morton, Alec (1999) 'Ethics in action research', *Systemic Practice and Action Research*, 12, 2, 219–22.

Mounce, H. (1997) *The Two Pragmatisms*, London, Routledge.

Muir, S. (2004) 'Not quite at home: field envy and new age ethnographic dis-ease', in Hume and Mulcock (eds).

Murphy, E. and Dingwall, R. (2001) 'The ethics of ethnography', in Atkinson, P., Coffey, A., Delamont, S., Lofland, J. and Lofland, L. (eds), *Handbook of Ethnography*, London, Sage.

Murphy, E. and Dingwall, R. (2007) 'Informed consent, anticipatory regulation and ethnographic practice', *Social Science and Medicine*, 65, 2223–34.

Nardi, P. (1999) 'Reclaiming the importance of Laud Humphreys's tearoom trade: impersonal sex in public places', in Leap, W. (ed.), *Public Sex, Gay Space*, New York, Columbia University Press.

Nehamas, A. (1985) *Nietzsche: Life as literature*, Cambridge, MA, Harvard University Press.

Nejelski, P. (ed.) (1976) *Social Research in Conflict with Law and Ethics*, Cambridge MA, Ballinger.

Nespor, J. (2000) 'Anonymity and place', *Qualitative Inquiry*, 6, 4, 564–9.

Newman, J. E. and Clarke, J. (2009) *Publics, Politics and Power: Remaking the public in public services*, London, Sage.

Nicolaus, M. (1968) 'Fat-cat sociology: Remarks at the American Sociological Association Convention', available at: www.colorado.edu/Sociology/gimenez/fatcat.html (accessed 10.9.10).

Nietzsche, F. (1886) *Beyond Good and Evil*, London, Penguin, 1990.

Nietzsche, F. (1887) *The Gay Science*, New York, Vintage, 1974.

Noddings, N. (1984) *Caring: A feminine approach to ethics and moral education*, Berkeley, CA, University of California Press.

Noddings, N. (2003) Preface to *Caring: A feminine approach to ethics and moral education*, second edition, Berkeley, CA, University of California Press.

Nolen, A. and Vander Putten, J. (2007) 'Action research in education: addressing gaps in ethical principles and practices', *Educational Researcher*, 36, 7, 401–7.

Norris, N. (1995) 'Contracts, control and evaluation', *Journal of Education Policy*, 10, 3, 271–85.

Noyes, A. (2008) 'Using video diaries to investigate learner trajectories: researching the "unknown unknowns"', in Thomson (ed.).

Nussbaum, M. (2000) 'Why practice needs ethical theory: particularism, principle, and bad behaviour', in Hooker and Little (eds).

Nutbrown, C. (2010) 'Naked by the pool? Blurring the image? Ethical issues in the portrayal of young children in arts-based educational research', *Qualitative Inquiry*, 17, 1, 3–14.

O'Brian, K. (2010) 'Inside "doorwork"', in Ryan-Flood and Gill (eds).

Oderberg, D. and Chappell, T. (eds) (2004) *Human Values*, Basingstoke, Palgrave Macmillan.

Oeye, C., Bjelland, A. and Skorpen, A. (2007) 'Doing participant observation in a psychiatric hospital – research ethics resumed', *Social Science and Medicine*, 65, 2296–306.

Okely, J. (1983) *The Traveller-Gypsies*, Cambridge, Cambridge University Press.

O'Leary, T. (2002) *Foucault and the Art of Ethics*, London, Continuum.

Oliver, M. (1992) 'Changing the social relations of research production?', *Disability, Handicap and Society*, 7, 2, 101–14.

Olson, G. and Worsham, L. (eds) (2004) *Postmodern Sophistry: Stanley Fish and the Critical Enterprise*, Albany, NY, State University of New York Press.

O'Neill, O. (2002) *Autonomy and Consent in Bioethics*, Cambridge, Cambridge University Press.

Opler, M. (1986) 'Comment on "engineering internment"', *American Ethnologist*, 14, 2, 383.

Orgad, S. (2009) 'How can researchers make sense of the issues involved in collecting and interpreting online and offline data?', in Markham and Baym (eds).

Paine, T. (1791) *The Rights of Man*, in Kuklick, B. (ed.), *Paine: Political writings*, Cambridge, Cambridge University Press.

Parrish, J. (2007) *Paradoxes of Political Ethics*, Cambridge, Cambridge University Press.

Parry, O. and Mauthner, N. (2004) 'Whose data are they anyway? Practical, legal and ethical issues in archiving qualitative research data', *Sociology*, 38, 1, 139–52.

Paton, H. J. (1948) *The Moral Law: Kant's groundwork of the metaphysic of morals*, London, Hutchinson.

Payne, G., Dingwall, R., Payne, J. and Carter, M. (1981) *Sociology and Social Research*, London, Routledge.

Pearson, G. (2009) 'The researcher as hooligan: where "participant" observation means breaking the law', *International Journal of Social Research Methodology*, 12, 3, 243–55.

Pels, D. (2003) *Unhastening Science*, Liverpool, Liverpool University Press.

Pels, P. (2000) 'The trickster's dilemma: ethics and the technologies of the anthropological self', in Strathern, M. (ed.), *Audit Cultures*, London, Routledge.

Pels, P. (2005) '"Where there aren't no ten commandments": Redefining ethics during the *Darkness in El Dorado* scandal', in Meskell and Pels (eds).

Peneff, J. (1985) 'Fieldwork in Algeria', *Qualitative Sociology*, 8, 65–78.

Pettigrew, M. (1994) 'Coming to terms with research: the contract business', in Halpin, D. and Troyna, B. (eds) *Researching Education Policy*, London, Falmer.

Pieterman, R. (2001) 'Culture in a risk society', *Zeitschrift für Rechtssoziologie* 22, 145–68.

Pink, S. (2004) 'Visual methods', in Seale, C., Gobo, G., Gubrium, J. and Silverman, D. (eds), *Qualitative Research Practice*, London, Sage.

Pink, S. (2007a) *Doing Visual Ethnography*, second edition, London, Sage.

Pink, S. (ed.) (2007b) *Visual Interventions*, Oxford, Berghahn.

Pinkard, T. (1982) 'Invasions of privacy in social science research', in Beauchamp et al. (eds).

Piper, H. and Sikes, P. (2010) 'All teachers are vulnerable but especially gay teachers: using composite fictions to protect research participants in pupil–teacher sex-related research', *Qualitative Inquiry*, 16, 7, 566–74.

Pippin, R. (1991) *Modernism as a Philosophical Problem*, Oxford, Blackwell.

Platt, J. (2003) *The British Sociological Association: A sociological history*, Durham, NC, Sociologypress.

Plummer, K. (1995) *Telling Sexual Stories*, London, Routledge.

Polanyi, M. (1962) 'The republic of science', *Minerva*, 1, 1, 54–73.

Pollner, M. (1987) *Mundane Reason: Reality in everyday and sociological discourse*. Cambridge: Cambridge University Press.

Polsky, N. (1969) *Hustlers, Beats, and Others*, Harmondsworth, Penguin.

Potter, J. (1996) *Representing Reality: Discourse, rhetoric and social construction*, London, Sage.

Price, D. (2008) *Anthropological Intelligence: The deployment and neglect of American anthropology in the Second World War*, Durham, NC, Duke University Press.

Pring, R. (2001) 'The virtues and vices of an educational researcher', *Journal of Philosophy of Education*, 35, 3, 407–21.

Prosser, J. (2000) 'The moral maze of image ethics', in Simons, H. and Usher, R. (eds), *Situated Ethics in Educational Research*, London: Routledge Falmer.

Putnam, H. (2002) 'Levinas and Judaism', in Critchley, S. and Bernasconi, R. (eds), *The Cambridge Companion to Levinas*, Cambridge, Cambridge University Press.

Reason, P. and Bradbury, H. (eds) (2008) *The SAGE Handbook of Action Research*, second edition, London, Sage.

Reiss, A. (1979) 'Government regulation of scientific inquiry: some paradoxical consequences', in Klockars, C. and O'Connor, F. (eds), *Deviance and Decency*, Beverly Hills, CA, Sage.

Renold, E., Holland, S., Ross, N. and Hillman, A. (2008) 'Becoming participant: problematizing "informed consent" in participatory research with young people in care', *Qualitative Social Work*, 7, 4, 431–51.

Renzetti, C. and Lee, R. (eds) (1993) *Researching Sensitive Topics*, Newbury Park, CA, Sage.

Reynolds, P. (1979) *Ethical Dilemmas and Social Science Research*, San Francisco, CA, Jossey-Bass.

Richardson, E. (1973) *The Teacher, the School and the Task of Management*, London, Heinemann.

Riecken, H. (1956) 'The unidentified observer', *American Journal of Sociology*, 62, 2, 210–12.

Riessman, C. (2008) *Narrative Analysis*, second edition, London, Sage.

Roberts, B. (2001) *Biographical Research*, Buckingham, Open University Press.

Rosenhan, D. (1973) 'On being sane in insane places', *Science*, 179, 4070, 250–8, available at: http://web.archive.org/web/20041117175255/http://web.cocc.edu/lminorevans/on_being_sane_in_insane_places.htm (accessed 10.8.11).

Ross, W. D. (1930) *The Right and the Good*, Oxford, Oxford University Press.

Roth, J. A. (1969) 'A codification of current prejudices', *American Sociologist*, 4, 2, 159.

Ruddick, S. (1989) *Maternal Thinking: Towards a Politics of Peace*, New York: Beacon Press.

Ryan-Flood, R. (2010) 'Keeping mum: secrecy and silence in research on lesbian parenthood', in Ryan-Flood and Gill (eds).

Ryan-Flood, R. and Gill, R. (eds) (2010) *Secrecy and Silence in the Research Process: Feminist reflections*, London, Routledge.

Sagarin, E. (1973) 'The research setting and the right not to be researched', *Social Problems*, 21, 1, 52–64.

Saguy, A. (2002) 'Sex, inequality, and ethnography: response to Erich Goode', *Qualitative Sociology*, 25, 4, 549–55.

Sanders, T. (2005) 'Researching the online sex work community', in Hine (ed.).

Sanders, T. (2006) 'Researching sex work: dynamics, difficulties and decisions', in Hobbs and Wright (eds).

Scarce, R. (1994) '(No) trial (but) tribulations: when courts and ethnography conflict', *Journal of Contemporary Ethnography*, 23, 2, 123–49.

Scarce, R. (1999) 'Good faith, bad ethics: when scholars go the distance and scholarly associations do not', *Law and Social Inquiry*, 24, 4, 1301–10.

Scheper-Hughes, N. (1979) *Saints, Scholars and Schizophrenics: Mental Illness in Rural Ireland*, Berkeley, CA, University of California Press.

Scheper-Hughes, N. (1995) 'The primacy of the ethical: propositions for a militant anthropology', *Current Anthropology*, 36, 3, 409–40.

Scheper-Hughes, N. (2000a) 'Ire in Ireland', *Ethnography*, 1, 1, 117–40.

Scheper-Hughes, N. (2000b) 'The global traffic in human organs', *Current Anthropology*, 41, 2, 191–224.

Scheper-Hughes, N. (2001) *Saints, Scholars and Schizophrenics: Mental Illness in Rural Ireland*, twentieth anniversary edition, Berkeley, CA, University of California Press.

Schilpp, P. and Friedman, M. (eds) (1967) *The Philosophy of Martin Buber*, La Salle, IL, Open Court.

Schutz, A. (1974) *Collected Papers*, Volume 1, The Hague, Martinus Nijhoff.

Scott, C. (1990) *The Question of Ethics: Nietzsche, Foucault, Heidegger*, Bloomington, IN, Indiana University Press.

Scott, G. (1983) *The Magicians*, New York, Irvington.

Seymour, J. and Ingleton, C. (1999) 'Ethical issues in qualitative research at the end of life', *International Journal of Palliative Nursing*, 5, 2, 65–73.

Shaffir, W. (1985) 'Some reflections on approaches to fieldwork in Hassidic communities', *Jewish Journal of Sociology*, 27, 2, 115–34.

Shils, E. (1956) *The Torment of Secrecy*, London, Heinemann.

Shils, E. (1959) 'Social inquiry and the autonomy of the individual', in Lerner, D. P. (ed.), *The Human Meaning of the Human Sciences*, New York, Meridian.

Shils, E. (1980) *The Calling of Sociology*, Chicago, University of Chicago Press.

Shils, E. (1997) 'The Academic Ethic', in *The Calling of Education*, Chicago, University of Chicago Press.

Shweder, R. (2004) 'Tuskegee re-examined', available at: www.spiked-online.com/articles/0000000CA34A.htm (accessed 13.9.10).

Shweder, R. (2005) 'When cultures collide: which rights, whose tradition of values? A critique of the global anti-FGM campaign', in Eisgruber, R. and Sajó, A. (eds), *Global Justice and the Bulwarks of Localism*, Leiden, Martinus Nijhof.

Sidgwick, H. (1967) *The Methods of Ethics*, seventh edition, London, Macmillan. (First published in 1874.)

Sikes, P. (2006a) 'Scandalous stories and dangerous liaisons: when male teachers and female pupils fall in love', *Sex Education*, 6, 3, 265–80.

Sikes, P. (2006b) 'Towards useful and dangerous theories', *Discourse*, 27, 1, 43–51.

Sikes, P. (2008) 'At the eye of the storm: an academic('s) experience of moral panic', *Qualitative Inquiry,* 14, 2, 235–53.

Sikes, P. (2010) 'Teacher–student sexual relations: key risks and ethical issues', *Ethnography and Education*, 5, 2, 143–57.

Sikes, P. and Piper, H. (2010) *Researching Sex and Lies in the Classroom: Allegations of sexual misconduct in schools*, London, Routledge/Falmer.

Simons, H. (2009) 'Whose data are they?', in *Case Study Research in Practice*, London, Sage.

Simons, H. and Usher, R. (eds) (2000) *Situated Ethics in Educational Research*, London, RoutledgeFalmer.

Singer, E. (1980) 'More on the limits of consent forms', *IRB: Ethics and Human Research*, 2, 3, 7.

Skinner, Q. (2000) *Machiavelli: A Very Short Introduction*, Oxford, Oxford University Press.

Skomal, S. (1993) 'The ethics of fieldwork', *Anthropology Newsletter*, 34, 1, 26.

Slote, M. (2000) 'Virtue ethics', in LaFollette, H. (ed.), *The Blackwell Guide to Ethical Theory*, Oxford, Blackwell.

Slote, M. (2007) *The Ethics of Care and Empathy*, London, Routledge.

Small, R. (2001) 'Codes are not enough: what philosophy can contribute to the ethics of educational research', *Journal of the Philosophy of Education*, 35, 3, 387–406.

Smith, J. K. (1987) *The Nature of Social and Educational Inquiry*, Norwood, NJ, Ablex.

Smith, L. (1999) *Decolonizing Methodologies: Research and indigenous peoples*, London, Zed.

Smith, L. (2005) 'On tricky ground: researching the native in the age of uncertainty', in Denzin and Lincoln (eds).

Solove, D. (2008) *Understanding Privacy*, Cambridge, MA, Harvard University Press.

Sparkes, A. (1995) 'Physical education teachers and the search for self: two cases of structured denial', in *New Directions in Physical Education*, third edition, ed. N. Armstrong (pp. 157–78), London, Cassell.

Spicker, P. (2007) 'Research without consent', *Social Research Update*, 51. Available at: http://sru.soc.surrey.ac.uk/SRU51.pdf

SRA (1995) *The Data Protection Act 1998: Guidelines for social research*, London, Social Research Association.

Stacey, J. (1988) 'Can there be a feminist ethnography?', *Women's Studies International Forum*, 2, 1, 21–7.

Stake, R. (1995) *The Art of Case Study Research*, Thousand Oaks, CA, Sage.

Stanley, L. (1995) *The Auto/Biographical I*, Manchester, Manchester University Press.

Stanley, L. and Wise, S. (2010) 'The ESRC's 2010 framework for research ethics: fit for research purpose?', *Sociological Research Online*, 15, 4, available at: www.socresonline.org.uk/15/4/12.html

Starn, O. (1986) 'Engineering internment: anthropologists and the War Relocation Authority', *American Ethnologist*, 13, 4, 700–20.

Stephenson, R. (1978) 'The CIA and the professor: a personal account', *American Sociologist*, 13, 128–33.

Stern, S. (2003) 'Encountering distressing information in online research: a consideration of legal and ethical responsibilities', *New Media and Society*, 5, 249–66.

Stern, S. (2009) 'How do various notions of privacy influence decisions in qualitative internet research: a response to Malin Sveningson', in Markham and Baym (eds).

Stocker, M. (1990) *Plural and Conflicting Values*, Oxford, Oxford University Press.

Stolyarova, G. (2011) 'Inventing the facts', *St Petersburg Times*, 1639, 19 January. Available at: www.sptimes.ru/index.php?action_id=2&story_id=33407 (accessed 24.5.11).

Strauss, L. (1987) 'Machiavelli', in Strauss, L. and Cropsey, J. (eds), *History of Political Philosophy*, third edition, Chicago, University of Chicago Press.

Sveningsson Elm, M. (2001) *Creating a sense of community. Experiences from a Swedish web chat*. Dissertation, Linkoping Studies in Art and Science.

Sveningsson Elm, M. (2009) 'How do various notions of privacy influence decisions in qualitative internet research?', in Markham and Baym (eds).

Thompson, P. (2003) 'Towards ethical practice in the use of archived transcripted interviews: a response', *Social Research Methodology*, 6, 4, 357–60.

Thomson, P. (ed.) (2008) *Doing Visual Research with Children and Young People*, London, Routledge.

Thorne, B. (1980) '"You still takin' notes?" Fieldwork and problems of informed consent', *Social Problems*, 27, 3, 284–97.

Tickle, L. (2001) 'Opening windows, closing doors: ethical dilemmas in educational action research', *Journal of Philosophy of Education*, 35, 1, 345–59.

Tierney, P. (2001) *Darkness in El Dorado*, New York, Norton.

Tight, M. (ed.) (1988) *Academic Freedom and Responsibility*, Milton Keynes, Open University Press.

Tolich, M. (2004) 'Internal confidentiality: when confidentiality assurances fail relational informants', *Qualitative Sociology*, 27, 1, 101–6.

Tourigny, S. (1993) *Helping to harm? The ethical dilemmas of managing politically sensitive data*, Kalamazoo, MI, Center for the Study of Ethics in Society, Western Michigan University.

Tourigny, S. (2004) '"Yo bitch…" and other challenges', in Hume and Mulcock (eds).

Traianou, A. (2007) 'Ethnography and the perils of the single case: an example from the sociocultural analysis of primary science expertise', *Ethnography and Education*. 2, 2, 209–20.

Traianou, A. and Hammersley, M. (2011a) 'Ethics and educational research', on ESRC Teaching and Learning Research Programme, Capacity Building Resources, website. Available at: www.tlrp.org/capacity/rm/wt/traianou/ and at www.bera.ac.uk/ethics-and-educational-research/

Troyna, B. and Carrington, B. (1989) 'Whose side are we on? Ethical dilemmas in research on "race" and education', in Burgess, R. (ed.), *The Ethics of Educational Research*, Lewes, Falmer.

Tuchman, G. (2009) *Wannabe U: Inside the corporate university*, Chicago, University of Chicago Press.

Tuck, R. (1979) *Natural Rights Theories*, Cambridge, Cambridge University Press.

Turner, R. H. (1956) 'Role taking, role standpoint and reference group behavior', *American Journal of Sociology*, 61, 316–28.

Turner, R. (1962) 'Role taking: process versus conformity', in Rose, A. (ed.), *Human Behavior and Social Processes*. Boston, Houghton Mifflin.

United Nations (1948) Universal Declaration of Human Rights, available at: www.hrweb.org/legal/udhr.html (accessed 17.11.10).

United Nations (1990) Convention on Rights of the Child, available at: www.unicef.org/crc/

Urmson, J. (1968) *The Emotive Theory of Ethics*, London, Hutchinson.

Usher, R. (2000) 'Deconstructive happening, ethical moment', in Simons and Usher (eds).

Vidich, A. and Bensman, J. (1958) *Small Town in Mass Society*, Princeton, NJ, Princeton University Press. (Revised edition, Champaign, IL, University of Illinois Press, 2000.)

Vidich, A. and Bensman, J. (1964) 'The Springdale case: academic bureaucrats and sensitive townspeople', in Vidich et al. (eds) (pp. 313–49).

Vidich, A., Bensman, J. and Stein, M. (eds) (1964) *Reflections on Community Studies*, New York, Wiley.

Wacks, R. (2010) *Privacy: A very short introduction*, Oxford, Oxford University Press.

Wakin, E. (ed.) (2008) *Anthropology Goes to War: Professional Ethics and Counterinsurgency in Thailand*, Madison, WI, University of Wisconsin Press.

Waldron, J. (1984) Introduction, in Waldron, J. (ed.), *Theories of Rights*, Oxford, Oxford University Press.

Walford, G. (2002) 'Why don't we name our research sites?', in Walford, G. (ed.), *Educational Ethnography and Methodology*, Amsterdam, JAI Press, pp. 95–105.

Walford, G. (2005) 'Research ethical guidelines and anonymity', *International Journal of Research and Method in Education*, 28, 1, 83–93.

Walford, G. (2008) 'Selecting sites, and gaining ethical and practical access', in Walford, G. (ed.), *How to do Educational Ethnography*, London, Tufnell.

Walker, R. (1993) 'The conduct of educational case studies: ethics, theory and procedures', in Hammersley, M. (ed.), *Controversies in Classroom Research*, second edition, Buckingham, Open University Press.

Walker, S., Eketone, A. and Gibbs, A. (2006) 'An exploration of kaupapa Maori research, its principles, processes and applications', *International Journal of Social Research Methodology*, 9, 4, 331–44.

Walsh, W. H. (1969) *Hegelian Ethics*, London, Macmillan.

Warren, S. and Brandeis, L. (1890) 'The right of privacy', *Harvard Law Review*, 4, 5, 193–220.

Warwick, D. (1982) 'Types of harm in social research', in Beauchamp et al. (eds).

Waskul, D. (1996) 'Ethics of online research: considerations for the study of computer-mediated forms of interaction', *The Information Society*, 12, 2, 129–40.

Wax, M. L. (1980) 'Paradoxes of "consent" to the practice of fieldwork', *Social Problems*, 27, 3, 272–83.

Weber, M. (1946) 'Science as a vocation', in Gerth, H. and Mills, C. W. (eds), *From Max Weber: Essays in Sociology* (pp. 129–56), New York: Oxford University Press. (First published in German in 1919.)

Wellings, K., Branigan, P. and Mitchell, K. (2000) 'Discomfort, discord and discontinuity as data: using focus groups to research sensitive topics', *Culture, Health and Sexuality*, 2, 3, 255–67.

West, W. G. (1980) 'Access to adolescent deviants and deviance', in Shaffir, W., Stebbins, R. and Turawetz, A. (eds), *Fieldwork Experience: Qualitative approaches to social research*, New York, St. Martins Press.

Westin, A. (1967) *Privacy and Freedom*, New York, Athenaum.

Wetherell, M., Taylor, S. and Yates, S. (eds) (2001) *Discourse Theory and Practice*, London: Sage.

White, M. (2002) 'Representations or people?', *Ethics and Information Technology*, 4, 249–66.

Whitt, L. (1999) 'Value bifurcation in bioscience: the rhetoric of research justification', *Perspectives on Science: Historical, Philosophical, Social*, 7, 4, 413–46.

Whyte, W. F. (1992) 'In defense of "street corner society"', *Journal of Contemporary Ethnography*, 21, 52–68.

Whyte, W. F. (1993a) *Street Corner Society*, fourth edition, Chicago, IL, University of Chicago Press. (First published 1943.)

Whyte, W. (1993b) 'Revisiting "street corner society"', *Sociological Forum*, 8, 2, 285–98.

Wiles, R., Heath, S., Crow, G. and Charles, V. (2005) *Informed Consent in Social Research: A literature review*, National Centre for Research Methods Review Paper.

Wiles, R., Crow, G., Heath, S. and Charles, V. (2008a) 'The management of confidentiality and anonymity in social research', *International Journal of Social Research Methodology*, 11, 5, 417–28.

Wiles, R., Prosser, J., Bagnoli, A., Clark, A., Davies, K., Holland, S. and Renold, E. (2008b) *Visual Ethics: Ethical issues in visual research*, ESRC National Centre for Research Methods Review Paper.

Willett, R. (2009) '"As soon as you get on Bebo you just go mad": young consumers and the discursive construction of teenagers online', *Young Consumers*, 10, 4, 283–96.

Williams, B. (1985) *Ethics and the Limits of Philosophy*, London, Fontana.

Williams, B. (2002) *Truth and Truthfulness*, Princeton, NJ, Princeton University Press.

Williams, C. (2002) 'To know me is to love me', *Qualitative Sociology*, 25, 4, 557–60.

Williams, M., Dicks, B., Coffey, A. and Mason, B. (2011) 'Methodological issues in qualitative data sharing and archiving. Briefing paper 2. Qualitative data archiving and reuse: mapping the ethical terrain', available at: www.cardiff.ac.uk/socsi/hyper/QUADS/guide.html (accessed 10.7.11).

Williamson, J. and Prosser, S. (2002) 'Action research: politics, ethics and participation', *Journal of Advanced Nursing*, 40, 5, 587–93.

Wilmott, P. (1980) 'A view from an independent research institute', in Cross, M. (ed.), *Social Research and Public Policy*, London, Social Research Association.

Wollstonecraft, M. (1792) *A Vindication of the Rights of Woman*, Cambridge, Cambridge University Press, 1995.

Wood, A. (1990) *Hegel's Ethical Thought*, Cambridge, Cambridge University Press.

Woolgar, S. and Pawluch, D. (1985) 'Ontological gerrymandering: the anatomy of social problems explanations', *Social Problems*, 32, 314–27.

Yuill, R. (2004) 'Letter: answering back', *Times Higher Education*, 3 December.

Zablocki, B. and Robbins, T. (eds) (2001) *Misunderstanding Cults: Searching for objectivity in a controversial field*, Toronto, University of Toronto Press.

Zussman, R. (2002) 'Editor's introduction: sex in research', *Qualitative Sociology*, 25, 4, 473–77.

INDEX

academic freedom *see* researcher autonomy
action research 38
Alcoholics Anonymous 9
Alderson, P. 106
American Anthropological Association 3, 4, 72
American Sociological Association 4
Angrosino, M. 124
anonymisation 14, 126–31
   and researcher responsibility/blame 10, 69, 70, 71
   strategies and concerns 126–9
     arguments against 129–31
anti-oppressive stance 12–13
anti-theory in ethics 32
Appell, G. 138–9
Aristotle 27, 28–9
Armstrong, G. 85
Atkinson, P. 85
autonomy 14, 75–6, 134–5
   individual freedom
     as an ideal 76–8
     fallacy of 78–9
   researcher's *see* independence
   the right not to be researched 80–2
   see also informed consent

Barnes, J. 95
Bauman, Z. 118
Beckerleg, S. 54
Belmont Report 2–3, 25, 26
benefit *vs* harm *see* cost–benefit
Benjamin, A. 81, 87, 91
Bentham, J. 23–4
Birckhead, J. 99
Bok, S. 105, 106, 109–10
British Sociological Association 4
Buber, M. 30, 31

Calvey, D. 83
Caplan, P. 4, 13
Caputo, J. 32, 63

care, ethics of *see* ethics of care
Carrier, J. 61
casuistry 26
categorical imperative 21–2
causal inference 69
Chagnon, N. 10, 107
Chambliss, W. 86
childhood studies 137
   and visual research 67–8
codes of ethics
   historical perspectives 2–8
   key principles 7
   problems with 142–3
Coggeshall, J. 60, 63, 123–4
Colic-Peisker, V. 89
Colvard, R. 130
commitment 46–7
communities
   access to 87–8
   marginalised groups 137
   rights of 78, 80–1
conclusions *see* publishing
confidentiality 14, 132
   professional and legal responsibilities
     121–3
   strategies for maintaining 123–6
conflicting imperatives 24–5
consent *see* informed consent
consequentialism 22–4, 35
constructionism 41–2
controversial studies 8–11
cost–benefit analysis
   applied to ethical judgment 23–4, 34
counterfactual inferences 70
covert observation 8, 10, 85–6, 106
Coxon, A. 109
criminal behaviour 8, 54–5, 138

Dalton, M. 87
Dancy, J. 27

data collection
  and privacy 113–14, 132
  see also online data
data protection 2, 121–3
  see also anonymisation; confidentiality
deception 9, 97, 98, 124
dedication 46–7
deontology 21–2, 35
Derrida, J. 18
determinism 79
Ditton, J. 72
Dixon-Woods, M. 5
Dodd, S-J. 66
Dodge, M. 107
duties
  conflicting 24–5
  and rights 21

Economic and Social Research Council (ESRC) 6,
  7, 49, 58
Ellis, C. 31
Emmet, D. 35–6
end of ethics 32
equity 15
ESRC *see* Economic and Social Research
  Council
ethical regulation *see* regulation
ethics 34
  definitions and meanings 16–20
  philosophical viewpoints 21–35, 139
  see also research ethics, as occupational ethics
ethics committees 2, 4
  problems with 143
  and public management ideology 6
ethics of care 29–31, 35, 36
evaluations, process of making 19–21
expressivism 31–2
extrinsic values
  defined and discussed 13–24, 37, 52–5
  researcher's moral stance 138–9
  shaping research 137, 142

Faden, R. 75, 76
feedback 125–6
Feinberg, J. 61, 64
feminism 12, 29; *see also* ethics of care
Festinger, L. 8, 106, 110, 114
film 67–8
findings *see* publishing
Fletcher, J. 26
Flewitt, R. 67–8
Forsey, M. 125–6
Forsythe, D. 59
Foster, J. 54
Foucault, M. 33
Framework for Research Ethics (ESRC) 6, 7
free-will 79

freedom
  as an ideal 76–8
  fallacy of 78–9
funding 49, 50

gatekeepers 50, 87–8
  and confidentiality 124, 125
Geros, P. 66, 83
Gilligan, C. 29–30
Gjessing, G. 12
goals *see* research goals
good and bad as concepts 17, 34
Goode, E. 10, 60–1
Grenz, S. 59
Grinyer, A. 129–30
guiding principles in ethics 27

harm 14, 57–8, 134–5
  assessing degree of 62–4, 72, 74
  benefits weighed against 58–61, 74
  definitions/types of 61–2
  difficulty of envisioning/predicting 64–7
  harm *vs* benefits of research 58–61; *see also*
    cost–benefit analysis
  methodological decisions 66
    visual research with children 67–8, 74
  participant observation 64–5
  payment and reciprocity 66
  responsibility and blame 68–9
  to the researcher or wider community 72–3, 74
Hegel, G. 18
Heidegger, M. 33
historical perspective on the development of
  research ethics 2–8
Holdaway, S. 54–5, 85
Holmes, R. 124–5
Homan, R. 4, 6, 9–10, 84, 85, 138
Hudson, C. 112
Hudson, J. 118–19
Hume, L. 106–7
human rights 17, 22, 103
Humphreys, L. 9, 71, 84, 109, 111

independence, researcher see researcher autonomy
individualism 77–8
informed consent 14, 68, 75, 76
  access and consent
    covert observation 85–6
    deciding if consent is needed 82–3, 138
    gatekeepers 86–8
    public areas 84
  individual consent
    agreeing and clarifying 88–91
    constraints and pressures 91–2
    providing non-misleading information 93–8
  online difficulties 120
  privacy issues 114–16

Institutional Review Boards 5
instrumentalism 42–3
Internet *see* online
intrinsic values 134
    defined 13, 36–7
    of knowledge 42–3
    professionalism/researcher virtues 46–52
I–It and *I–Thou* relations 30

Janovicek, N. 129
Josselson, R. 125
journalism, investigative 123, 141–2, 144
judgements, ethical 19–21, 34
    desire to minimise role of 24
    as legitimate compromises in research 135–6
    and reflexivity 33

Kant, I. 21–2, 24, 34, 79, 102
Kelly, A. 88
Kelly, P. 53, 60, 124
Kierkagaard, S. 18
knowledge
    fallibility of/scepticism about 40–2,
        58–9
    instrumental *vs* intrinsic value of 42–3
    relevance of 51–2
    research as pursuit of 37–9, 134
    synonymous with truth 38–9
Kurotani, S. 54, 112

Laerke, A. 73
legislation *see* regulation
Levinas, E. 30–1
Levinson, M. 53, 60, 92–3
Lewis, J. 120
liberal individualism 77–8
Lofland, J. 9, 73, 85

McGuinniss, J. 116
Machiavellianism 139
MacIntyre, A. 104, 108–9
Malcolm, J. 101, 102, 116, 141–2
managerialism in higher education 50
marginalised groups 137
Marzano, M. 85
Masson, J. 86
McKeganey, N. 65–6, 107
media 100–1, 103
    and anonymisation 128
medical regulations 4–5
Messenger, J. 131
Mill, J. S. 24, 76, 77
Mitchell, R. 55, 60
Moore, H. 65
moral licence 50–1, 139–41; *see also* researcher
    autonomy
moral realism and expressivism 31–2

moralism
    definition and forms of 136
    misrepresenting research goals/roles 137–8
    research values and ethical absolutism
        138–42
    problematic nature of regulation 142–3
morality
    researcher's moral stance 138–9
    synonym for ethics 17–18
    unrealistic overemphasis on *see* moralism
Muir, S. 48, 90

National Association for the Advancement of Fat
    Americans (NAAFA) 10
natural rights 23; *see also* human rights
NHS Research Governance Framework 5
Nietzsche, F. 33
Noddings, N. 29
Nuremburg Code 2

O'Brien, K. 65
O'Neill, O. 95, 96
objectivity 47–9
obligations *see* researcher obligations
observation
    covert 8, 10, 85–6, 106
    public *vs* private places 84–6, 111–13
    see also participant observation
occupational ethics 13, 36, 133–4
Okely, J. 59, 96
online data 117–21
    and anonymisation 128
    audience and accessibility 119
    informing and gaining consent 120–1
    public *vs* private content 118–19

participant observation
    and harm 65–6
    incidental benefits of 59–60
    notion of benefiting those studied 137
    trust and privacy 106–7, 116
particularism in ethics 26–7
partnership research 81, 137
payment 11, 65–6
Payne, C. 4
peer review 44
Pels, P. 4
philosophical viewpoints
    ethics 21–34, 139
    freedom 76–8
photography 67–8
Plummer, K. 59
Peneff, J. 60
politics/political dimension 18–19
Polsky, N. 54
practical research 44–5
principles, guiding 27

privacy 14
  general aspects of 99–100, 131–2
    contrast with publicity 100–2
    demands for/attitudes to 103–4
  online data 117–21
  in qualitative research
    conflicting interests 105–8
    eliciting accounts 113–14
    informed consent 114–16
    private vs public places 84, 111–13
    research design 110–13
    sensitive topics 108–10
  see also anonymisation; confidentiality
professional autonomy see independence
professional codes see codes of ethics
professionalism
  intrinsic obligations and virtues 36, 45,
    46–51
  see also independence
Project Camelot 3
pseudonyms 128, 129
public areas 84, 104
publicity 100–3
publishing and reporting 44–5, 125
Putnam, H. 31

qualitative research
  character and general nature of 1, 7,
    64–5
    critical debate about 11–13, 39–40
  overview of controversial studies 8–11
  task and purpose of 37–8, 134
    demands of publishing 43–5
    moralism misrepresenting 137–8
quantitative research 11

Rashomon effect 41
reciprocity 15
reflexive judgment 33
regulation, ethical
  development of 4–6
  mismatch with qualitative research 7
  reflecting concern for harm 58
  unethical/damaging aspects of 142–3
  see also codes of ethics
relational ethics 29–31, 35, 76; see also ethics of care
religion
  casuistical traditions 26
  deontology 21
Renzetti, C. 66, 108
reporting and publishing 44–5, 125
research design 110–11
research ethics
  historical developments 2–8
  key principles specified 7
  mismatch with qualitative work 7

research ethics cont.
  as occupational ethics 36–7, 133–4
  transformation by critical debate 11–13
  research goals 13, 37–8
  and moralism 137–8
Research Governance Framework (NHS) 5
Research Ethics Framework (ESRC) see
    Framework for Research Ethics (ESRC)
researcher autonomy 49–51, 78, 135, 143
researcher obligations 36, 45
  cultivation of research virtues 46–52
responsibility, assigning 68–72
Reynolds, P. 17
right and wrong as concepts see good and bad
rights and duties 21; see also human rights;
    natural rights
roles, social 36
Rosenhahn, D. 85
Ross, D. 25
Ryan-Flood, R. 59

Sanders, T. 116
scepticism, epistemological 40–2, 44
Schaffir, W. 85
Scheper-Hughes, N. 10, 128, 130
secrecy 100, 102, 124
sensitive topics 108–10
sexual relationships 10, 11, 60–1
Seymour, J. 91, 129
Shils, E. 36, 38–9, 46, 85, 94, 101–2, 103, 104, 105,
    107, 115, 121
Sidgwick, H. 24, 102
Sikes, P. 11, 73, 108
situationism 24–7, 35
  anti-theory 32
  situation ethics 26
Society of Applied Anthropology 3
Svenningsson Elm, M. 117, 118, 120

taboos 108, 110
television 100–2
therapeutic research 59
Thorne, B. 93–4
Tierney, P. 10–11
Tourigney, S. 25, 72–3
Traianou, A. 66
trust and trustworthiness 15, 106–7
truth
  empirical propositional truth 39–40
  synonymous with knowldge 38–9
  see also knowledge

utilitarianism 23–4

value-neutrality 38
values see extrinsic values; intrinsic values

video 67–8; *see also* visual data
    and mass media 100–2
Vidich, A. 9, 127
virtue ethics 27–9, 34, 35
virtues, research 46–52
visual data 67–8
    and mass media 100–2
voyeurism 12

Walford, G. 131
Warwick, D. 57–8, 61, 62–3, 73
Weber, M. 38, 139
Whyte, W. F. 8
Williams, B. 17–18
Willett, R. 119

Yanomamö 11